CW00868831

Sacred Stairway

The Story of the Shrine of the Báb
Volume III
1963–2001

He, verily, loveth the spot which hath been made the seat of His throne, which His footsteps have trodden, which hath been honoured by His presence, from which He raised His call, and upon which He shed His tears.

Bahá'u'lláh[1]

From the bottom of the mountain to the Shrine there will be nine terraces, and nine more terraces will be built from the Shrine to the top of the mountain. Gardens with colourful flowers will be laid down on all these terraces.

'Abdu'l-Bahá[2]

This beautiful and majestic path which extends from the Shrine of the Báb to the City of Haifa in line with the greatest avenue in that blessed city... will subsequently be converted, as foreshadowed by the Centre of the Covenant, into the Highway of the Kings and Rulers of the World.

Shoghi Effendi[3]

The beauty and magnificence of the Gardens and Terraces . . . are symbolic of the nature of the transformation which is destined to occur both within the hearts of the world's peoples and in the physical environment of the planet.

The Universal House of Justice[4]

Sacred Stairway

The Story of the Shrine of the Báb
Volume III
1963–2001

Michael V. Day

GEORGE RONALD
OXFORD

GEORGE RONALD, PUBLISHER
Oxford
www.grbooks.com

© Michael V. Day 2019
All Rights Reserved

A catalogue record for this book is available from the British Library

ISBN 978-0-85398-622-5

Cover design: William McGuire

CONTENTS

1986–1999: BUILDING THE TERRACES OF LIGHT

LIST OF ILLUSTRATIONS

Bahá'ís assembled on the Arc, 25 May 2001

The President of the Republic of the Marshall Islands, Mr Kessai Note, on an official visit in 2005

The gardens team and the tour guides

Details of the terraces: benches, fountains, paths

Pool next to the wall that conceals the Afnán reservoir built by 'Abdu'l-Bahá

Shoghi Effendi's feat of entwining bougainvillea on a jacaranda tree near the Shrine, producing a stunning display of colour

Between pages 170 and 171

The Shrine of the Báb takes pride of place in this aerial photograph of the completed Terraces

Teitei vou (A new garden), 2009, by artists Robin White, Leba Toki and Bale Jione

A talented creative team: Fariborz and Golnar Sahba

The architect and project manager with his deputy, Steve Drake

Portraits of some of those who worked on the Terraces project: Saad Al-Jassar, Robert Pilbrow, Samandar Milani, Nancy Markovich, Daniel Caillaud, Andrew Blake, Eliza Rasiwala, Tony White, Wendy Marshall, Hooshang Yazdani, Abdul Jarrah, Ernie Lopez

Cover placed over the dome and drum of the Shrine of the Báb during its restoration

Saeid Samadi and colleague examine the plans for the restoration of the Shrine

Perched above the bottom lip of the dome, a worker repairs spots damaged from 50 years of exposure to the elements

Workers restore the panels above the balustrade

Newly gilded pinnacles and balustrade after the restoration

The beauty of the design by William Sutherland Maxwell

Interior lighting enables the full beauty of the windows of the drum to be visible

Unveiling the Queen of Carmel one glorious morning in 2011

Dedicated to
Douglas Moore
an inspiring leader and loving friend,
and to the happy band[5] who served with him and the author from
2003 to 2006 as staff members of the Office of Public Information at
the Bahá'í World Centre

And in fond memory of
Murray Smith and Eliza Rasiwala
my dear friends and colleagues, both of whom loved the Shrine and its
Terraces and who proclaimed the Bahá'í teachings in those most holy,
those most beautiful precincts

My affectionate and sincere gratitude is again extended
to a former custodian of the Shrine
Fuad Izadinia
whose constancy of expert and personal support is matched in his
contribution to this book and its predecessors only by his wisdom and
his inspiring love of the Shrine of the Báb

PREFACE

This final volume in the trilogy telling the story of the Shrine of the Báb describes the project that fulfilled 'Abdu'l-Bahá's vision of 19 garden terraces stretching up Mount Carmel.

It is a story of the magnificent leadership of the Universal House of Justice and the beautiful design of the architect commissioned to design and project-manage the construction. It is also a story of the dedication, professional expertise and hard work of a team of devoted Bahá'í volunteers as well as contractors and their staff. Reminiscences of some of the volunteers involved in the Terraces project are included in Annex I.

This volume also describes the support of the residents and officials of Haifa, who continue to celebrate this treasure in the heart of their city. The outcome of the project is a creation so stunningly beautiful that the description 'a wonder of the world' cannot be considered an exaggeration.

Other contributions to the Shrine and its environment will no doubt continue for centuries to come. In Annex II to this volume there is a description of the successful refurbishment of the Shrine building and its surrounds that came to a glorious conclusion with the unveiling of the new golden tiles in 2011.

The first phase of the Shrine project was conducted between 1850 and 1921 mainly by eastern Bahá'ís, as described in *Journey to a Mountain*, the first volume of the trilogy. Between 1922 and 1963, as told in the second volume, *Coronation on Carmel*, most of those involved in the completion of the Shrine building were from the West. How wonderful that the Terraces were built in the closing decade of the 20th century by a team symbolizing a united world through the inclusion of people from many national and ethnic backgrounds.

The Shrine, founded by Bahá'u'lláh Himself, is a spiritual dynamo that drives the Bahá'í administration forward in its mission to spiritualize a united world society. It is also a holy place that assists us all, whether present in the Shrine or turning our minds toward it.

Shoghi Effendi said that the core of religious faith is that 'mystic feeling' which unites individuals with God: 'This state of spiritual communion can be brought about and maintained by means of meditation and prayer.' As well as being a spiritual dynamo and a beacon of world unity and peace, the Shrine of the Báb inspires the most profound meditation and prayer, bringing us further along on our eternal journey towards our Creator.

ACKNOWLEDGEMENTS

When I assisted a colleague at the Bahá'í World Centre, Yin Thing Ming, as she escorted visitors down the upper terraces of the Shrine of the Báb, I rejoiced in the privilege. What earthly paradise could compare with the Terraces in their sheer beauty? What atmosphere could compare with being on that stairway, breathing in a breeze of contentment and happiness emanating up from the Shrine, a spiritual zephyr that seemed to transform our guests into the best versions of themselves?

For the opportunity to serve in such a way, I thank the Universal House of Justice. I again extend my gratitude for that esteemed institution's assurance of prayers in the Holy Shrines that my endeavours in the service of the Cause be 'blessed and confirmed'. How more blessed and confirmed could I be than to complete, however imperfectly, a trilogy of the story of the Shrine of the Báb with an account that focuses mainly upon the building of the Terraces?

And how blessed and confirmed I feel to have had the assistance of one so closely associated with this project, Mr 'Alí Nakhjavání. Those blessings and confirmations kept on coming as the architect of the magnificent spiritual ladder to the Throne of Carmel, Fariborz Sahba, generously agreed to assist me as I attempted to describe how the spiritual muses inspired his creation. After I chronicled in detail the years of construction, Mr Sahba corrected one or two things in the text, and then scanned photographs from his vast collection. He gave me a rare and precious volume of *Vineyard of the Lord*, the contemporary chronicle of most of the years of the project. I acknowledge his trust in me, and the hospitality and conversations when I stayed with him in his home.

Any time I called upon Fuad Izadinia, who has assisted me with all volumes of this trilogy, he would quickly and thoroughly answer, no matter how nit-picking or repetitive my inquiry, and whether on matters spiritual, practical or personal. This has been his generous practice for more than seven years. I am also grateful to the assistance of his brother, the scholar Faruq Izadinia.

My deep appreciation goes to the eminent architect Hossein Amanat, for his answers to my questions about his beautiful design of the Seat of the Universal House of Justice. I am also grateful to Saied Samadi for the information he gave me on the restoration of the Shrine, and to his colleague Samira Rahimi. Richard Armbruster also assisted me with the history of the ideas for restoration.

I approached some of those who served on the Terraces project and they were kind enough to indulge my questions, despite sometimes feeling awkward about describing their efforts due, as it seemed to me, to their selfless mindsets. Special thanks are due to Andrew Blake, who also helped with the previous two volumes, and also to Steve Drake and Nancy Markovich. Michael Hughey, whose calligraphic contributions to the Shrine have helped elevate the experience there of so many pilgrims and visitors, was generous in his support, comments and gifts. Jo Hill provided memories and some great photographs.

I also want to thank the following for their encouragement: Dr Janet Khan, Paul Toloui-Wallace, Sahba Abedian, Judy Hassall, Edward Broomhall, Derek Brown, Alan Manifold, June Perkins, Lisa Jackson, Ian Hallmond, Thelma Batchelor, Ariana Ali, Richard Rawlings, Keith McDonald, Venus Khalessi, Natalie Mobini, Riadh Ali, Jalal Mills, Daniel Schaubacher, Thor Henning Lerstad, Keith Thorpe, Saied Rezaie and the other members of the Yaran, Lee Tate, the late Mehroo Mihrshahi, the late Tiffany Haldoupis, and the late Mary O'Neill, whose advice bore fruit. All those who have helped me and undeservedly are not listed, please forgive me as you take a bow.

During the final stages of this project, I was blessed to be able to visit the grave in Buenos Aires of May Maxwell, a donor to the Shrine, the wife of the architect of the arcade and superstructure and the mother of the consort of Shoghi Effendi. I thank the Hon. Rimbink Pato MP, for giving me that opportunity. I also took many opportunities to pray at the grave in Brisbane of Dr Peter Khan, his resting place not far from the spot where he gave me advice about my project before I started in earnest.

The late Eliza Rasiwala provided me with information that was of great help to this book and I am sorry she is not on this earthly plane to see this volume appear. Belatedly, I thank Abdu'l-Rauf Rowhani, a gardener for Shoghi Effendi, who gave me priceless help with *Coronation on Carmel*.

Dr Marjorie Tidman once again assisted with preliminary editing, fulfilling an unsolicited promise she made years ago to assist me, a contribution she wanted me not to acknowledge. I normally follow her suggestions but I have joyfully not acceded to her suggestion, and even quoted her in the text of the book.

Working with editor May Hofman meant I could cast my protective worries about my text aside because May's light touch is that of an editing artist who refines and polishes while correcting glitches, and who gives expert suggestions based on long experience and deep knowledge of the Bahá'í Faith and its history.

Erica and Angharad Leith and Carmel and Wendi Momen are the reassuring, cheery, and informative folk at George Ronald Publisher, just the kind a solitary writer likes to hear from. How thrilled I was when Wendi told me my books would be published in Spanish.

William McGuire provided the beautiful design for the cover, worked with me to select the photographs, and cleaned or enhanced them when necessary, making the book so attractive to the eye. Together with Shahnaz Hoveydai he also arranged a presentation on *Coronation on Carmel*, a very pleasant experience. I am also grateful to the New Zealand and Queensland Bahá'í communities for their invitation to speak about the story of the Shrine of the Báb at their summer schools.

I thank my late parents, Noel and Win Day, for my upbringing and spiritual education.

It is more than eight years since I embarked on this thrilling project. Throughout it all, my wife, Dr Chris Day, paid nearly all of our bills, and reinforced in me the feeling that the books will be valued down the years.

I extend my loving appreciation to my current and future readers for spending time with my books, particularly when on the stairway to the Shrine.

THE STORY SO FAR

As told in *Journey to a Mountain* and *Coronation on Carmel*,
Volumes I and II of the story of the Shrine of the Báb

A small band of the followers of the Báb, the great spiritual leader executed in 1850, walk across Persia, carrying His sacred remains in a 'running throne', a palanquin for holy objects. The small casket encasing those remains had been concealed in various places for nearly five decades until the journey begins in 1898. The men carry their precious trust over the mountains to Baghdad, and then tread the long and difficult path over vast stretches of desert to Damascus and on to Beirut.

In 1899, the casket arrives by boat in the Holy Land where 'Abdu'l-Bahá is obeying the direction of Bahá'u'lláh, the Prophet-Founder of the Bahá'í Faith, by building a Shrine on Mount Carmel in Haifa. As head of the Faith, He inters the sacred remains in the Shrine in a moving ceremony in 1909. Twelve years later, 'Abdu'l-Bahá passes away and is Himself interred in the Shrine.

In 1953, after decades of patience and planning, Shoghi Effendi, the head of the Faith, completes a beautiful superstructure and arcade for the Shrine of the Báb. An exquisite golden-tiled dome soars over mysteriously charming gardens.

Only one task remains to fulfil the vision described by 'Abdu'l-Bahá and empowered by the Tablet of Carmel, the foundation scripture for the Shrine. The Universal House of Justice, the elected governing body of the Faith, takes on that task. In 1987, the House of Justice announces a project to build nine garden terraces from the base of Mount Carmel to the Shrine of the Báb, and another nine above it.

The story of this arduous project is about to begin.

Pathway

WONDROUS RESULT

Just after sunset, the sky above Mount Carmel turned a rosy hue.

Orchestral music accompanying the prophetic words of the Tablet of Carmel reached its stirring crescendo. The lights on each of the 19 Terraces of the Shrine of the Báb came on, one terrace at a time, illuminating the steep mountain slope. Onlookers thrilled to the vision, many audibly expressing their wonder and delight.

It was 22 May 2001, and this was the inauguration ceremony in Haifa, Israel, of the Terraces which had been completed in December 2000 under the direction of the Universal House of Justice, the governing body of the Bahá'í Faith.

Nearly nine decades previously, on 14 February 1914, 'Abdu'l-Bahá, while seated at the window of the Eastern Pilgrim House, had said: 'Mount Carmel itself, from top to bottom, will be submerged in a sea of lights.'[1] His vision had come stunningly to life in front of the peoples of the world, a microcosm fortunate to be seated in a temporary amphitheatre at the base of Mount Carmel, and countless others watching on television and via the Internet in many countries around the globe.

The 16-metre-tall amphitheatre, with capacity for 4,500, provided easily enough seats for the more than 2,500 Bahá'ís, including two Hands of the Cause, 650 special guests, and about 100 members of the national and international media. Also present were ambassadors from more than 30 countries, Israeli government ministers and deputy ministers, members of the Knesset and three Supreme Court justices. Other dignitaries who had accepted invitations were the mayors of Haifa and Acre, and as well as local political and religious leaders.

Members of the Universal House of the Justice also took their seats. The message from the Bahá'í world governing council on which they served was delivered by the Secretary-General of the Bahá'í International Community, Dr Albert Lincoln, who spoke as he stood in the entrance plaza, facing the amphitheatre and the bank of cameras of the world's media. That message said in part:

> We are met not to lament the tragedy of the Báb's martyrdom and the persecutions that followed; rather have we come to celebrate the culmination and acknowledge the meaning of an unprecedented project that had its beginning over a century ago. It was then that Bahá'u'lláh, Whom the Ottoman authorities had banished to Acre to serve out His days in confinement, visited Mount Carmel and selected the spot where the remains of His Herald would be interred.
> We humbly trust that the wondrous result achieved by the completion of the nineteen terraced gardens, at the heart of which rises the Shrine of the Báb, is a fitting fulfilment of the vision initiated by Bahá'u'lláh.[2]

The large gathering of Bahá'í attendees from around the world, many wearing national dress, had begun to arrive at 3.30 p.m., well in time for the commencement of the inauguration ceremony. They had shaded their eyes from the westering sun to take in the breathtaking view that encompassed the exquisite marble entrance plaza, and the pathway of the kings and rulers with its flower-adorned terraces flanked by emerald lawns, cypresses and palms.

And there, in the centre of the middle ground, the gold and white Shrine of the Báb rose imposing yet beautiful, massive yet delicate. Its dome, because of the perspective, appeared to be above the crest of the holy mountain itself.

At the direction of Bahá'u'lláh, 'Abdu'l-Bahá had built the initial mausoleum, the rough texture of its exterior stone so pleasant to the touch.

Shoghi Effendi, His successor as head of the Faith, had completed the Shrine with an arcade and superstructure that blended East and West, and set it in perfumed gardens of 'peculiar charm'.[3]

The task taken on by the Universal House of Justice was to embellish the Shrine with the terraces which had been spoken of by the Master and which had links to terraces in Persia where Bahá'u'lláh Himself had once delivered majestic words of spiritual inspiration.

The massive project, to construct terraces stretching nearly a kilometre from the base to the summit of Mount Carmel, had been supported by voluntary, confidential donations and prayers from Bahá'ís in villages, on farms, in towns, and in cities – in countries ranging from the poorest on the planet to the wealthiest. A volunteer band of Bahá'ís had come from around the world and worked alongside local staff and contractors who did the actual physical work[4] of building the terraces, a project driven by an assertive, talented and conscientious project manager, who also was the architect.

All this happened during a decade of crises all over the world. War erupted and later subsided in the Balkans and Iraq. In Israel, violent civil unrest called the *intifada* caused havoc at times. Dramas affected political leaders and celebrities. There were convictions, exposés and premature deaths.

But there were also great achievements in the arts and in the sciences, most noticeably as technology produced new inventions which had a huge impact. The Internet arrived into the lives of people in the economically advanced countries, although its full impact in such areas as media, education and entertainment were still some time off. Mobile (cell) phones were initially in the shape of a small brick but started to shrink. Instead of posting letters, increasing numbers of people were starting to use electronic mail. In the Bahá'í world the Institute process was evolving into a world-wide training programme. Amatu'l-Bahá Rúḥíyyih Khánum, the last direct Bahá'í link to the Guardian of the Bahá'í Faith, had passed away just 16 months earlier. Persecution of the Bahá'í community in Iran was still occurring, yet less severe than in the 1980s and not as systematic as it was to become in the first decade of the new century.

In a 10-year period many changes happen in the lives of ordinary people – births, marriages and deaths – but for the Bahá'í community these took place against the backdrop of a seemingly never-ending construction programme. Not only were the Terraces being built at the Bahá'í World Centre, but simultaneously two huge marble buildings were rising as wide-ranging work took place on nearby land on Mount Carmel.[5]

From design to completion, the Universal House of Justice supervised the implementation of its decision to build the Terraces.

How the House of Justice came to this decision had its roots in 1963, a century after Bahá'u'lláh's declaration that He was the bearer of a divine message – the fulfilment of the promise of the Báb and a line of Prophets stretching back millennia. It was in that momentous year that the Universal House of Justice came into being. It was in that year that the Shrine of the Báb, the holiest Bahá'í shrine in the world after the Shrine of Bahá'u'lláh, became its responsibility.

To learn how the supreme body of the Bahá'í Faith fulfilled its onerous responsibility in the years leading up to the inauguration of the Terraces on that glorious night in May 2001, it is necessary to venture back in time to the very early days of its existence.

2

THE 1960s

What needed to be done was clear from the Master's stirring description of the glorious future of the Shrine and its precincts: 'From the bottom of the mountain to the Shrine there will be nine terraces, and nine more terraces will be built from the Shrine to the top of the mountain. Gardens will be made with flowers of different hues.'[1]

Nobody could have predicted just when the Universal House of Justice would bring that vision into reality, yet within four decades of its inauguration it was to present to the world terraces of such ravishing beauty that increasing numbers of people, Bahá'ís and others alike, would salute them as a new wonder of the world.

How the House of Justice came to that triumphant achievement is a drama pulsating with mind-bending challenges, timely decisions, frightening wars, heart-rending sorrows, artistic inspiration, heroic self-sacrifice, hard work and spiritual exultation – all elements that had characterized the story of the Shrine in earlier decades

It was to be almost two-and-a-half decades after the inauguration of the House of Justice that the international governing body made firm plans to build the terraces, about the same length of time Shoghi Effendi had waited from the beginning of his ministry until he took deliberate steps to build the superstructure of the Shrine.

In the first years of its existence the House of Justice placed a priority on 'the basic, minimum essentials of undertaking repairs to the holy places'[2] but it also had its eyes firmly set on the need to develop its precincts. In its message addressed to the Bahá'ís at their national conventions in May 1963 it said that the plan to be embarked upon in a year's time would include, among other projects, 'the extension and embellishment of the endowments at the World Centre'.[3]

In June 1963, the House of Justice said that its decision to occupy the entire former Western Pilgrim House made it necessary to find other accommodation for Western pilgrims. 'We have therefore established one Pilgrim House, at the Bahá'í gardens on Mount Carmel,' the House of Justice said.[4] That began the intermingling of eastern and western pilgrims in what had been known as the Eastern Pilgrim House.

The House of Justice started a process of planning the extension of the gardens and the beautification of the Shrine's surroundings, but made it clear that any resulting programme could take years to implement.[5]

It was obvious that more money was vital for any substantial work in and near the Shrine. In December that year, the House of Justice called upon local and national communities to contribute substantially to the International Fund to enable the House to, among other things, carry forward the work of beautifying the land surrounding the holy Shrines.[6]

Certainly something had to be done. There were external pressures for the development of the extensive Bahá'í property behind the Shrine leading up to the peak of the mountain. The area of the Bahá'í properties on Mount Carmel was extensive, and except for the limited number of terraces provisionally created by Shoghi Effendi, the rest of the slope of the mountain was barren. The Mayor of Haifa and local residents would often ask the Bahá'ís what plans they had for the mountainside.[7] The city was growing, and vacant land was at a premium.

Even though the House of Justice did not have the resources to develop the site at the time, it did make plans. Among the tasks it listed in a nine-year plan presented to the worldwide Bahá'í community in 1964 were 'the preparation of a plan for the befitting development and beautification of the entire area of Bahá'í property surrounding the holy shrines' and 'the extension of the existing gardens on Mount Carmel'.[8]

In that same year, in its desire to offer reassurances to the city that this area would be developed and that plans for the terraces were not just an empty hope, the House of Justice invited a distinguished Bahá'í architect, Robert W. McLaughlin Jnr, Dean of the School of Architecture at Princeton University in the United States,[9] to come to the Holy Land to prepare a concept for the extension of the gardens above the Shrine of the Báb and the Archives Building.

Professor McLaughlin was familiar with the issues because two years previously he had provided advice to the International Bahá'í Council after the Haifa authorities had proposed to 'improve' existing roads running through Bahá'í properties on Mount Carmel and to add new ones. That risk of dividing up the land needed for the terraces had not entirely dissipated.

In 1965 Professor McLaughlin submitted to the House of Justice a rudimentary plan, based on a photogrammetric survey, which was a process of making measurements from photographs.[10] It is reported that his plan was primarily aimed at showing how the surface and texture of the slopes of the mountain would lend themselves to the construction of nine terraces down from the top of the mountain to the terrace of the Shrine, and nine other terraces from the Shrine to an open space leading to Hagefen Street at the base of the mountain.[11]

Based on these tentative plans, the Bahá'í World Centre then made representations to the Haifa Municipality and the Government of the Israel towards the adoption of definite plans in line with Shoghi Effendi's wishes.[12] In the associated meetings, Professor McLaughlin, with his gentle manner and deep knowledge of city planning, helped convince the authorities, at least for the time being, that 'the long term interests of Haifa would be better served by a verdant and beautiful Bahá'í World Centre, open to all, than by a series of little roads that would do little to alleviate the city's growing traffic problems'.[13] The Mayor was satisfied that the Bahá'ís were serious about the development of the face of Mount Carmel, and that they were considering preliminary possibilities. However, the potential for roads was still contained in the city's town planning scheme.

The work of Professor McLaughlin, however, was not to play a role in the future design of the terraces by their architect Mr Fariborz Sahba.[14]

In its Riḍván message of 1966 the Universal House of Justice re-emphasized the need for funds, without which nothing much could be done to significantly enhance the area: 'All the goals assigned to the World Centre of the Faith, and particularly those dealing with the development and beautification of the properties surrounding the holy shrines and the extension of the gardens on Mount Carmel, entail heavy expenditures.'[15]

Less than a year later, in March 1967, the House of Justice called for a greater flow of funds, saying it was vital to undertake extensive beautification of the sacred endowments surrounding the Shrines of the Báb and Bahá'u'lláh 'both for its own sake and for the protection of these lands which are situated within the boundaries of rapidly expanding cities'. It also said that pilgrimage arrangements 'may have to be greatly expanded to provide for the ever-increasing number of applications from East and West'.[16]

In its Riḍván message a month later the House of Justice said the development and extension of the holy Shrines in both Haifa and Bahjí were continuing.[17] There was a range of projects undertaken, including an extension of floodlighting of the Shrine and repairs to its flat roof. Repairing a retaining wall that had collapsed at the eastern wing of the Shrine's terrace also made it onto the work schedule. The Pilgrim House got a new roof, and there was extensive painting and gilding of the ornamentation on the Shrine as well as on the gates and ornaments in the gardens.

In 1968 another change occurred. Until then, vehicles could enter the Bahá'í gardens via the main gate on Hatzionut Street directly south of the Pilgrim House, the way the Guardian had arrived and departed in his car.[18] Now that there was a steady increase in the number of visitors, that route was no longer suitable for vehicles; only foot traffic was now permitted. The House of Justice established a parking lot and associated gardens near the Pilgrim House, the entrance off Shifra Street, which flanked the eastern side of the Shrine property.

Other projects in those years included: building a wall and an extension to the sidewalk adjacent to the Bahá'í gardens along UNO Avenue (formerly known as Mountain Road and later Hatzionut Avenue); adding new soil to gardens in the higher reaches of the gardens where there had been erosion; the rewiring of all electrical circuits in the gardens; the fencing of property on Mount Carmel; and the paving of the path that drew a curve on the face of Mount Carmel just southeast of the Shrine, a place known by Bahá'ís as 'the Arc'.

The climbing of the terraces

In the heat of August 1968, Bahá'ís climbed the terraces from the base of the mountain to the Shrine itself. This event occurred 100 years after Bahá'u'lláh had first set foot in Haifa and where, 23 years later, He would point out the site for the Shrine of His Herald, the Báb.

Some 2,000 Bahá'ís had attended a conference in Palermo, Sicily, and then came to Haifa for the commemoration events – the experience of a lifetime. *The Bahá'í World* reported:

Golden jewel on black velvet. The Shrine of the Báb sits resplendent in the centre of lights that give intimations of circles surrounding it

© Bahá'í World News Service

The Terraces of the Shrine of the Báb illuminated at the climax of the Terraces of Light oratorio on 22 May 2001

Bottom left: *Violinist Bijan Khadem-Missagh was one of the soloists for the* Terraces of Light *oratorio. His son, Vahid, and his daughter, Martha, also played their violins at the event*

Bottom right: *The statement of the Universal House of Justice for the opening of the Terraces on Mount Carmel was read by the Secretary-General of the Bahá'í International Community, Albert Lincoln*

© Bahá'í World News Service

© Bahá'í World News Service

© Bahá'í World News Centre

In August 1968, one hundred years after Bahá'u'lláh arrived in Haifa, Bahá'ís climbed the lower terraces to the Shrine. They had been at a Bahá'í conference in Palermo, Sicily

Photos: Courtesy of Bruce Hancock

Beverly Rennie and Bruce Hancock, both from New Zealand, inside the octagon of the Shrine, applying gold leaf to the new finial of the Shrine of the Báb

In 1980, staff replaced the finial that had been hit and broken by lightning. Left to right: Max Hancock and his son Bruce Hancock, both from New Zealand, and Eric Anderson, from the United Kingdom

The seat of the Universal House of Justice, designed by Hossein Amanat

Architect Hossein Amanat with a model depicting buildings he designed for the Arc at the Bahá'í World Centre

Photo: Montecristo magazine

Hossein Amanat in later years

At the foot of the mountain, only blocks from the home of 'Abdu'l-Bahá and from the headquarters of the Universal House of Justice, the pilgrims assembled starting the ascent in the early morning heat of Haifa. Looking far up to the magnificent Shrine of the Báb above and looking back occasionally to the streets and the harbour below, the friends – the old and the young – mounted the steep path lined by towering cypress trees and bougainvillaea along the wall. Photographers along the way recorded the climb for a film that will seek to convey the beauty, the uniqueness and the universality of our beloved Faith.[19]

A similar event was not to take place again until 24 years later.

Grief and anxiety

During the 1960s one event brought grief to those at the Bahá'í World Centre, and another induced great anxiety.

On 22 July 1965, an historic figure associated with the Shrine passed away. Hand of the Cause Leroy Ioas, aged 69, died in Haifa, and the next day was buried next to a comrade-in-arms, the Hand of the Cause Amelia Collins.

The grieving House of Justice paid tribute to the man who had been the project manager for the construction of the drum and dome of the Shrine and who had successfully negotiated the purchase of key properties on Mount Carmel on behalf of the Guardian. It saluted him as an 'outstanding' Hand of the Cause, whose name the Guardian had given to the octagon door, and whose services would ensure that his name would appear in the immortal annals of the Faith.[20]

Nearly two years later, in June 1967, a frightening conflict erupted in the Holy Land. Israel and its Arab neighbours engaged in what came to be known as the Six Day War. It was a perilous time, but fortunately fighting did not occur near Haifa. Peace soon returned.

The irony, one which was to continue down the decades, was that in this region under contention by armed combatants there was a special emblem of peace. It was a Shrine that was the object of close and loving attention by the institution whose sacred duty was to protect, maintain and embellish it.

3

THE 1970s AND 1980s

The 1970s began with victory after victory for the Faith, as many people around the world joined the religion.

But at the end of the decade, in accord with a process so often described in Bahá'í scripture and commentary, alongside the victories came a crisis of extreme proportions. A savage persecution erupted in Iran as a clergy-dominated regime began to torture and execute Bahá'ís, steal their possessions, deny them education, desecrate their cemeteries and plot the extinction of the community. It led to a halt of pilgrim groups from Iran coming to the Bahá'í World Centre.

Influx

In the 1960s and 1970s there was an influx into the Faith as many people, particularly in Western society, searched for new spiritual meaning and purpose. The new Bahá'ís found it easier than those before them to come on pilgrimage because international travel was becoming cheaper with the arrival of the jumbo jet.

To cope with the increased requests by Bahá'ís to come on pilgrimage, the Universal House of Justice in 1969 quadrupled the size and increased the number of pilgrim groups. It said this would give many more people the opportunity 'to pray in the Shrines of the Central Figures of their Faith, to visit the places hallowed by the footsteps, sufferings and triumphs of Bahá'u'lláh and 'Abdu'l-Bahá, and to meditate in the tranquillity of these sacred precincts, beautified with so much loving care by our beloved Guardian.' Beginning in October 1969, the House of Justice said, the numbers arriving would be nearly six times greater than before.[1]

In 1971, the precincts of the Shrine of the Báb expanded in size when the House of Justice supervised the establishment of a formal garden at the southwest corner of the property surrounding the edifice, to the west of the path established by the Master seven decades previously.[2] This opened up a beautiful new view of the Shrine from UNO Avenue, formerly known as Mountain Road and now as Hatzionut Avenue.

A star design adorned the central areas of its lawn. Shrubs and trees studded the area and a row of trees flanked its southern border.[3] Globe-like lamps, a signature of the gardens, sat atop the stone gateposts and adjoining wall. A double wrought-iron gate leading to the Master's path shone in gold and black, the gilding picking out the initials 'B' (one reversed) in wheel-like designs forming both sections of the gate. Gilded eight-pointed stars sat at the tips of four of the spokes. A stylized fleur-de-lis surmounted the ironwork.

The steady progress of the work at the Bahá'í World Centre took place in anxious times. In 1973 another war erupted in the Holy Land, but this time the fighting was not so far away from Haifa as it had been seven years earlier. Israel prevailed in the conflict and peace resumed.

In the second half of the 1970s the House of Justice further extended and beautified some small informal gardens on the upper slopes of the mountain facing the Shrine.

In the 1980s, the emphasis in the precincts of the Shrine was mostly on maintenance and improvement. Between 1979 and 1983, gardeners replaced overgrown trees around the Shrine and did extensive work in the garden bordering Hagefen Street at the foot of Mount Carmel, the spot where Bahá'u'lláh had once pitched His tent.

In 1980 new lights on poles discreetly concealed in trees below and above the Shrine illuminated the building with such effect that just after their installation, the Hand of the Cause Paul Haney, who was escorting pilgrims out of the Shrine at dusk, exclaimed with delight at the sight.[4]

Bahá'ís who were professional gardeners replaced some cypress trees near the Shrine. From 1983 they were able to obtain most of the plants and trees required from a local plant-production facility that had begun operating that year. Plans for a comprehensive irrigation project and professional pest control were under way.[5]

The political upheaval and intense persecution in Iran that continued and worsened from 1979 prevented most Persian Bahá'ís from coming on pilgrimage, so the Universal House of Justice filled their places with others from around the world. From 1984 the House of Justice increased the places from 80 to 100 per group. Twenty pilgrimage groups came every year.

Those who arrived in the late 1970s and early 1980s were in for a treat because an exciting development was taking place on the Arc, just a few hundred metres from the Shrine.

Under the wings of the Shrine

On 7 June 1972, the House of Justice made an historic announcement. It said that before the completion of the Nine Year Plan it would begin the procedure to choose an architect to design a building that would be the seat of the Universal House of Justice as envisaged by Shoghi Effendi on the Arc on Mount Carmel, centering on the resting places of the sister, mother and brother of 'Abdu'l-Bahá.[6] It would be the second building on the Arc which, as the Guardian had said, was 'under the wings of the Báb's overshadowing Sepulchre'.[7] The first had been the International Archives Building completed in 1957.

The House of Justice said in its message that the range and acceleration in the growth of the Faith at local and national levels and the resultant expansion of activities at the World Centre had impelled it to make its decision to erect the building.

There was nowhere near adequate space in its offices at 10 Haparsim Street for the continuing expansion of the work of the House of Justice. A desperate need arose for enough room for the ever-increasing staff numbers and for filing and storing the mounting number of documents. Even the transformation of a water reservoir into office space did not meet the current needs.

Some Bahá'ís speculated on whether there was a spiritual reason for the decision. In the Tablet referred to as 'Seven Candles of Unity', 'Abdu'l-Bahá had written:

> The fifth candle is the unity of nations – a unity which in this century will be securely established, causing all the peoples of the world[8] to regard themselves as citizens of one common fatherland.[9]

Many Bahá'ís saw this as referring to the establishment of the Lesser Peace. There were a number of pilgrim notes attributed to Shoghi

Effendi which said that the Lesser Peace would be established by the end of the 'century', and that the building of the Arc would have to be finished by then. But there was always a doubt – even if the pilgrim notes had been correct – whether the Guardian had meant the Gregorian century, or the second Bahá'í century.

Essentially the decision was taken because the building was needed.[10] In fact, the timing of the Lesser Peace was still somewhat of a mystery, and it was not a motivating factor in the decision to proceed with the building, although the House of Justice (as well as the architect) linked it to the fulfilment of a prophecy in the Tablet of Carmel.[11]

The construction of the new building would be the first major step, the House of Justice pointed out, in the development of the area near the Shrine since the completion of the International Archives Building 15 years previously. A little over a year later, on 17 September 1973, the House of Justice told the Bahá'í world whom it had chosen to design its permanent Seat: 'Delighted announce appointment Ḥusayn Amánat young Bahá'í architect cradle Faith as architect of building for Universal House of Justice.'[12]

At the age of 30, Mr Amanat was already prominent in his profession, having won the national competition in Iran to design the Shahyad Monument in Tehran, now a symbol of the country.[13]

His brief for the new building was that it had to last for many years, be functional and able to accommodate future technology. He was living in Iran at the time,[14] and wasted no time producing two designs. He wrote: 'Initially in the schemes proposed to the Universal House of Justice were included a design in the modern style[15] with consideration given to classical proportions and principles, and one of pure classical style, which was accepted.'[16]

Asked later about his inspiration for the design, Mr Amanat said: 'As they say, you do not know the source of a poem. It comes to you.'[17] The design in the classical Greek tradition would clearly live up to the prescription of Shoghi Effendi who had said the edifices of the Arc would follow 'a harmonizing style of architecture'.

In February 1974, only five months after the announcement of his appointment, the Universal House of Justice said that it had accepted his design and that a decision had been taken to proceed with contracts for its construction.[18]

The building, which would be at the very apex of the Arc, would have a dome capping the central core, whose heart was the Council Chamber of the House of Justice. Mr Amanat wrote that the dome was 'deliberately not designed in a more prominent form in order not to compete with the Shrine of the Báb'.[19] He said the design of the superstructure of the Shrine did not influence his design of the Seat and other Arc buildings: 'I was only aware not to dominate the Shrine and be respectful to it.' At about 39 metres from the ground, the dome of the Shrine of the Báb was some 14 metres taller than the dome of the Seat of the Universal House of Justice. Mr Amanat wrote: 'Like many domes in eastern architecture, the dome of this building is based on an octagon[20] in the heart of the building itself . . .'[21]

More than 20 years earlier, a well-known Bahá'í living in Haifa, Jessie Revell,[22] had reported that the Guardian had said that when he thought of the Shrine's dome, he also thought of the International House of Justice, the Institution of the Guardianship and the Hands of the Cause.[23] Now those connections were to be symbolically embodied in a structure.

The marble for the building was Pentelikon stone quarried near Athens. As had been the case more than two decades earlier for the different kind of stone for the Shrine, artisans in Italy carved and cut it before ships carried it to Haifa.[24]

Excavation began on the site on 17 June 1975 and was completed by Naw-Rúz, 21 March 1976. Mr Amanat was the official project manager for the building but, having design responsibilities for his office in Canada, he asked for cooperation from Azizu'lláh Khabirpour of Luxembourg to closely oversee the day-to-day construction on his behalf and in coordination with him.[25] They travelled together to Italy about a dozen times to select and order the marble.[26]

On 28 April 1978 at the dedication of the Seat, nearly five years before its occupation, Amatu'l-Bahá Rúḥíyyih Khánum placed a casket containing dust from the Shrine of Bahá'u'lláh and the Shrine of the Báb in a niche of the Council Chamber's outer wall. The inauguration took place on 17 July 1982 in association with a seminar on the 50th anniversary of the passing of the Greatest Holy Leaf.[27]

The completion and occupation of the magnificent six-storey marble-clad building, with its 58 fluted Corinthian columns adorning the arcade, took place in 1983. The House of Justice members transferred their offices there in the last two weeks of January. The House of Justice said the auspicious event signalized another phase in the process of the fulfilment of 'sailing God's ark on [the] mountain of the Lord' as anticipated in the Tablet of Carmel.[28] As a prominent Bahá'í historian David Ruhe has pointed out, the Seat of the Universal House of Justice was in a commanding position 'but still in the shadow of the jewel-like Shrine of the Báb'.[29]

The House of Justice also gave Mr Amanat the tasks to prepare plans for three buildings that would stand on the Arc under the 'wings' of the Shrine: the Centre for the Study of the Texts and the buildings for the International Teaching Centre and the International Bahá'í Library.[30] He produced a series of concepts and in mid-1985 the House of Justice asked that he prepare a conceptual report of the project in which he would take into account the many factors that needed to be resolved before work could begin. At that time there was no thought given to a Terraces project proceeding at the same time.[31]

The House of Justice approved Mr Amanat's plans in general terms. He then refined them and resubmitted them in early 1986. The House of Justice then accepted them in their specifics.

The future architect of the Terraces of the Shrine of the Báb, Fariborz Sahba, had been the associate architect working with Mr Amanat[32] during the design phase of the Seat project and then had gone on to build a spectacular new Bahá'í Temple in the country with the world's largest Bahá'í population.

4

THE TEMPLE AND THE TERRACES

In December 1986 in India's capital city, New Delhi, a new Bahá'í
House of Worship opened its doors to humanity. It was in the shape of
a lotus, a bloom with deep spiritual significance to the peoples of the
subcontinent.

On the morning of 23 December, Amatu'l-Bahá Rúḥíyyih Khánum
ascended a nine-metre high stage to place a silver casket holding dust
gathered from the Shrine of Bahá'u'lláh and the Shrine of the Báb in a
niche under the marble slab at the apex of the arch. She later gave an
address in which she spoke about the significance of that dust, a gift
from the Universal House of Justice.[1]

The exquisite Temple was soon to become the most visited building
in India, and later was said to be among the most visited in the world.

The Temple's architect was Iranian-born Fariborz Sahba, who had
moved from England to India with his wife, Golnar, a talented designer,
and their children. Mr Sahba took on the role as project manager, an
enormous challenge in an environment in the days when an experienced local workforce was in short supply and where there were many
other hurdles to a major construction project.

Born in 1948, Mr Sahba had grown up listening to his mother's
description of the Bahá'í Temple in Ashqabat. She said: 'If you become
an architect, you too can build a House of Worship.' In 1972, he grad-
uated with a Master's degree in architecture from Tehran University,
winning his faculty's highest honour, and went on to design prestigious
buildings and also to obtain government recognition for a low-cost
housing system.[2] In 1976 the House of Justice selected him to design
the Temple in India.

In 1986, after the Temple opened, Mr Sahba and his family were
invited by the House of Justice to come to the Holy Land for pilgrimage, rest and consultation for one month. It was at that time that he

was informed of the decision of that body that a project to build the Terraces should proceed simultaneously with the Arc projects. It was clear that the Terraces – unlike the Arc buildings – would be open to the public, would attract domestic and international tourists and be a 'green lung' for the city.

These factors were to significantly contribute to the relationship between the Bahá'ís and Haifa residents during years of disruption to the city caused by the building development on Mount Carmel. It was to turn out, too, that a big advantage in having the two projects under way at once was that the massive excavations required for the three Arc buildings would produce the necessary amount of earth fill to adjust the levels of the slope for the Terraces, which were higher on the west than the east.

Other developments were clearing the way for the project ahead. At the end of April 1987 the House of Justice announced in a letter to Bahá'ís throughout the world that a status agreement had been signed with the Government of the State of Israel in which the legal position of the Faith in Israel was clarified and recognized.[3] The weighty responsibility of winning official recognition had taken some 35 years. The agreement recognized, among other things, that the Universal House of Justice was the Trustee of the Bahá'í International Community for the Holy Places of the Faith in Israel. The House of Justice said the agreement 'brings us within reach of the realization of the beloved Guardian's vision for the Arc on God's Holy Mountain', formidable obstacles having been thus removed.

In the same message the Universal House of Justice also said:

> In the meantime, we are happy to announce that the architect of the India Temple, Mr Fariborz Sahba, has been assigned the task of designing the Terraces to be situated below and above the Shrine of the Báb; he has also been appointed Project Manager[4] to execute the design already adopted for the three remaining buildings on the Arc.

After ten years working on the Indian Temple project, Mr Sahba, his wife and three children would soon shift their place of residence to Haifa.

On 31 August 1987, the House of Justice outlined in a letter to the Bahá'ís the history of the Shrine and the Guardian's plans for the Arc, and then spoke of the future:

Five closely related projects demand our attention: the erection of the three remaining buildings on the Arc and, added now to these, the construction of the terraces of the Shrine of the Báb and the extension of the International Archives Building.

The letter described the Terraces of the Shrine of the Báb:

In His plans for the development of Mount Carmel, 'Abdu'l-Bahá envisaged nineteen monumental terraces from the foot of the mountain to its crest, nine leading to the terrace on which the Shrine of the Báb itself stands, and nine above it. These plans were often referred to by Shoghi Effendi, and he completed in preliminary form the nine terraces constituting the approach to the Shrine from the central avenue of the former German Templer Colony.

. . . It is impossible at this stage to give an accurate estimate of the cost of these projects. All that we can now say is that in the immediate future two objectives have to be met: to accumulate rapidly a reserve of fifty million dollars on which plans for the construction can realistically begin to be implemented, and to provide an income of between twenty and twenty-five million dollars for the Bahá'í International Fund for each of the next ten years. As the work proceeds, contracts are signed and costs can be accurately determined, further information will be announced.

The great work of constructing the terraces, landscaping their surroundings, and erecting the remaining buildings of the Arc will bring into being a vastly augmented World Centre structure which will be capable of meeting the challenges of coming centuries and of the tremendous growth of the Bahá'í community which the beloved Guardian has told us to expect . . .[5]

How would these Terraces look? For Fariborz Sahba it would have been a daunting enough task to follow up a Temple design that had entranced the Bahá'ís, captivated the people of India and attracted millions of visitors. But his commission had an extra dimension of challenge. He had to produce a design that the Universal House of Justice would accept as one that would befittingly embellish the resting place of the Báb, the holiest place on earth for the Bahá'í Faith after the Shrine of Bahá'u'lláh.

Moreover, it was a project involving construction on a challenging site in a country with its own existential issues, and which had to be done to a strict timeline and in accordance with a budget relying on voluntary donations. Waiting to be solved were complex issues relating to town planning, land ownership, building permits and funds.

On 8 August 1988 Mr Sahba arrived in the Holy Land and established the office of Mount Carmel Bahá'í Projects (MCBP) to complete the design of the Terraces and to take up the task of project management of the Arc buildings.

A key move approved by the House of Justice was to separate the MCBP management from that of the departmental administration of the Bahá'í World Centre. That enabled a singular focus on the construction and allowed the departments and the construction team to be free from what would have been the difficult task of efficiently incorporating the new enterprise into existing procedures.

The MCBP office was to become the liaison between the House of Justice and consultants and contractors, and soon had on board a wide variety of talented specialists such as architects, horticulturists, mechanical and electrical engineers, site supervisors, gardeners and also volunteers.

To ensure the efficient management of the funds that would be donated for the project, Mr Sahba established his own finance team, and engaged an Israeli chartered accounting firm to ensure a constant auditing of the accounts. Based on a detailed assessment by a quantity surveyor,[6] the cost of the Arc and Terraces projects combined was estimated at US$250 million. The cost of the actual construction of the two Arc buildings would be $60 million each and the cost of the Terraces would also be $60 million. But in addition there was the cost of $70 million which was for such items as inflation, building permit and municipal fees, land purchases, consultants' fees, project management and supervision.

For the Terraces project, in the absence of a general contractor the MCBP became the construction manager. Due to the large scale of the Mount Carmel Projects, the progressive completion of the working drawings, the ongoing approvals of the town planning schemes and the issuing of building permits by the authorities, as well as land-ownership issues, the MCBP divided the project into seven distinct phases.[7]

The MCBP office was to approach each phase of the work and determine the most cost-and-time-effective way to complete it. This meant at times that MCBP would arrange for a local factory to work exclusively for the project, or it would provide the materials and employ specialists, or employ subcontractors on unit rates. The Bahá'ís did not carry out the bulk of the physical tasks. The MCBP would engage the necessary skilled staff members to supervise the work on both the Arc and the Terraces.[8]

5

PRELUDE AND INSPIRATION

The first known plan for the Terraces, a design by Haifa city engineer Dr Assaf Ciffrin in 1920, had won the approval of 'Abdu'l-Bahá, but his idea for a 'monumental stairway and cypress avenue' from the Templer Boulevard to the Shrine never became a reality and may not even have been committed to paper.

When prominent Bahá'í architect Charles Mason Remey visited him in 1922, Dr Ciffrin explained to him his project in general terms and gave him a tracing of the survey of the site but no design for the stairway. At the request of the Guardian, Mr Remey prepared a design. His plan for parallel terraces from top to bottom, with a tower at the top, appeared in a *Bahá'í World* volume,[1] but although Shoghi Effendi had published that design, it was not considered a plan that had to be followed when it came to the Terraces project decades later.[2]

In 1937 when William Sutherland Maxwell was in Haifa, Shoghi Effendi discussed with him a physical model[3] of stairways for the terraces leading down from the Shrine, and also spoke about a drawing of an iron gate that the Guardian was considering for the bottom terrace.

Two years later, in response to a request from Shoghi Effendi, Mr Maxwell drew a general design for the lower terraces – a front and side view – and also produced beautiful designs for an entrance plaza, including a gate and a fountain. The Guardian admired them but the scheme was never carried out because no agreement could be made with the Municipality.[4]

In the 1960s, the US architect Robert W. McLaughlin prepared some sketches but they were intended to show the long-term plans for the development of the steep rear slope of the mountain, not to propose a design. Fariborz Sahba had not seen any such sketches.

In 1987 Mr Sahba began work on his design in Vancouver, Canada where he had opened an office while completing arrangements for he and his family to become citizens of that country.

The brief was daunting. It was for a site on a 'challenging and dramatic' landscape that stretched over nearly a kilometre, starting at near sea level and gaining a height of some 225 metres, the slope reaching some 60 degrees in places. Mr Sahba remembered an injunction of the Báb's that when someone builds an edifice they should elevate it to the utmost state of perfection.[5] He prayed, meditated, and looked at Persian and Western traditions and other designs.[6]

'Any design starts with all of that as well as confusion and anxiety,' he recalled later.[7] 'However, before anything, I was looking for a story, something to start with and which could give me inspiration and be the reason for whatever would be my design. More than anything I was looking at the history and writings of the Báb and references to the Shrine.'

He contemplated the 'tragic and moving' life of the Báb, especially the last seven years between His declaration and His martyrdom. 'The whole history of this period – the execution of thousands of His followers, their heroic and dramatic martyrdom– is something that will remain the source of inspiration for artists for centuries to come,' he said.[8]

The architect kept in his office a photograph of the prison of Máh-Kú, a site he described as a 'bleak and sad castle at the top of a rocky cliff with no greenery'. That place of imprisonment influenced his eventual design: 'It is in memory of those dark nights in the prison of Máh-Kú, which the Báb described as not having even one lamp in His presence,[9] that this mountain has been flooded with light.'

Mr Sahba saw the contrast between the image in the photograph of Máh-Kú and the Shrine. 'They imprisoned this spiritual Sun in such a dark dungeon in the hope that His light would be extinguished. But that Sun rose from the other side of the world on this magnificent and beautiful Mount Carmel, in such a colourful and dramatic landscape in such a heavenly garden, so appropriately named "Vineyard of the Lord".'[10]

He was inspired by a prayer of the Báb revealed while He was in that mountain prison:

How can I praise Thee, O Lord, for the evidences of Thy mighty splendour . . .? Thou hast watched over Me in the heart of this mountain where I am compassed by mountains on all sides. One hangeth above Me, others stand on My right and My left and yet another riseth in front of Me . . . How often have I seen rocks from the mountain hurtling down upon Me, and Thou didst protect Me therefrom . . . Thou didst turn it [the prison] into a garden of Paradise for Me . . .'[11]

The architect also considered the Báb's references in the Persian Bayán,[12] revealed in Máh-Kú, to the Letters of the Living and to '18 mosques' in their names. He considered the meaning of the word 'mosque' (a place of prostration) and linked that to the Terraces. He saw the Shrine and its 18 terraces as symbolically representing the Báb surrounded by His 18 disciples, the Letters of the Living.[13] He also pondered the Báb's reference to '2001 lanterns'. This led him to design lights in the shape of hanging lanterns rather than as those found on lampposts. He thought of 'terraces of lights, lights upon lights', words conveying the vision of the Master.[14]

Mr Sahba contemplated a quotation from the Bible's Book of Revelation: 'Then the angel showed me the river of the water of life, as clear as crystal, flowing from the throne of God and of the Lamb.'[15] An outcome of this was a design for water runnels along the side of the stairway. It was also to influence his design of the entrance plaza, where water would appear to be flowing down from the Shrine of the Báb, the throne of God.[16]

The architect deeply pondered a reference by Shoghi Effendi in a message penned more than three and half decades previously. The Guardian had seen the Shrine as being in the midst of nine concentric circles, two outer circles being the planet and the Holy Land but all the others being on Mount Carmel itself. Mr Sahba's mind was drawn to the Guardian's reference to these circles existing in the visible plane, and sought to embody them physically in his design so that intimations of circles could be seen from below.[17]

Another source of inspiration was the design of the superstructure of the Shrine: 'It is so elegant and special. It has blended the architecture of the east and west in such a unique and extraordinary manner that it really touches the heart of the visitor.' And so it became clear to the architect as he meditated upon his design that the Terraces 'had to be in harmony with the Shrine of the Báb, and blend the architectural styles of the east and the west'.[18]

'The gardens around the Shrine of the Báb, originally designed by Shoghi Effendi, are also most inspiring because of their simplicity, elegance and order,' he said. 'All these elements together create a very special spiritual atmosphere,' he added, noting the 'wonderful display of the colour green . . . Green, in fact, was the colour of the Báb Himself, the colour He always dressed in.'

The gardens, Mr Sahba said, were a magnificent blend of the landscape of east and west. 'They bring the fragrance of the gardens of Shiraz, where the Báb was born, the symbol of which is cypress trees and orange blossoms, the magnificent geometry and order of the gardens of Kashmir, and at the same time reflect the beautiful English gardens all in one place.'

All these influences gave Fariborz Sahba the inspiration for the preliminary design of the garden Terraces.

Was there an 'eureka moment'? Mr Sahba: 'There were several moments that parts of the design came to me part by part.'[19]

It took him one year to make the overall model of the concept design: 'The first model was approved [by the Universal House of Justice] in general but different parts were approved in stages: the Shrine and its first five lower Terraces; Panorama road and its entrance plaza; Hatzionut bridge and Terrace 11 entrance plaza.'[20] Images of models, drawings and a photographic montage appeared in a small, glossy booklet, *Mountain of the Lord*.[21] It was intended to stimulate support for the project amongst the Bahá'ís of the world. There was no time at this stage for the architect to attend to details such as the fountains. The pools in the shape of nine-pointed stars as seen in that booklet were not intended to be final but as just a part of the schematic concept that gave an overall impression.

What stood out in that publication, though, was the stunning image of the Shrine at the centre of circles produced by the terraces closest to it, with intimations of circles created by the curved shapes of the upper and lower terraces. The architect said: 'The terraces are in fact a tribute to the Shrine of the Báb, a prelude and approach to it. They are supposed to complement and enhance the Shrine,[22] and direct one towards it. If the Shrine can be considered a jewel, a diamond, the terraces are supposed to provide the most beautiful golden ring that will bring the beauty of the diamond to the fore, and provide a perfect setting for it . . . I consider the terraces a symbol of beauty, perfection and hope, the way the Báb described and wished life to be for the people of the world.'[23]

The House of Justice had made it clear to the architect that there was no deadline and that MCBP should work according to what were the reasonable requirements of the project. Mr Sahba set December 2000, the end of the 20th century, as the deadline, and the team supported the idea.[24]

6

THE DESIGN IN DETAIL

It was clear from the Master's description and the Guardian's construction that any new design would be for a stairway to go up to the Shrine through a series of nine terraces and then to continue behind the Shrine via another series of nine terraces to the peak. Accordingly Mr Sahba produced such a plan, with entrance plazas at the base and the summit.

As he was working on his design, he had to overcome the problem caused by the fact that a major road, Hatzionut Avenue, crossed the slope behind the Shrine. At first sight, this would have prevented a continuity of terraces from the base of Mount Carmel to its summit. An elevated bridge, with steps up to it from the garden behind the Shrine, and down on the other side, would not be a good solution. The architect came up with the idea of lowering the road instead.

Shoghi Effendi had thrown a bridge over Abbas Street in the 1930s but Hatzionut Avenue was a much busier and more significant thoroughfare and was lined with a myriad of communication, water and sewage lines. However, there would be an advantage to the Municipality if the road were lowered just behind the Shrine. As it existed, there was a traffic hazard caused by the road being steep before and after that flat section. If that 'bump' in the more or less constant slope were removed and the road lowered by almost five metres, it would become safer.

Not only that, but it later became evident that this would also allow for the widening of the road by an extra lane on the southern edge, a plan of the city since the time of the British Mandate. And it could be done without interfering with the Bahá'í gardens. It would also allow for the 'Pathway of the Kings' to continue uninterrupted over the bridge. The task was to convince the Municipality. After an extremely enthusiastic presentation of the idea by Mr Sahba to a city official in the presence of two other Bahá'ís, that official successfully recommended the idea.[1]

There was another problem too. The slope on the upper part of the mountain was dauntingly steep, so how could a stairway work? A solution arrived: providing two symmetrical flights of stairs on the outer curved borders of the terraces above the Shrine rather than going straight ahead like the terraces below, which would have created impossibly steep stairways. In addition, curved stairways when illuminated would create a halo effect over the Shrine at night. The places where there would be a single stairway on this rear section would maintain the continuity of the centre-line of the Terraces and the sense that there is a staircase going directly to the peak.

The Terraces

There were two possible ways to build the Terraces: to build walls and backfill behind to create a platform, as in the design published in the *Bahá'í World* volume in the 1920s, or to cut into the mountain. Mr Sahba chose the latter. That avoided creating an ascending series of high walls that could take away attention from the Shrine. Instead, with only a small wall in front to indicate the presence of a terrace, he saw the Terraces as sacrificing themselves for the Shrine.

The Terraces would be concave, built into the mountain, and this shape would be extended to the east and west through lines of cypresses interspersed with lanterns. This would create curved lines similar to parts of a circle, the upper terraces hinting at being the top of the circle, the lower terraces the bottom.

In all, they create the impression that if extended they would form nine concentric circles that seem to emanate from the Shrine, yet with the effect of directing attention to the building that is at the very centre. The architect was inspired by these words of the Guardian:

> For, just as in the realm of the spirit, the reality of the Báb has been hailed by the Author of the Bahá'í Revelation as 'The Point round Whom the realities of the Prophets and Messengers revolve,' so, on this visible plane, His sacred remains constitute the heart and centre of what may be regarded as nine concentric circles, paralleling thereby, and adding further emphasis to the central position accorded by the Founder of our Faith to One 'from Whom God hath caused to proceed the knowledge of all that was and shall

be,' 'the Primal Point from which have been generated all created things.'[2]

The stairway enters each terrace through ornamental iron gates, flanked by fluted-stone gateposts with ornaments and balustrades whose carved design echoes that of the lancet windows on the drum of the Shrine.

The fountains on the lower terraces are deliberately set to the side so that the stairway leads arrow-like to the Shrine with no obstacle in front of those ascending.

Although each terrace has similarities, they all have unique features, such as special fountains, paving design, benches or ornaments, and incorporate the idea that, although the 18 Letters of the Living together with the Báb would create one '*váhid*' – a unit of 19 as described in the Bayán, the Báb's most holy Book – yet each one was an individual with unique character. The architect pondered whether each terrace should be linked to an individual Letter of the Living but did not proceed with the idea. This decision was confirmed by the Universal House of Justice in 1994.[3]

The Terraces each have three distinct zones. The first is a formal central zone which is accessible to pilgrims and visitors, who can have close-up views of seasonal flowers and ornamental plants of lower height. The formal zone requires maximum care. The second zone to the east and west is a transition area, planted mainly with hardy, drought-resistant groundcover and bushes of medium height, and requires minimum irrigation. This zone then gradually merges with the third zone of high trees and natural forest with no need of any irrigation. This combination provided an overall impression of a vast green area while only a very small portion of it requires irrigation.

In the formal centre section, the staircase arrives at a paved area in an embellished rectangular design. Low fountains and pools flank this paved section. Each terrace has a fountain or fountains, ochre gravel areas with islands of formal gardens of lawn, flowers, shrubs, two canary palm trees[4] and lamp-posts reminiscent of those near the Shrine. There are carved stone benches for visitors.

Signature features of the gardens created by Shoghi Effendi are present on the side of the staircase, in the form of duranta hedges, vases of vermilion red geraniums, and globe-shaped lamps. Narrow-stepped channels or runnels carry water down both sides of the stairway, which is lined by cypress trees. Lawns on the sides are shaped in ways to complement and echo the forms of the Terraces.

The bridge over Abbas Street is a platform of the staircase. Cypresses and garden areas adorn its edges. Its garden is very similar to the gardens of the Terraces, and has eight-pointed stars on the lawn.

Five special elements

The architect has spoken of the special elements of the design: light, colour, water, stone and ornaments.[5]

Light

'The whole concept of the design is centred around light,' he said. The placement of the lanterns along the Terraces produces the intended impression of waves of light emanating from the highly-illuminated Shrine and creates the nine concentric circles around the edifice, the line of cypresses creating that impression during the day.

The design, he said, with its curved parallel surface of emerald-green lawns, and its rows of dark-green cypresses and the cold grey-green of the olives, sets up the palate on which the sunlight can paint its pictures, the images changing as the day moves on:

> The deliberate order and rhythm that have been used in all parallel concentric circles provide the comfort and relaxation that will contribute to the creation of a spiritual feeling. While walking towards the terraces all the lines appear to accompany the visitor. They are all in agreement with the visitor, there is no argument, no resistance, only continuity of space. One space merges with another endlessly. The same principle of water and rhythm is created by the lights at night. Waves of light emanating from the Shrine make them appear as 'terraces of light, light upon light'.[6]

The lanterns lining the stairway lead the viewer up to the very source of spiritual illumination, the Shrine of the Báb. And the Shrine with its dome, the architect said, has a magnificent relationship with the sky and with light, 'and this combination provides different displays of light generating different feelings at every hour of the day'.[7]

Colour

Colour, being the expression of light, is a vital part of the design, which incorporates seasonal flowers, groundcover, shrubs and trees chosen after a special study of colour combinations.

> For example, when jacaranda trees are in bloom, convolvulus has been chosen to complement as ground cover. This creates a purple season for the mountain, and the most beautiful display of purple combines with other colours that are in harmony or in decided contrast with purple.[8]

This colour design enables there to be a red season and a yellow and pink season. The two colours used most extensively are red, symbolizing the martyrdom of the Báb, and green, the colour He used in his clothing and which depicted his lineage.[9]

Water

A central element in the great gardens of ancient and modern Persia was water. The very foundation of those gardens reaches back to the time of Cyrus the Great (558–528 BC), who created a garden in his capital northeast of present-day Shiraz.

Although there is no actual description of that place, it was likely to be similar to another one belonging to Artaxerxes, described more than a century later by Xenophon. It was said to be the first where there were gravity-fed water rills and basins arranged in a geometric system.[10] The design that emerged from the mind of the architect of the Terraces is an interpretation of that ancient pattern, but this time on a steep slope instead of on the flat surface as in ancient Persia.

Rills, or runnels, carry water alongside the stairway and create the impression of water running from the top of the mountain to the base, although that is not the case. Along the way there are cascades formed by water enclosed in wide marble basins of pleasing geometric shapes overflowing to basins below. Fountains are a signature of the Terraces.

Water features also create a stunning entrance to the Terraces. A fountain sends water overflowing into surrounding ponds which form a nine-pointed star. Above that there is a cascade formed by water running down a ladder of carved marble, an inspiration from the Mughal gardens as seen in Kashmir.[11] Embedded lights illuminate it, creating an ethereal vision.

Stone

When Shoghi Effendi was planning to build the superstructure of the Shrine as designed by Mr Maxwell, he had hoped to use stone from the Holy Land. The conditions that prevented him from doing so had changed by the time the Terraces project was being planned.

The architect decided upon stone from the Galilee in his bid to maintain the overall appearance of the mountain, and for the gardens to be in keeping with the city. The stone would be like that found in the old buildings in the Templer colony below, and trees and plants would be mostly those already present on Mount Carmel. He chose a beige stone known as *sajur* for the balustrades and the walls, while for the steps and paved areas he selected tough *jatt* stone, named after the village where it was quarried.

A large range of stone was tested before selection. Jatt proved highly abrasion-resistant and would not wear out to produce the scallop-like appearance at the entrance of some old buildings. Ideal for stairways, jatt is also darker and not so reflective of light. Sajur had the lowest water absorption rating the architect and his team could find. It was suitable for decorative features. By not taking in moisture the stone would not go black through absorbing polluted moisture, as could be seen with other stone elsewhere in Haifa.

Ornaments

The ornaments gracing the Terraces are inspired by those that Shoghi Effendi had selected for the gardens he established in Haifa and in Acre. There is the signature eagle of the design of the one that stands on guard near Bahá'u'lláh's resting place at Bahjí, and the pedestals and vase-like planters have a familiar feel. The gates with their beautiful designs are in harmony with those put in place by the Guardian. However, there are great innovations in many aspects of the designs such as for the balustrades, the theme being harmony between eastern and western traditions.

1986–1999
Building the Terraces of Light

7

DUAL PROJECTS

The scope of the project to build the Terraces of the Shrine of the Báb was enormous, daunting in its physical dimensions alone.

The staircase with its terraces would climb about one kilometre up Mount Carmel, reaching a height of 225 metres. Its accompanying landscaping would span the mountain to widths ranging from 60 to 300 metres. At 41 metres in diameter, the upper terraces would be about six metres wider than those below the Shrine.

The project was also daunting because of the momentous decision to proceed simultaneously with both the Arc and Terraces projects. That would result in a construction site one kilometre wide along the mountain. Fortunately that decision brought its advantages, as the project manager pointed out: 'It represents savings in overheads, supervision costs and the utilisation of hundreds of tons of cubic metres of excavated material of the Arc project in the terraces.'[1]

The availability of that excavated material would prove vital in meeting the first of four significant challenges facing the MCBP team. This challenge was that the slope of the mountain behind the Shrine was not symmetrical, being higher on the western side. Great shiftings of earth would have to take place to level out the sides so that the upper terraces would be in line with the Shrine and the lower terraces.

The second challenge was the instability of the mountain on its upper slopes. The mountain is made of fractured boulders of lime and chalk. Boulders, stones and other material covered the slope. Excavation and stabilization measures were vital before the Terraces and their stairway could be pinned to the mountain, never to shift.

The MCBP team paid immense attention to this factor. Mount Carmel is on an earthquake fault line, more or less straight and continuous on both sides of the Bahá'í property on Mount Carmel. Fortunately, however, the fault becomes fractured within the property, which is a big advantage for the safety of construction and the stability of the buildings because of the distribution of force from any movement.

The third challenge was that for the 'Pathway of the Kings' to be continuous, the major thoroughfare of Hatzionut Avenue had to be lowered and a bridge built, all without interrupting the flow of the traffic.

The fourth was to keep the public onside. Considerable emphasis on public relations would be vital. A ten-year project creating jackhammer noise, dust and scars across a wide section of a beautiful city would test anybody's goodwill. Had the project involved just the Arc buildings, Haifa residents might have become restive because, although impressed by the beauty and dignity of the administration buildings, they knew those buildings would not be open to them for visits. However, the relationship with the Haifa residents did not sour, mainly because they realized that the construction of the Terraces would result in a public asset, beautifying their city. Locals would be able to visit them, as would tourists from all over the world.

The public support that emerged reinforced the resolve of the civic authorities to find solutions to town planning problems to assist the project, and it encouraged the Haifa Tourist Board to restore the German Templer Colony at the foot of Mount Carmel in harmony with the Terraces.

There was another factor that made the work challenging. The first *intifada*, a rising of Palestinians against the Israeli authorities, began in 1987 and lasted until 1993. The second such uprising began in 2000. The conflicts and tensions that arose were to hinder the supply of stone and the obtaining of permits from city and district offices, which were overwhelmed with the situation. Security became a real issue for the MCBP team. Due to travel restrictions it was impossible to hire West Bank labourers to work on the site. There were, however, many Arab Israelis working there, and labourers were recruited from Turkey, Romania and China.

Adding to the difficulties, the Bahá'í World Centre did not own all the property needed for the project. Long and patient negotiations were inevitable.

Fortunately, in October 1989, after strenuous and detailed negotiations led by Mr Sahba for MCBP, the local town planning committee and the city council of Haifa approved a town planning scheme that was essential for the Mount Carmel projects to begin. The granting of approvals was linked to the Bahá'í commitment to immediately start work.

The scheme, which was then to go before the district planning commission for final approval, included cancellation of two roads previously approved to cross Bahá'í lands and the lowering of the level of Hatzionut Avenue, and thereby permitted the construction of the terraces that would link the Shrine of the Báb with those adjacent to the Archives Building.[2]

And then there was the issue of funds, referred to by the House of Justice when it told the National Spiritual Assemblies in April 1989 that it rejoiced to announce the commencement of a geological survey that was an essential preliminary step towards the implementation of the Mount Carmel Projects.

The announcement said that the survey had sharpened the need for the accumulation of the US$50 million-dollar reserve called for to permit the initiation of major works. One third of that amount had so far been contributed. By about the end of the year, the survey was complete and more than half the required funds had been received.[3] The project was now ready to be carried out in its phases.[4]

8

1990: WORK BEGINS

In 1990 the Universal House of Justice made a major announcement to the Bahá'ís of the world relating to the 'stupendous collective undertaking'[1] on Mount Carmel:

> WITH FEELINGS OF PROFOUND JOY ANNOUNCE TO FOLLOWERS OF BAHÁ'U'LLÁH IN EVERY LAND THAT ON MORNING OF TWENTY-THIRD MAY, ONE HUNDRED AND FORTY-SIX YEARS AFTER THE DECLARATION OF THE BÁB, WORK ON EXTENSION TERRACES COMMENCED. THIS HISTORIC OCCASION MARKED BY VISIT HIS SHRINE AND SHRINE OF 'ABDU'L-BAHÁ BY THE HANDS OF THE CAUSE OF GOD AMATU'L-BAHÁ RÚḤÍYYIH KHÁNUM AND 'ALÍ-AKBAR FURÚTAN, THE MEMBERS OF THE UNIVERSAL HOUSE OF JUSTICE AND COUNSELLOR MEMBERS OF THE INTERNATIONAL TEACHING CENTRE WITH FARIBURZ SAHBA, ARCHITECT OF TERRACES AND MANAGER OF ARC PROJECT, TO PRAY FOR DIVINE CONFIRMATIONS ENABLE UNINTERRUPTED PROSECUTION THIS MAJESTIC ENTERPRISE.[2]

There was special historical significance in the presence of the Hands of the Cause in the Shrine on that occasion described by the House of Justice. Amatu'l-Bahá Rúḥíyyih Khánum had personally worked on the project established by the Guardian, her husband, to build the super-structure that had been designed by her father – himself appointed a Hand of the Cause in 1951. Mr Furútan, when he was a pilgrim 49 years previously, had walked with Shoghi Effendi in the gardens near the Shrine and had heard him say that in the future there would be nine additional terraces from the Shrine to the top of the mountain, each illuminated at night, a vision of 'light upon light'.[3]

Now, 37 years after the superstructure had been completed, the next major Shrine project had begun. Phase 1 started with the central terrace, Terrace 10, the one which had been the focus of so much Bahá'í history in the decades stretching back to the ministry of 'Abdu'l-Bahá.

There was no need to obtain a building permit to do work on that terrace, nor the terraces immediately below it, because it fitted under a landscaping category.[4] Under the direction of the MCBP team, a local firm extended and reinforced Terrace 10, working on the base and the facing of the 200-metre long retaining wall which Shoghi Effendi had built but which had begun to erode. The extensive restoration work on the wall involved injecting hundreds of tons of concrete and strengthening it with anchors. In addition, the team constructed a 1,000-square-metre storage building underneath, and extended the gardens eastward over it, making the terrace symmetrical on both sides of the Shrine.[5]

As had happened before in the history of this Holy Place, progress was taking place during a time of armed conflict in the region. In August 1990, war erupted 1,230 kilometres to the east when the military forces of Iraq invaded and annexed Kuwait. The government in Baghdad said that if any nation attacked Iraq it would retaliate against Israel.

In response, the Israeli authorities adopted civil defence measures, and in that context the Universal House of Justice looked at actions that could protect the Bahá'í Holy Places and those serving at the Bahá'í World Centre. Soon staff were learning about the use of gas masks, how to establish 'safe rooms' in their apartments, and what to do in case of air raids.

In October the Universal House of Justice said the Bahá'í World Centre would 'continue to function as usual, as it has during all the previous disturbances which have threatened or shaken the Holy Land.'[6]

The flow of Bahá'í pilgrims to the Shrine of the Báb halted after the House of Justice postponed pilgrimages in November and December, and later cancelled them until the end of March 1991.

9

THE GENERAL AND HIS TEAM

Increasing numbers of volunteers from Baháʾí communities in more than 30 nations around the world were putting their hands up to serve on the mighty project to build the Terraces of the Shrine of the Báb, the enterprise that originated from – and was directed and ultimately brought to victory by – the Universal House of Justice.[1] They were arriving to work in connection with contractors and labourers who were not members of the Faith and who did the actual physical construction work – these came not only from Israel but other countries as well.

Fariborz Sahba was the unquestioned general of this volunteer army and those with whom they worked. He not only had designed the Terraces but had the energy, single-minded determination and charisma to drive his team forward. He led from the front in his dedication to meet what he referred to as 'divine deadlines'. Seemingly ever-present on the site, he paid such attention to safety issues that there were no major injuries in the decade-long project, a record perhaps unparalleled on construction sites in similar difficult terrain. As one who served as his secretary recalled:

> Mr Sahba was an unbelievable taskmaster. He had no patience for slackness; he wanted things done right, and on schedule. In one of our staff meetings he said that he knew everyone was trying to work hard and do their best, but had received complaints about 'not enough family time' . . . He knew it required a lot of hard work and dedication and sacrifices for families, his own included, and basically said, 'If you can't stand the heat, get out of the kitchen!' He stated that none of us were irreplaceable.[2]

The writer Eliza Rasiwala, who chronicled the project, wrote:

The Shrine of the Báb and its environs before the Terraces project began

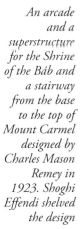

An arcade and a superstructure for the Shrine of the Báb and a stairway from the base to the top of Mount Carmel designed by Charles Mason Remey in 1923. Shoghi Effendi shelved the design

Photo: The Bahá'í World, vol. V (1932–1934), p. 241

At a door to the Shrine of the Báb are former member of the Universal House of Justice Dr Lotfullah Hakim and author Gloria Faizi (née 'Alá'í). In an obituary, Mrs Faizi's husband, the Hand of the Cause Abu'l-Qásim Faizi, wrote that Dr Hakim 'would accompany the pilgrims to the Holy Shrines, urging them to pray also for the friends who were not there'. Dr Hakim attended the funeral ceremony of 'Abdu'l-Bahá at the Shrine in 1921

Fariborz Sahba, the architect of the Terraces of the Shrine of the Báb, and the project manager for their construction. Behind him are some early drawings of his design

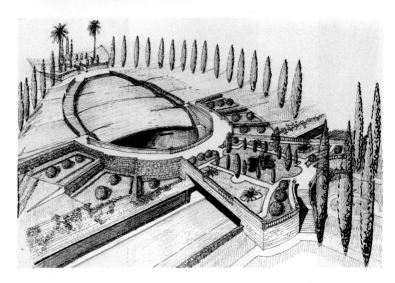

An early concept drawing of the Hatzionut bridge before modifications

A beautiful early depiction of Terrace 9

Photos: Courtesy of Fariborz Sahba

Early models of preliminary designs for the Terraces

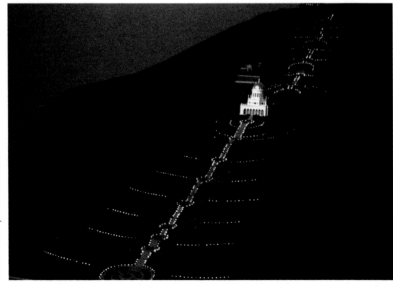

Photos: Courtesy of Fariborz Sahba

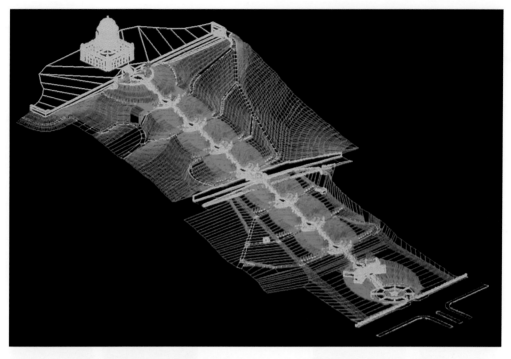

A computer depiction of the Shrine, the lower terraces and the entrance plaza

A computer rendition of the design for the lower terraces and Abbas Street bridge

Photos: Courtesy of Fariborz Sahba

The top of the entrance plaza and some of the lower terraces, a computer design

Terrace as designed on a computer

Terrace as designed on a computer

Photos: Courtesy of Fariborz Sahba

Hands of the Cause Amatu'l-Bahá Rúhíyyih Khánum and 'Alí-Akbar Furútan are with Members of the Universal House of Justice and the International Teaching Centre as Fariborz Sahba points to aspects of the Mount Carmel projects he is managing

Members of the Universal House of Justice looking at plans, with Fariborz Sahba and Hossein Amanat

Israeli statesman Shimon Peres is shown the model of the Terraces by the architect

Architect Fariborz Sahba and a colleague examine a drawing of the Terraces prior to construction

Photos: Courtesy of Fariborz Sahba

Hand of the Cause Amatu'l-Bahá Rúḥíyyih Khánum, members of the International Teaching Centre and others listen as Fariborz Sahba describes aspects of the Terraces project

At the factory owned by Mr Noufi outside Nazareth, Fariborz Sahba inspects one of the ornaments for the terraces

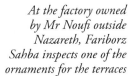

At Bahjí, Fariborz Sahba measures an urn to assist with similar decorative features on the terraces of the Shrine of the Báb

Photos: Courtesy of Fariborz Sahba

In the early days of the project, the site of the future Terraces was mostly bare earth, but canary palms are visible on the lower terraces. The Abbas Street bridge is under way

Work began first on the lower terraces. In April 1992, the foundations of the steps up which will proceed the kings and rulers were still visible

Preparing to build the Abbas Street bridge. Canary palms are in place on the terraces leading down from the Shrine

Mr Sahba comes across as a reserved and dignified person to those briefly acquainted with him. But to those who know him well, he can be charming, expressive and humorous. But the overriding impression he gives is that of a strong personality, a man with a mind of his own. Mr Sahba is passionate about his work and absolutely dedicated to his profession, an architect par excellence.

Never one to shirk responsibility, he was a workaholic who drove his team hard. A perfectionist to the core, Mr Sahba could not tolerate sub-standard work. And perhaps for this reason he was not the most popular man around . . . Mr Sahba always drove a hard bargain. He particularly demanded quality work at reasonable prices, and always maintained a tight grip on quality control.

The scale of the projects was such that it was inevitable that the citizens of Haifa would be inconvenienced by the dust, noise and disruption in traffic resulting in unhappiness while the projects were underway. Here Mr Sahba's excellent skills in public relations came to the rescue in minimizing adverse reactions.

Also, despite most of the team members being volunteers, Mr Sahba was able to extract commitment to complete tasks before finishing their term of service ensuring that no delays would occur because of the changing workforce.[3]

Mr Sahba explained in later years how he coped with the personal stress:

It [the stress] was beyond imagination but I would comfort myself by the fact that we were tools to fulfil the divine vision of our beloved Guardian who understood the great Vision of Bahá'u'lláh for the Mountain of the Lord.[4]

His headquarters were in the building next to the resting place of the Greatest Holy Leaf. It was that house that the Master's wife, Muním Khánum, had built for a girls' school but never used as such. For three weeks in 1939 it had hosted the remains of the son and wife of Bahá'u'lláh prior to their reinterment on the Arc. It had also been an office for the Guardian of the Faith when he visited the precincts of the Shrine to carry out his work.

In that office the project manager saw contractors for meetings which were often fiery. Using funds donated sacrificially by Bahá'ís around the world, Mr Sahba would not tolerate any attempts to overcharge or mislead and would convey this vigorously and directly to some contractors, who would reply in similar style. Relations with other contractors were cordial and over the years contractors of all stripes came to respect the man who had exacting standards, who could neither be cowed nor conned, but who would always pay fairly.

The deputy project manager and chief quantity surveyor was Stephen (Steve) Drake, a New Zealand Bahá'í who had previously worked on building the Bahá'í Temple in Samoa, a beautiful structure designed by Hossein Amanat. Mr Drake had worked not for the Bahá'ís but for the firm which was constructing the Temple. He was initially engaged as a quantity surveyor for the Arc buildings and the Terraces, but later in 1995 was appointed by Mr Sahba as his deputy, and then as work became more intense on the Terraces he focused more and more on that project.[5]

Mr Sahba took steps to ensure that should anything happen to him, the project could continue by means of an emergency plan. Mr Drake would take on the responsibility of the project management and Mrs Sahba would oversee the execution of the design.

Mr Drake's roles included responsibility for details of contracts. He kept the accounts in various foreign currencies and authorized all payments. He was responsible for estimates, budget control, financial reports and ordering of materials both local and overseas. He liaised directly with the local stonemasons, checking every stone that was cut and sent to Italy for machining into balustrade pieces. On site, Mr Drake measured the work to ensure it was accurate and complete. As deputy to Mr Sahba, he was his 'wing man' in negotiations, giving him the facts he needed and attending to the paperwork. Of his boss, he said he was 'born for the project', was a very creative designer, would make tough decisions, was incredibly astute and an amazing negotiator, was no micro-manager, and cared for his staff.[6]

Also in the main office was a talented designer, Golnar Sahba (née Rafiei), the wife of the architect. She had worked on the India Temple project, contributing to the design of fences, gates and benches, and had worked on the content and graphic design of the panels in the Temple's information centre.

Mrs Sahba worked closely with the architect on the Terraces projects. Her exquisite design contributions can be seen in the gates, fountains, ornaments, paving, tiles, balustrades and other features. At the conclusion of the project, the architect said: 'She has not only been the support and inspiration for me throughout these difficult years, but as a designer has worked closely with me and we have consulted upon almost every aspect of the design.'[7]

Soon the team, which included design and supervision as well as facility and maintenance personnel, built up to about 100 staff from many nationalities, with departures and arrivals over the years. There were experts in irrigation, structural and mechanical engineering, architecture, management, gardening, horticulture, design and sculpture.

MCBP staff often collaborated with the contractors as if they were working for them, but no actual construction work was taken on by the Bahá'ís themselves. On some occasions MCBP acted as a contractor by employing workers and machinery to work for the office instead of a contractor. Occasionally MCBP provided material and expertise to contractors who could not find them at fair prices.

Like most Bahá'ís, the volunteer staff were familiar with the sacred Writings about the Báb and His Shrine and also with the remarks that 'Abdu'l-Bahá and Shoghi Effendi had made about the project to complete its precincts with terraces above and below the holy spot.

MCBP staff had decided to forgo the salaries they could have been earning in their homelands, and instead, like all other staff at the Bahá'í World Centre, they worked for no monetary compensation, receiving only the recompense for the daily expenses of moderate living in Haifa. Staff meetings led by the project manager were usually about deadlines and high standards, but there were also morale-boosting events with dinners and parties for the whole staff where often some members of the Universal House of Justice were also present. Often, though, some staff were so busy they could not attend.

The workload was heavy and the hours were long. A few staff were present throughout the project, others for varying lengths of time. They found the work mentally and physically challenging yet inspiring. Morale was high, with the team conscious that they were all working on something of immense historical importance and of great value to humanity. There was humour too. At an interdepartmental beach party, the MCBP staff took along a movie banner, designed by Steve Drake. It had photos of the staff on it.[8] In a play on the popular 1981 film *Raiders of the Lost Ark*, the banner was labelled 'Builders of the Last Arc'. Mr

Sahba was depicted as the main character of the movie, Indiana Jones, and wielding Indiana's trademark whip.

These Bahá'í volunteers worked tirelessly for long hours and with meticulous attention to quality, and drove themselves forward to meet what seemed to others to be impossible deadlines. They did so with good spirit and forged good relations with others. They were to achieve the goal set for them by the Universal House of Justice in accordance with the vision of the Master.

10

1991: WORKING DESPITE WAR

At the start of 1991 it was clear that war was on the horizon. On 17 January, staff at the Bahá'í World Centre received instructions to have their gas masks with them at all times. Two days later, after the armed forces of 34 nations led by the United States began to wage war against Iraq, all work on the site was suspended. About 3.15 a.m. the next day, staff woke up to the sound of explosions and air-raid sirens as Iraq launched its retaliation, firing rockets at targets near Haifa. Again the Bahá'ís suspended work.[1]

During the war, which ran from 17 January to 28 February 1991, six missiles landed in the Haifa and Acre areas, damaging property but not people. The Shrine of the Báb and all other Bahá'í properties remained untouched. There were only four days on which the Bahá'ís suspended work, and only eight days when they reduced their working hours.

Although office staff worked part-time, the MCBP team – their gas masks with them – maintained normal hours, surprising and impressing the local authorities.[2] They provided rudimentary safe rooms on the site, containers with a plastic sheet over the front doors.[3]

By the time the war ended, most of the work on Terrace 10 was complete, including the restoration of the water cistern built by 'Abdu'l-Bahá at its northwestern base and the building of a small pool adjacent to it.[4]

Good news came on the financial front. Donations flowing in from Bahá'ís around the world had reached the US$50 million reserve which the House of Justice had set before any major construction could start.[5]

The Shrine building itself soon became the focus of attention. High up on scaffolding, staff plastered the ceiling of the colonnade, work which had not been completed at the time of its construction.

The colonnade of the Shrine had long been dimly lit, but that was to change. The design for its lights made by architect William Sutherland Maxwell was located and sent to Spain for the fabrication of its beautiful brass fixtures.[6] When these arrived, the team affixed the new lights, illuminating the promenade around the Shrine. They also washed the superstructure and repainted the inside of the dome.

There was clearly a need to stop rainwater seeping into the interior via the small cracks between the joints of the tiles and where the tiles joined the ribs.[7] The team injected the interior with a special jelly-like glue that would be impermeable under the plaster, stopping the water but not providing a permanent solution. They also built scaffolding inside the dome to improve access to both its interior and exterior.

The plan was to complete the lower terraces before those on the steep slopes behind the Shrine. Accordingly, on 17 June, Phase II began with work on the construction of Terraces 9 down to Terrace 3.

Olive trees on the lower terraces had been removed and planted in rows on the Temple site in Haifa. Years later they were replanted back on the terraces.[8]

1992: FOCUS ON LOWER TERRACES

In 1992 earthworks continued right down from Terrace 9 to Terrace 5, bringing big changes to the appearance of the slope below the Shrine.

On Terraces 6 and 7 the MCBP team made a surprising discovery – a small cave with three old terracotta coffins. They immediately stopped the earthworks and reported the find to official Israeli antiquity experts. Specialists arrived and with great care opened the cave and the coffins, which were of a child and two adults. They were dated as being from Byzantine times. Within a week, the coffins were removed and taken away for further study, and work continued.

The MCBP set up an experimental garden to the side of Terrace 8 to test various types of grass so as to find those best suited to a site that faced the sea, where plants grew slowly, needed minimum water and would not lose their green colour during a cold winter or hot summer. In addition, in this experimental garden they tested various types of hedges, groundcover and flowers.

A Holy Year began in April to mark the centenary of the passing of Bahá'u'lláh. It was the second Holy Year in the Faith's history, and it revived memories among elderly Bahá'ís of the first in 1952–1953 when the golden dome of the Shrine of the Báb had been brought to glorious completion.

Some 3,000 Bahá'ís attended commemoration events at Bahjí at the end of May. Among the invited participants were those people named 'Knights of Bahá'u'lláh' for being the first to introduce the Faith to various countries and territories during that Holy Year. All participants had the opportunity to ascend Mount Carmel from its foot and to then circumambulate the Shrine, the first such ascent by a large group of Bahá'ís since 1968. For them, it was also an opportunity to view the first stages of the Terraces project and to get an eye-witness under-standing of its magnitude. When they returned home they spread the word about the wondrous vision unfolding on Mount Carmel.

Other memories too stirred among some older Bahá'ís when work began that year on Terraces 4 and 5. This major construction entailed building a new bridge over Abbas Street, the road which bisects the slope below the Shrine and which had been named after the Master. Shoghi Effendi had directed similar work more than five decades previously when he had built a bridge over that same road to enable him to continue building a line of terraces down Mount Carmel.[1]

Mr Drake described the demolition, which was carried out at night: 'All the neighbours turned out to supervise the demolition work, and after a lot of shouting and the customary arm-waving, everyone instructed the bulldozer driver what to do. The driver, under a blaze of floodlights, ignored everyone and demolished the bridge his way, in just over 20 minutes.'[2]

In modern times, the narrow road had been busy with traffic. The new bridge was constructed with minimum traffic disturbance. Soon vehicles passed under the bridge, which initially had a raw look until later beautifully dressed with sajur stone.

The architect clearly had a special affection for this part of the project: 'Because of the name of the street and its connection to 'Abdu'l-Bahá, Who was dearly loved by the people of His era, I wanted this bridge to look very friendly and romantic as a part of a secret garden of Eden,' he said.[3]

In November some 27,000 people attended the second Bahá'í World Congress in New York City, making it the biggest gathering of Bahá'ís ever to assemble. Fariborz Sahba gave repeated presentations on the Terraces and Arc projects to packed audiences. The enthusiasm generated boosted understanding and support for the historic enterprise.

In the last month of the year, contracts were signed to allow work to begin on the daunting steep upper face of the mountain. This involved developing the top five terraces, from Terrace 15 right up to 19 at the crest.

As part of this Phase III of the Mount Carmel projects, massive excavations were taking place at the eastern end of the Arc on the site of the future International Teaching Centre building, following equally extensive work the year before on the western side. The material excavated was to prove very useful on the Terraces project a few hundred metres to the west.

12

1993: UPPER TERRACES

In April, in its annual Riḍván message, the Universal House of Justice announced a three-year worldwide plan for the Baháʼís in which it said the World Centre would be 'pursuing with deliberate speed the gigantic building projects on God's Holy Mountain' and that by the end of the plan seven terraces below the Shrine would have been completed. It said these projects 'constitute part of a process clearly perceived by Shoghi Effendi as synchronizing with two no less significant developments: the establishment of the Lesser Peace and the evolution of Baháʼí national and local institutions'.[1]

By this time, the face of the mountain overlooking Ben Gurion Avenue was a giant construction site. Moving thousands of cubic metres of earth through the narrow streets around the Arc and the Shrine to where it was needed for the terraces would inevitably involve dust, noise and traffic disruption for the local residents. Public support was an important component of the project, so Mr Sahba took time to explain to those living in areas neighbouring the site, and to city representatives, how the work would be done and what would be the eventual result. He presented a slide programme in a public hall in Haifa to a capacity audience and answered questions from the public.

By May 1993 the residents of Haifa had some indication of what was to come. After the grading and structuring of Terrace 9 down to Terrace 5, there were plantings of grass and trees. They soon produced what appeared 'lush green carpets',[2] giving the first real hint of their future beauty.

The upper terraces, however, were unrelieved by vegetation. There was a huge expanse of earth and rock. It became an active site of excavation and grading as the MCBP team rebalanced the slope. Trucks hauled to the site an initial 10,000[3] and then another 50,000 cubic metres of rock,[4] which had been excavated from the Arc sites and would now help support and balance the levels. This fill material shaped stretches of about 100 metres on both sides.[5]

It was also vital to reinforce the slope. Mount Carmel is composed mostly of soft and fractured limestone, which is prone to crumble under heavy weight.[6] The design ensured that the Terraces would sit on huge quantities of concrete and boulder walls, called debish walls. These were unreinforced, concrete, pyramidal structures in which there was no steel reinforcing because steel would rust and affect the life of the structure. The stability provided by these walls protected the delicate carved stone and fountains from the constant movement of the mountain.

Funds

As the physical work gathered speed, so did the appeals for funds.

In June, the Universal House of Justice sent a letter to the Bahá'ís of the world in which it said the development of the terraces was 'proceeding apace'. But the House of Justice also said that to ensure the uninterrupted progress of the rapidly accelerating construction work, a sacrificial effort was needed from all the Bahá'ís to contribute to the US$74 million Arc Projects Fund during the current Three Year Plan.[7]

Another letter sent to the Bahá'ís of the world in October on behalf of the Universal House of Justice described the priority for various funds of the Bahá'í Faith, and made it clear that the most challenging and urgent of the tasks facing the Bahá'í community was 'the completion of the Mount Carmel Projects – the Terraces of the Shrine of the Báb and the raising of the three new structures of the Administrative Centre of the Cause.'[8] It was a major challenge, the letter said, but one 'well within our capacity to meet – and the time for the completion of these projects is now'. The letter continued:

> It is inevitable that in a project of such size, a large portion of the money will have to come from those Bahá'ís who are endowed with wealth, whether this be to a moderate degree or of a considerable magnitude. The US$74,000,000 called for during the years of the Three Year Plan is a sum that is difficult for many friends to visualise. Some have written to suggest means of making the contribution of this large sum manageable.
>
> One suggested the idea of breaking it into units. Thus, to assist

in visualizing this sum one can regard it as being a little over eight thousand units of $9,000 each. Individuals with means can use this as a measure of whether they feel able, with sacrifice, to give one or more units of $9,000 in this time. Local communities or other groups may wish to set collective goals on such a unit basis. This may be helpful but, of course, contributions of any size will constitute a vital part of the stream of means for the accomplishment of this historic enterprise.[9]

The first unit of this endeavour came from the staff of the Mount Carmel Bahá'í Projects.[10] Then, throughout the world, in communities big and small, Bahá'ís consulted on how to raise the funds and then went ahead and made their contributions.

City visitors and plans

In December, Israeli officials visited the site. Among them was the Mayor of Haifa, Mr Aryeh Gurel, who had been an enthusiastic and visionary supporter of the project throughout the complicated years of its inception.[11] He was within a few days of the expiration of his term in office. Shortly afterwards, on 8 December, his successor, Mr Amram Mitzna, together with his deputy, the city engineer and the general manager of the Haifa Tourist Board, viewed the progress and received a two-hour presentation on the developments from the project manager. Mr Mitzna, like his predecessor, was to become an ardent advocate of the Terraces project.

Another important visit was by the Director-General of the Israel Government tourist corporation, who came with nine members of his office and local officials. Other prominent visitors to the Shrine of the Báb in 1993 included the Deputy Prime Minister of Papua New Guinea, later Prime Minister, Sir Julius Chan.[12]

A week before the end of the year, a Haifa weekly newspaper broke the news that, largely for tourism purposes, the Haifa Municipality would be developing the 'German colony', which was one of the oldest developments in Haifa. It would restore this area, centred around Ben Gurion Avenue, to how it was just after the arrival of the German Templers, the time immediately before Bahá'u'lláh first came there in 1868. The Municipality would link this project with the Bahá'í developments.

A steering committee of the Municipality invited Mr Sahba to become one of its members. Others included the Haifa city engineer and senior representatives of the Ministry of Tourism and the Israel Land Authority.

In fact, Mr Sahba had initiated discussions about the restoration of the German colony with local officials shortly after he arrived in Haifa. Together with distinguished Israeli historian Professor Alex Carmel, he had presented a seminar called 'From Mountain to Sea', in which he had incorporated the vision of 'Abdu'l-Bahá.

He was soon to successfully propose as an initial step the aligning of the centreline of Ben Gurion Avenue with the Shrine of the Báb, a change from its then current deviation of 1.86 metres. A survey had found that the buildings of the German colony were not built on very straight lines and it was impossible to align the complete length of Ben Gurion Avenue with the Shrine, so it was decided to align the beginning of it near Hagefen Street and gradually merge it to the old centreline of the colony. As a result Ben Gurion Avenue became a gradual curve.[13]

13

1994: SACRIFICIAL OUTPOURING

In the first week of 1994, as the Terraces project was gathering momentum, the Universal House of Justice sent out a rousing message in which it called upon the Bahá'ís of the world to sustain 'this vast collective enterprise' through 'a sacrificial outpouring of material resources' and through their dedication to the work of the Faith.

In its message, drawing especially on the explanations of Shoghi Effendi, the House of Justice put into spiritual and historical perspective the raising of buildings and construction of the Terraces, which were, it said, of 'profound significance' and were 'central to the work of the Faith in eradicating the cause of the appalling suffering now afflicting humanity'. The message noted that 'the crisis now engulfing every part of the planet is essentially spiritual', and proclaimed that the construction projects were part of the pattern of a world order that would resolve the problems affecting humankind.

The House of Justice said the edifices on the Arc and the Terraces under construction were also an expression of the Faith's emergence from obscurity and of the determining role it was ordained to play in the affairs of humanity. It then gave the worldwide Bahá'í community a mighty vision that would often be quoted in the years to come:

> The future significance of the Terraces is evident from their characterization by Shoghi Effendi as 'the Pathway of the Kings and Rulers of the World'.[1] The beauty and magnificence of the Gardens and Terraces now under development are symbolic of the nature of the transformation which is destined to occur both within the hearts of the world's peoples and in the physical environment of the planet.
>
> Mount Carmel was extolled by the prophet Isaiah almost three thousand years ago, when he announced that 'it shall come to pass in the last days, that the mountain of the Lord's house shall be

established in the top of the mountains, and shall be exalted above the hills; and all nations shall flow unto it'. Now, with the coming of the Lord of Hosts, His devoted servants throughout the world have been summoned to the momentous undertaking with which the fulfilment of this ancient promise is associated. As they dedicate themselves to this mighty task, let them draw inspiration from these Words of Bahá'u'lláh: 'Carmel, in the Book of God, hath been designated as the Hill of God, and His Vineyard. It is here that, by the grace of the Lord of Revelation, the Tabernacle of Glory hath been raised. Happy are they that attain thereunto; happy they that set their faces towards it'.[2]

Funds flooded in, more than US$7.5 million in the three months from February to April 1994. There was about $58 million still required to reach the goal. The House of Justice expressed its confidence that the Bahá'ís would achieve it.[3]

Excerpts from the House of Justice's message received front page coverage in a new publication that MCBP launched that same month, *Vineyard of the Lord.* Fariborz Sahba, who had publishing experience in Iran and India, was the managing editor; Eliza Rasiwala was the reporter and writer; and Ruhi Vargha the photographer. For the next seven years the publication would take the news and photographs of the Mount Carmel projects to eager Bahá'í readers around the world.

Planning

To enable the whole Terraces project to go ahead, the secular local and national authorities in the Holy Land had to give their blessing by way of planning permission.

Negotiations involving Mr Sahba had been under way with the planning authorities since 1988 to ensure that the old town planning scheme, instituted in the days of the Guardian, would be replaced with one that recognized the Bahá'í development projects on Mount Carmel. The old scheme had caused concerns for Shoghi Effendi in the 1940s and 1950s. He had recorded his objection to that scheme because it could have allowed key areas of the slope to be bisected by new roads (for example, a road crossing the mountain above the site where now sits the seat of the Universal House of Justice) or used for other buildings. The scheme also allowed the widening of existing roads, including Hatzionut Avenue. Had these provisions been enforced they would have prevented the construction of the upper terraces and the buildings on the Arc.[4]

In February 1994, the District Committee of Galilee approved the town planning scheme the Bahá'í World Centre submitted. Its draft had appeared some months earlier in the Official Gazette of the Government of Israel. This gave the Bahá'ís great satisfaction. *Vineyard of the Lord* summed up the significance:

> The modified Town Planning scheme not only incorporates the Bahá'í plans for construction, but also resolves the problems of road extensions and traffic, recognises the spiritual significance of the Bahá'í endowments, avoids intrusions into the Bahá'í properties and addresses the code of behaviour for the general public while approaching these sites.[5]

On 10 May 1994, the Mayor of Haifa told the MCBP office that Israeli Prime Minister Yitzhak Rabin had affixed his ceremonial signature to the scheme in his role as acting Minister of the Interior.

Rabin's signature, reported *Vineyard of the Lord*, was 'the final stamp of authority' and it paved the way for the 'uninterrupted implementation' of the Terraces and Arc buildings:

> This approval brings with it not only protection to our Holy Shrines, and recognition by the Government of Israel of the extraordinary significance of the gardens surrounding the Shine of the Báb and the Mount Carmel Bahá'í projects, but in a way, reinforces the recognition of special status conceded to all Bahá'í Holy Places.[6]

In June, Prime Minister Rabin, accompanied by the Mayor, visited the site of the Terraces project where Mr Sahba described the work. The Prime Minister also visited the Pilgrim House. The architect showed him a model of the project on display there, and then escorted him to Terrace 9 where he viewed the lower terraces and expressed interest in the linkage of the project with the restoration of the German Templer colony below. In August the Israeli Foreign Minister of Israel, Shimon Peres, after being briefed and viewing the models, visited the construction site to see for himself the progress being made.

Another prominent visitor was the Egyptian Minister of Tourism, Mamdouh Lel Beltagi, his viewing of the project organized in response to a request by the Mayor of Haifa.[7]

Upper terraces

Meanwhile, the eastern edges of the upper terraces were getting a new look. Staff planted trees there, some 300 years old, and sowed the seeds of wild flowers.

Nurseries at the Bahá'í Temple site on Mount Carmel, at Bahjí and in the Riḍván gardens, grew trees and a variety of plants to help satisfy the ongoing requirement for more trees, shrubs and flowers. Some 700 cypress trees had been propagated, and in an experimental section nursery staff were testing different plant and flower species for their variety of colours, and to see how they handled water conservation, seasonal changes and disease on the slope of Mount Carmel.[8]

The MCBP team removed a labyrinth-style garden area which years before Fujita, the well-known Japanese assistant to the Master and the Guardian, had made to the west of the International Archives Building.

The failure of winter rains caused problems for local residents but was a blessing for the Terraces project, allaying fears that the topsoil would be eroded, and allowing work to continue with few hours lost. Trucks transported in some 5,000 square metres of lawn, which had been grown outside Haifa on a farm. The team put the lawn in place on the lower terraces.

From the city below, the general shape of the terraces was becoming apparent. Way up near the top, concrete steps were in place on Terraces 17 and 18. They sat on top of underground walls made of rubble and concrete, walls which went down as far as 12 metres. Below that, on Terraces 15 to 18, the work continued to be particularly difficult and required special access paths.

It was easier to get to the other levels. There was access to Terrace 19 from Yefe Nof Street. Terraces 12, 13 and 14 could be reached via Crusader Road, which came across to the Bahá'í property through a residential area to the west. Access to Terrace 11 was from Hatzionut Avenue.

To catch any material that might roll down the slope, the team used the ancient techniques of building rubble walls at intervals, but even more than that was needed on those upper reaches of the site where precariously perched excavators worked on slopes as steep as 30 to 45 degrees. The team erected net fences to catch the rocks and rubble that inevitably tumbled down the slopes and which otherwise could smash into workers and machinery on the site and, further down, hit pedestrians and traffic on Hatzionut Avenue. The capturing of runaway rock and stones, especially as they started to gather speed, was a dramatic sight.

Down below, the earthworks were now complete on Terraces 3 and 4 and retaining walls were in place.

Underground rooms

On the western side of all but one terrace, the team built underground mechanical rooms to a depth of seven metres, a huge task mostly completed by the middle of 1994.[9] The rooms housed the fountains' mechanical systems, as well as the controls for lighting the terraces and the pools. On Terrace 18 they built the room on the eastern side.

On the lower terraces these rooms were two-storeyed, the upper section used to store tools and supplies. It took one of the largest cranes in Israel to install a big transformer in the mechanical room on Terrace 6.

Stone

Ships sailed from Haifa to Italy carrying jatt stone that had been quarried in the Galilee and cut into workable blocks in a factory near Nazareth owned by a Catholic Arab, Mr Noufi.[10] Once the stone was unpacked, the artisans of the Margraf Spa factory[11] shaped it into balustrades for the terraces. In conjunction with the MCBP team, they created a new stone-cutting process employing a machine that had a computer disc which would enable it to cut in three dimensions. Then, as in the days of the superstructure construction more than 40 years earlier, ships took the carved stone from Italy to Haifa. By March, they had delivered 700 of the 2,400 balustrades required, each one costing about US$600.

Meanwhile, workers in Noufi's factory bush-hammered the jatt stone to texturize it to make it slip-resistant for use on the stairways. They used small hammers to create two sorts of finish, one fine and one coarse.[12]

By the middle of 1994, the factory was a hive of activity. In about ten working sheds, the artisans were working on the sajur stone mantles of the fountains for Terraces 9 to 6. Stone for the project seemed to be everywhere in the 10,000-square-metre premises.

Sculptures

In a shed-cum-studio at the western side of the property on the top of Mount Carmel, staff of the MCBP's ornaments workshop carried out their task to create the eagles, some 200 urns and other items that were to adorn the terraces.

Mr Sahba had led a team to Bahjí[13] and measured items such as the urns to obtain ideas for the type suitable for the Terraces project. He selected a sculpted eagle near the Shrine as the model for the majestic sculptures standing guard on the posts of the wrought-iron gates leading to every terrace.

The first step for the sculptor was to draw the items, take positive rubber moulds of the existing stone ornaments, sharpen up the details, and then create a master copy in plaster-of-paris. Step two was to wrap a six-piece mould of fibreglass around the model, remove the plaster and then assemble the mould.

The team crushed sajur stone off-cuts from the work on the terraces into specific grades, from dust to pea-size. They added white cement, some yellow oxide, water, silica sand and a plasticizer and then poured it into the mould and vibrated it for half an hour. After 12 hours, when the stone was cured, they removed the mould to find the completed object. A colour-matched mix filled any air bubbles. Hand-sanding was the last task undertaken to produce the final item.

The ornaments workshop provided large bronze urns for each side of the fountain pools, stone planter urns for the balustrades where they would contain variegated flowers, and stone and bronze urns for each side of the stairway. Altogether, the team produced about 500 stone items for the terraces and a further 50 bronzes, including the urns, eagles, peacocks and light fittings. Graphite paste smeared into the bronzes made them blend with the lead items in the gardens that Shoghi Effendi had obtained from Europe.[14]

A few special eagles were carved in Italy out of Carrara marble and they were placed in the main plaza and near the Shrine.

Visitors

Among the prominent visitors to the Shrine of the Báb in 1994 was the Dalai Lama, the most senior head of another religion to enter that Holy Place. He meditated in the Shrine and then placed a traditional white scarf on the threshold, an act of his deep respect.

14

1995: ACCELERATION ON ALL FRONTS

By early 1995 the people of Haifa were getting a better picture of how the Terraces would eventually appear.

Lower terraces

Diners in the outdoor cafés and restaurants on Ben Gurion Avenue, the boulevard leading to the base of the mountain, could see three great green curves immediately below the Shrine created by grass sods which had been laid on both sides of Terraces 9 down to 6.[1] Trees also dotted the landscape to the east of those terraces.

Terrace 9, directly below the Shrine, was presenting an example of what the other terraces might look like. Some lights were now in place. Planter urns sat at intervals on a balustrade, which had balusters of an appealing design and which stood upon the rough-edged stone contour walls. The pools had their stonework in place although their fountain bowls were still being built.[2]

As it turned out, the only problems the project had with the construction of the fountains was when two carved in Italy from Venetian stone and placed on Terrace 9 began to show faults, with efflorescence leading to rough deposits on its base. The MCBP raised this with the supplier who agreed to replace them with the best available Carrara marble, which was white and without veins. The old ones were later used as vases in the gardens at Bahjí.

The steps called by the Guardian 'the Pathway of the Kings and Rulers of the World', referred to in an abbreviated form as 'the Kings' Pathway', were in place down to the Abbas Street bridge.

Upper terraces

Work was well under way on the upper terraces. The team established a site office at the peak to avoid a long steep climb or a circuitous drive to keep returning to the crest. People down below on Ben Gurion could spot the excavator machines doing the preparatory work to build Terrace 19, the most complex of the new terraces.

By this time, the rudimentary curved staircases leading to Terraces 17 and 18 were in place, presenting a view resembling big stone brackets – elsewhere the central staircase bisected the steep concave sections. A close-up view of those upper terraces revealed scenes somewhat reminiscent of the early days of the lower terrace construction by the Master, as boulders were piled on top of each other to create gravity walls. This time, though, there was concrete to keep them all together. These walls were in addition to the underground retaining walls.

On the outer eastern slopes, tree planting and the building of stone rockeries had begun. The spreading of topsoil and planting had also started in the central slopes of those upper terraces. It was an eye-catching sight as workers placed grass sod on steep slopes, some lying down to do the work and others leaning over from wooden ladders that stretched from one contour to the other.

Because Terraces 13, 15 and 17 were very steep, the design did not incorporate grass as it did elsewhere, because grass would require mowing. Instead the crew planted English Ivy, a short groundcover that had been selected after long experimentation. From a distance it gave the same effect as grass.[3]

Underneath the vegetation was an ingenious erosion control system comprised of stair-stepped boulders. Plastic panels with honeycombed cells, which were filled with topsoil, were anchored to the very large boulders to prevent soil movement; they were spread through the uppermost section of the topsoil to provide a stabilizing structure and to prevent surface runoff.

To ensure that surface rainwater would not waterlog and damage the terraces in the future, the team had also carried out the design requirements for major drainage work on the eastern side and inner zone. A series of drains at the bottom of the slope of every terrace collected the water runoff. Meanwhile, on the western side, the order of the day was to work on irrigation lines and electrical duct banks.

A Haifa Municipality walkway known as the Louis Promenade ran along the southern side of Yefe Nof (Panorama) Street, the road next to Terrace 19 at the top of Mount Carmel. Mr Sahba's cordial discussions with Paul Goldschmidt,[4] who had funded the Louis Promenade, had led to a mutual agreement on how the terraces could join that walkway. By mid-year the team had built a reinforced concrete pedestrian tunnel from Terrace 19 under the street to the promenade. The architect saw this as fulfilling part of the vision of 'Abdu'l-Bahá, enabling pilgrims to ascend to the summit and to enjoy the beauty of the mountain from that point.

Right next to the roadside entrance, above Terrace 19, the team built a three-metre-wide promenade, with concrete beams tied to micropiles drilled down nine metres and filled with reinforced concrete. This design preserved the Bahá'í property while allowing the widening of Yefe Nof Street.[5]

The design called for a 900-metre fence at the top of the property with trees at intervals along its entire length. For this fence, artisans at Noufi's factory were making 55 pedestals of sajur stone. Staff at the Bahá'í World Centre workshop fabricated the iron railings that would fit between the pedestals.

Demolition

Dramatic events took place at the end of March when it came time to clear the way to complete the lower terraces.

Forty years previously, Shoghi Effendi through the services of his lieutenant, the Hand of the Cause Leroy Ioas, had bought five houses that lined the path leading up what was then the end of the terraces. The houses now needed to be removed so as to provide the space to build the entrance plaza and Terraces 1 and 2.

In the week after Naw-Rúz 1995, staff of various departments at the Bahá'í World Centre removed windows, doors, floor tiles and other usable items such as furniture from the houses.

Staff had parked their cars overnight in the street and had removed them early in the morning to provide access for heavy machinery and trucks. At 8 a.m. on 31 March the demolition operation began. Crews using three hydraulic jackhammers worked quickly and carefully to raze the buildings.[6] By 2 p.m., five large buildings were gone. Later that day, Amatu'l-Bahá Rúḥíyyih Khánum and a member of the Universal House of Justice visited the site and expressed amazement at how quick and thorough the demolition had been.[7]

In a message to the National Spiritual Assemblies on 4 April 1995, the Universal House of Justice noted that

> the action taken with the full co-operation of the city authorities harmonises with the intention of the beloved Guardian; it clears the site for the monumental entrance to the majestic path leading from the southern end of Ben Gurion Avenue up to the central edifice of the Shrine and beyond to the crest of God's Holy Mountain.[8]

There was one building left to demolish, but that would not occur until the year 2000.

Irrigation system

The system to provide irrigation, drainage and plumbing had a price tag of US$10 million. The irrigation budget alone was $2 million.[9]

The irrigation system was to be one of four different lines in the main pipe network, the others being for fire protection, potable water and fertilizer injection. The potable water and irrigation lines were kept separate in order to cater for a potential alternative source of water such as treated wastewater or bore water.[10]

The challenges for those designing an environmentally sustainable irrigation system for the terraces included accounting for: the range in elevation from 60 metres above sea level to 225 metres; slopes that rose to a maximum of 63 degrees; and arid weather with occasional torrential rains.

The key criterion, which was to make the most efficient use of water as possible, led to the decision to have multiple ways of distribution – sprinklers, sprayers and drippers. There were many different kinds of hydrozones, all of which had different water requirements and so needed different water application rates. The zones included lawns on slopes, lawns on flat areas, hedges, flower beds, pot plants, trees, and gardens in the outer areas.

For easy access, the team put the supply lines only one metre below ground and sublines down between 30 and 40 cm. By May 1995 the network, involving kilometres of lines, was in place for Terraces 9 down to 3, 15 up to 18, and a small section in the Shrine gardens. Upgrading work took place in the irrigation systems in the rest of the gardens around the Shrine as well as in the Monument and Arc gardens.

The system had special 'back flow preventer devices' to stop mixing of the water and to allow for any future use of 'grey water' (recycled water). A centralized fertilizer injection system was incorporated.

Although fully automated and radio controlled, a manual override option was also available. Central monitoring computers would send out emergency messages if soil moisture sensors and an associated weather station provided data that warranted quick action. An alarm would be activated in case of excessive flows due to leaks or a burst pipe, or if the flow was too low due to low pressure or blockages of the drippers.

There were no wells to draw upon at this stage.[11] The water came from the municipal system via five water supply points and two pumping stations. The team restored a tank in the vacated former army camp to the west of the upper terraces. If there were a fire in the Shrine area and at the same time no power to operate the pump that had been installed in the Afnán cistern (the underground water reservoir under Terrace 10 that 'Abdu'l-Bahá had built), then gravity would bring the water from that tank high up the slope to the fire-fighting points below.[12]

Funding crisis

In March 1995 the Universal House of Justice issued an urgent message in which it expressed deep concern that the flow of contributions to the Arc Fund had become 'lamentably low' and, unless accelerated, the goal of completion on time would not be attained. Forty million dollars was needed that very year, the last year of the Three Year Plan. The House of Justice announced that it was sending out one of its members, Mr 'Alí Nakhjavání, to a series of meetings with the Bahá'ís.[13]

During a punishing 35-day schedule, the 75-year-old Mr Nakhjavání addressed large audiences in London, New York City, Washington DC, Dallas, Los Angeles, Vancouver, Toronto, Chicago, Brussels and Frankfurt am Main. As one who had been in Haifa during many years of the ministry of Shoghi Effendi, Mr Nakhjavání could draw on his own experiences and inspire the audiences with stories about the Bahá'ís who, in the days of Guardian, had made great sacrifices for the Faith.

An eloquent speaker, and a widely-loved and respected Bahá'í, Mr Nakhjavání reminded the Bahá'ís of their privilege and obligation to contribute to the funds. He explained why the project needed to be completed at this time and reminded them of the prophecies about the project.[14]

The Bahá'ís responded in amazing fashion. On 20 June the House of Justice told the National Spiritual Assemblies that the entire sum of US$40 million had been ensured 'through immediate contributions, firm pledges, and donations in kind, enabling this vital enterprise, which is proceeding with full force to proceed without any need to interrupt the construction work'.[15]

Amid the joy of such a huge response to the call for funds, the House of Justice also pointed out that from the conclusion of the Three Year Plan in 1996, there would be a need for about US$10 million annually. It was a big challenge, but one the worldwide Bahá'í community was to take on and make huge efforts to meet.

Reports were coming in of all sorts of innovative ways to raise funds. For example, some Bahá'ís made an 'Arc bag' which would be a daily reminder of the project as well as a place to drop spare change. An engaged couple asked guests to make donations to the Arc fund rather than buy them wedding presents. A poor farmer in Ghana donated what he could, retirees stretched their resources to make donations, and some people sold their jewellery to obtain funds to donate.

Terrace 11 and the bridge

Towards the end of the year, the area under Terrace 11 on the southern side of busy Hatzionut Street became a place of intense activity. It was the site for the 2,000-square-metre underground building for the Office of Public Information and Office of Security as well as a court-yard entrance. A three-month project to remove 28,000 cubic metres of rock required excavator machines working around the clock, their operators using spotlights at night.

Publications

Publicity within the worldwide Bahá'í community encouraged and reflected interest in the mighty projects under way on Mount Carmel.

A book by Jacqueline Mehrabi called *Mount Carmel: Whatever is Happening?* explained the projects to youth and children in editions published in English, French, Dutch, Norwegian, Spanish and Swedish. A third set of 'The Arc and Terraces Slides' was made available, following on from those that had come out in 1993 and 1994. Videos included one of the presentation that the architect had delivered about the project at the 1992 World Congress in New York, a 30-minute video produced in 1994 called *Vineyard of the Lord* and one made in 1994 called *The Ancient Promise*, which was about the historic significance of the projects and their relationship to the needs of suffering humanity.

External publicity was starting to happen. A 14-page beautifully illustrated article in the prestigious *Architecture of Israel* magazine said the 'hanging Gardens' would not only be one of Haifa's significant urban projects but would also be the most protected 'green lung' in the country. It pointed out that the public would have access in an organized way to the terraces which the Bahá'ís owned, and which had been designed, built, budgeted and maintained without the help of the government.

The article included responses by the architect to a range of questions. Asked if he regarded architecture as art, he said he had always thought that to be the case, and that, more than any other type of art, it communicated with the public.

Posed the question of whether he could operate outside the Bahá'í environment, he said the Faith was a way of life and an inseparable part of him but that his religion did not dictate the way he designed:

> None of my projects were designed solely for the Bahá'ís. In fact, my biggest challenge is to build something suitable for the general public, without any connection to faith, origin or belonging. My loyalty is to the location . . .

In reply to a question about whether the Bahá'í religion allowed him sufficient freedom for self-expression, he replied:

> You might as well ask if a kite is any freer without its string. The Bahá'í believer acts according to his personal conscience, and according to his understanding of the Bahá'í teachings. Self-expression and

freedom of expression is one of the important principles of the faith, and a person cannot force his opinion and desires on others. Nevertheless, there is no doubt that the philosophy and faith of a believer will be reflected in his art, thoughts and way of life. The blossom of the tree comes from within the tree. It cannot be glued to it from outside. Freedom of expression, nevertheless, does not mean that you live only for yourself. As in a game, every player is important. The result comes from the quality of teamwork.[16]

Guest visits

In its Riḍván message in April 1995, the Universal House of Justice observed that there had been a 'sharp increase' in the number of visits to the Bahá'í World Centre by high-ranking government officials, other dignitaries and media representatives. The House of Justice said this was underscoring 'a trend towards a greater familiarity of the governments of the nations with the evolving centre of a World Faith'. It linked that increase in awareness with Shoghi Effendi's vision for Mt Carmel and with the need for the completion of the projects as scheduled.[17]

In June, many thousands of people viewed the models of the Terraces at the 'Haifa 2000' exhibition organized by, among others, the Chamber of Commerce and Industry of Haifa. The event coincided with two international conferences. Among those attending the exhibition and who viewed the Bahá'í display was Israel's Foreign Minister Shimon Peres. Others included the United Kingdom's Minister for Housing and many business people and local residents.

The Mayor of Haifa, who escorted prominent individuals on several visits to the Bahá'í property, explained the Terraces project to his guests, and also said it was important for the people of Haifa to see the models and to support the project. That was especially the case before the Mount Carmel crews started to build the bridge over busy Hatzionut Street, a task which would cause disruption to traffic.

The Bahá'í volunteers reported that a common question was: 'When will the project be completed and will it be open to the public?' The Bahá'ís could answer: 'By 2001', and 'Yes'.

Bahá'í visits

On 1 October, during the celebration of the Holy Day of the Declaration of the Báb, Bahá'í visitors became the beneficiaries of a decision by the House of Justice to briefly open Terrace 9 just for them. Before that day dawned, the team bent to the tasks of providing the finishing touches and completing the inner landscaping.

Eliza Rasiwala, the staff writer for *Vineyard of the Lord*, described the scene: 'There was a tangible sense of elation among the friends as they thronged the terrace, walking along the tiled[18] paths, admiring the beauty around them.'[19]

Two months later, in December 1995, some 80 participants attending a conference of the Bahá'í Continental Board of Counsellors in Haifa also had an unexpected treat when they stood on the 'Kings' Pathway' on the completed terraces below the Shrine, by then lined with tall, candle-like cypresses and lush lawns.[20]

The seven terraces below the Shrine were, in fact, nearing completion. The central paving on the terraces was a combination of sajur and jatt stone, the motifs different for each terrace, and there were stone benches on which the Bahá'ís could rest. Here they could contemplate the extraordinary environment into which they had entered, and notice details such as the beautiful designs on the covers of the water runnels around the fountains. The covers had patterns produced by computer-aided machinery which used high-pressure water to make the cuts by firing out fine sand. Planting had accompanied the construction of each stage, so once the building of each terrace was complete, so were their gardens.

After they had moved through the gate between Terraces 9 and 8, the Bahá'ís passed between the apple-green duranta hedges on both sides of the stairway. The hedge had historic associations because Shoghi Effendi had himself chosen that plant for the gardens above. The hedges would grow to be one metre tall, 50 cm wide and with surfaces scalloped by gardeners. They would fulfil the criteria for the hedges, which due to their high visibility needed to repeat the rhythm of the water cascades and concentric circles, be dense, have full coverage from ground to the top, and shear well.

15

1996: TAPESTRY OF BEAUTY

'A watchful public is awed at the tapestry of beauty spreading over the mountainside,' the Universal House of Justice told the Bahá'í world in a stirring message during the holy festival of Riḍván in April 1996.

The House of Justice said that 'the magnificent progress of the projects on Mount Carmel' was preeminent among the measurable Bahá'í achievements of the past year: 'Seven terraces below the Shrine of the Báb are now completed, foreshowing the unfolding splendour from the foot to the ridge of God's Holy Mountain.' There had been 'numerous difficulties', yet the work was on schedule:

> The physical reality of the progress thus far so marvellously realised is proof of an even more profound achievement, namely, the unity of purpose effected throughout our global community in the pursuit of this gigantic, collective enterprise.

The intensity of interest and support as expressed 'in an unprecedented outpouring of contributions' was a reflection of 'a level of sacrifice that bespeaks the quality of faith and generosity of heart' of Bahá'ís throughout the planet.

> That contributions towards the Mount Carmel Projects have met the three-year goal of seventy-four million dollars marks yet another measurable and exceptional achievement, inspiring confidence that the necessary financial support for these projects will continue until their completion by the end of the century.

The House of Justice projected that in four years' time, April 2000, the broad connecting bridge above the Shrine gardens would have been built, five of the upper terraces would be completed and the remaining four upper terraces and the two at the foot of the mountain would be in an advanced stage of development.[1]

The Riḍván message came at a time when work had begun in earnest on the Hatzionut bridge part of the project and while work continued on the lower terraces.

Hatzionut bridge

Excavation at the bridge site had taken place in the last month of 1995. From early in 1996, it became time to tackle the construction of the bridge which was to connect Terrace 10 and the beautiful garden behind the Shrine to the upper terraces. It was one of the major challenges of the project.

Originally named Mountain Road and later UNO Avenue, Hatzionut Avenue was a major thoroughfare in Haifa so any work on it would inevitably involve major disruption. A challenge for MCBP was to minimize that disruption and keep the vehicles moving.

Mr Sahba had spent about two years consulting with, and making presentations to, the city and district authorities on the detailed step-by-step plan of the proposed operation to build the bridge. About ten different departments examined the plan in detail, looking especially at safety and convenience issues. All of them had to agree before the plan was approved. The architect recalled: 'No one including our best friends in the city believed this plan would pass.'[2] But pass it did.

It was a project that would be carried out while the traffic was directed into different lanes as required. The plan was to lower the road by a maximum of five metres, widening it from three to four lanes, while at the same time lowering all the service lines, such as sewer, water and communication lines, all of which should continue to function without any interruption while the road was being constructed.

It would involve excavations prior to building the several hundreds of metres of the retaining wall along the gardens bordering both sides of the road, and would employ rock engineering techniques to maintain the stability of the mountain behind the walls. The bridge was to accommodate a garden above the road while allowing a pedestrian walkway below. To do this the design called for building dozens of beams commonly known as 'deadman beams' behind the southern edge of the wall. They supported the cantilevered garden.

The bridge is formed with several concrete beams which together form a five-pointed 'Star of Haykal', which can be easily observed by pedestrians underneath. The star, which represents the Manifestation of God, was used by the Báb. Bahá'u'lláh also described the Haykal.[3] It is not only a spiritual symbol on the bridge, but it also camouflages the fact that the centreline of the bridge – in fact the centreline of the Terraces – is not perpendicular to the centre of the street which passes under it.[4] The first part of the project was to lower the road – an extra advantage for the city was that this would remove a major blind spot traffic hazard – and to widen it to four lanes, the extra lane being on the southern side. This would also combine with the construction of a pedestrian tunnel on the western side of the planned bridge.

On 9 February,[5] representatives of MCBP and a Haifa contractor signed a contract for the lowering of the avenue, the construction of the pedestrian tunnel, and the building of retaining walls for the bridge. A billboard on Hatzionut Avenue depicted the planned bridge.

In association with the relevant city utility departments, the complicated task began to lower telephone lines and electrical and TV cables, as well as water, sewage and stormwater pipes, which continued to function normally throughout the project. Vehicles were directed to the south side of the road so that the preparatory work could begin on the northern side. This involved removing trees that bordered the road, reducing the northern pedestrian sidewalk to 1.5 metres, relocating lamp posts, traffic lights and bus stops, and undertaking the preparatory piling for a pedestrian tunnel.

Traffic was then directed into two lanes on the northern two-thirds of the tarmac to allow four excavators to dig five metres below the original street level on the southern third of the road.

There was a fortunate end to a dramatic incident. A city truck full of gravel lost its brakes at the top of the hill to the west of the site, and the driver crashed it into concrete barriers to try to slow it down. It arrived at the open trench across the road and did a complete flip, landed on its roof and broke into pieces. Mr Sahba quickly arrived at the scene and thought the driver was dead. In fact, although bleeding, he was only concussed and was discharged from hospital next day.[6] There was no damage done to any other person or property.

Once the excavations were complete, structural work for the bridge began with the casting of the foundations for the nine columns upon which it was to rest, and which also formed part of the Information and Security building. Excavators had previously provided the space for that big building. Its foundations were completed in May. A bonus in terms of time and cost was that the rock uncovered during the excavation of the road proved sturdier than expected and so reduced the need for extensive shoring-in work.

By September, it was time to excavate the middle of Hatzionut Avenue. Downhill traffic moved to the south side, travelling along the lowered level next to the Information building. Uphill vehicles stuck to the north.

By November large sections of the 300-metre retaining wall on the south side of the Bahá'í property were in place.[7] Fortunately there were no delays in installing storm-drain pipes to cope with the inevitable winter rains that would pound down on to the road.

Lower terraces

On one glorious day, 22 April, pilgrims descended from the Shrine to experience the wonder and the beauty of Terraces 9 to 5. They were the first in a stream that would soon turn into a river of delighted Bahá'ís, and their experience came about as a result of a decision by the House of Justice to open the terraces to pilgrims and visitors.

In preparation for that event, the MCBP team had worked fever-ishly in and around Terrace 9 and also in the inner areas that lined the Kings' Pathway. By then most of the major structural work and stone ornamentation was complete on the lower terraces right down to, and including, Terrace 3.

The main focus of the work on the lower terraces in 1996 was the landscaping. It was time to put in place the distinctive plants that would give a visual lift to the whole scene. A typical terrace had two types of planted beds. One was of grass, bordered with a low, greyish-blue santolina hedge. The other was horse-shoe shaped, the sides made of vine-covered stones. Annual flower blooms appeared among shrubs sculpted into shapes such as cones and balls. Canary palms sat at both ends.

By this time the wildflower plantings were complete in the area to the east of Terraces 9 down to 5. Among those flowers were the red flowering native corn poppy, the blue globe thistle, and lupins with

Without its later cladding and adornments, the bridge over Abbas Street, named after 'Abbás Effendi, known to Bahá'ís as 'Abdu'l-Bahá

The completed bridge

Workmen toil on the terraces that lead down from the Shrine

Newly inserted canary palms in freshly laid lawns on the lower terraces give a hint of what is to come, but the site of the future upper terraces is unrelieved by vegetation

Very early stages in the construction of the entrance plaza

Newly planted olive trees stud the side of the lower terraces.
The earthworks on the upper terraces are now well under way

In March 1997, demolition
took place near Hagefen Street
to open up the site for the
completion of the terraces

View from the top of the dome to
the garden to the east of the Shrine
of the Báb. The Eastern Pilgrim
House is at right, rear

Sheltered from the intense heat, a skilled tradesman prepares stone for the stairway

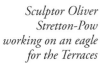

Sculptor Oliver Stretton-Pow working on an eagle for the Terraces

Photo: Courtesy of Josephine Hill

Above: *Dawn delivers its rosy rays on to an uncompleted terrace*

Left: *Lowering a fountain bowl on Terrace 9 needs to be done with care*

Gardens staff join Fariborz and Goli Sahba at the rear of the Shrine. At back left wearing a wide-brimmed hat is horticulturalist and Bahá'í gardens historian Andrew Blake

Beautiful curved lawns seem to emanate out from the Shrine

An aerial view shows the complexity of the project to build the Hatzionut bridge

Traffic proceeds down the lowered southern lane of Hatzionut Avenue but the northern half of the road remains at its original height

Preparations for the building of the bridge over Hatzionut Avenue

Preparations are still under way for the mighty task of building the bridge over Hatzionut Avenue connecting the Terrace of the Shrine of the Báb (Terrace 10) with those above, so there is a clear view into the courtyard outside the future Offices of Public Information (right) and Security. Terrace 11 is yet to be finished. Four skylights of the Office of Public Information underneath it can be seen just to the right of the bridge and adjacent to the road. The two new buildings on the Arc, on either side of the Seat of the Universal House of Justice, appear complete.

On 15 January 1998 a truck travelling down Hatzionut Avenue crashed and broke into pieces at the site for the bridge, but fortunately there was no loss of life or serious injury. No damage was done to the preparation work for the bridge

The beautiful garden on top of the Hatzionut bridge is flanked at left by the courtyard of the Offices of Public Information and Security and at right by the carpet-like garden behind the Shrine of the Báb, and the circle of cypress trees. The four skylights in a row on the southern side of the road to the west of the bridge are above the offices

Fariborz Sahba (pointing westward) had the daunting responsibility of project managing the construction of the Terraces as well as the buildings on the Arc. Next to him, as he explains the work to members of the Universal House of Justice, is the architect of the Arc buildings, Hossein Amanat (arm raised). The clearly visible House of Justice members are from left to right: Dr Peter Khan, Mr Glenford Mitchell, Dr David Ruhe, Mr David Hofman, Mr 'Alí Na<u>kh</u>javání, Mr Hugh Chance and Mr Hushmand Fatheazam, with Mr Borrah Kavelin behind Mr Sahba

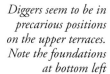

Diggers seem to be in precarious positions on the upper terraces. Note the foundations at bottom left

From the air in 1998, the southern entrance to the tunnel under Yefe Nof Street leading to the upper terraces is clearly visible, as is the uncompleted bridge over Hatzionut Avenue behind the Shrine of the Báb

their dark blue spikes. Their home was an attractive area of rockeries, olive trees, groundcover and stone pathways. Mid-year saw the completion of similar extensive plantings on the western side.

The beauty kept coming. In August and September the gardeners set out more than 20,000 plants, completing the inner and outer areas of Terraces 9 down to 5. Haifa residents and visitors viewing the lower terraces from below on Ben Gurion Avenue were enjoying increasingly lovely sights. There were green geometric curves sweeping across the mountain face. The Kings' Pathway, flanked by its cypress sentries, led to balustrades, with their white globe-like lamps and ornaments.

Meanwhile, the committee involved in redeveloping the Templer colony agreed that the new design of Ben Gurion Avenue, including its lighting, should be in harmony with the Terraces project. As a result, for example, the height of the lamp posts on Ben Gurion Avenue was lowered significantly so that their lights would not detract from the illumination of the terraces at night.

Upper terraces

By February 1996, the major structural work on the promenade adjoining Terrace 19 was complete, so it was possible for two-way traffic to resume on Yefe Nof (Panorama) Street, which had been reduced to a single lane the previous year.

There was plenty left to do on the complex structure of Terrace 19, which was different from the others. On each of its two levels there was a balcony approached by flights of stairs on each side. Also associated were 17 arches of varying height and width. In addition, the plans had called for 700 square metres of building space to be used for irrigation and mechanical rooms, a security station and storage.

By November 1996 substantial stonework on that uppermost section was finished, a major achievement. That level was connected to the now completed pedestrian tunnel linking it to both Panorama Street and beyond to the existing Louis Promenade.

Outside the boundary, immediately adjacent to the road, the team had virtually completed a 300-metre promenade. It was a wide stone path, separated from the Bahá'í property by a fence of ornamental iron railings and 53 pedestals. From that path visitors would soon be able to obtain spectacular views of the work below. By the end of the year, red-flowering Australian bottle brush shrubs added decorative finishing touches.

As the structural work continued, there were simultaneous plantings on the upper terraces. By mid-year the inner landscaping had begun with the first pair of palm trees put in place on Terraces 18, 17 and 15. Where the area was too steep for grass, the gardeners planted English ivy and Natal plum. Grading work on the eastern side provided areas for wildflower planting.

Media

Journalists played an important role in letting the local people understand more about the projects. Three major newspapers reported the nature of the work and the changes to the traffic arrangements in the section of Hatzionut Avenue which adjoined the Bahá'í properties.

When important officials visited, there was usually media coverage, as happened in May, when Minister Yossi Beilin from the office of the Prime Minister visited the site.

But the main media exposure occurred when Israeli television's commercial Channel 2 screened a programme that included footage of the gardens and the seat of the Universal House of Justice as well as aerial views of all the projects. There were interviews on Terrace 9 with Mr Sahba and with Haifa Mayor Amran Mitzna, who said the project was unique and would attract people from all around the world. 'I don't think there is any other city in the world to receive such a large gift, invested so correctly,' Mr Mitzna said.[8]

Lights that dazzled

On 16 October 1996 there was a surprising and dazzling display for all those residents, visitors and Bahá'ís who just happened to be below Mount Carmel on Ben Gurion Avenue that evening. After months of strenuous work by the electrical team, it was time to test the lights on the lower terraces so they could determine the final configuration of the illumination for the stone balustrades and contour walls.

When the lights went on, brightening the previously darkened slope, enthralled onlookers rushed to take photographs or just admire the lovely sight, and the traffic stopped for a few minutes. They saw the lamps lining the Kings' Pathway, and lanterns with hanging globes illuminating the great curves sweeping across the face of the mountain. On each terrace, the ornate lampposts shone out. Behind them, soft lights glowed over the fountain pools.

The test had given the architect and the electrical staff the information they needed to continue on with their work, and it provided the residents of Haifa an indication of how beautiful the Terraces and Shrine would appear in the evenings during the years to come.

16

1997: CHANGE IN ORGANIZATION

A major change in the management of the Terraces project took place after a dramatic event in early 1997. The main commercial contractor in charge of the upper terraces and Hatzionut bridge projects stopped work due to serious 'financial and internal complication within his organisation'.[1] He declared bankruptcy, and his contract was terminated.

The contractor had been working under the overall direction of the MCBP's Office of the Project Manager but he had control over the workers, equipment, programming of work, purchasing, and other aspects associated with the execution of construction work. In the midst of such a major construction project on a particularly challenging terrain, an event like this could have been a severe blow to the progress of the work.

However, in April,[2] the Office of the Project Manager took a big decision, one that was to have profound effects on the speed and cost of the Terraces project. The office decided to take on construction management itself – it would act as the main contractor. It bought all the heavy machinery from the contractor as well as all the supply materials. It used the services of labour contractors and subcontracted out various areas of work for all work on the upper and lower terraces and the bridge.

An amazing turnaround resulted. Rather than causing huge problems, the change in management led to more flexibility in the programming of work and saw improved quality control. It also provided opportunities to make up for delays.

There was another highly significant outcome. Economy and quality control had been guiding principles since the start of the project, but now with direct control over purchasing, there could be a reduction in costs, which turned out to amount to millions of dollars. This was a very important result in a project financed by donations from Bahá'ís around the world.

Purchases arranged by the Office of the Project Manager through Bahá'ís meant there could be considerable discounts over even the wholesale prices. Added on to those reductions were savings in the normal percentage of the profits and overhead costs going to the contractors, which were between 30 to 50 per cent of the market price. In effect, the purchase prices for the project often dropped to about half of what would have been paid had the contractor still been involved.[3]

Locally, too, the costs dropped. The Office of the Project Manager had won a reputation among the building trades for trustworthiness, financial stability and paying on time, so considerable discounts came the way of MCBP for the big bulk orders.

The use of the principles of value engineering also led to large savings. This involved a review of the design of particular features and the preparation of a budget for alternative ways of doing things or for using different materials and design solutions. It would ensure that although the original design concept was met, savings would result.

For example, the original plan for the promenade adjacent to Terrace 19 was for foundations, columns, beams and floor slabs. But a review led to the use of micropiles and precast concrete slabs. The promenade effectively emerged as originally designed, but the costs were greatly reduced.[4]

The change also boosted the atmosphere of teamwork and close cooperation with the subcontractors, and that in turn led to speedier progress and cost savings. A pickup in momentum was clearly evident by the middle of the year,[5] work accelerating on all fronts.

Hatzionut bridge

By the end of 1996 the roadwork was mostly complete on the southern side of the road, so in the winter months of the new year it was time to switch attention to the excavation of the northern side of the road, the third and final phase of lowering the thoroughfare.

Near the construction area behind the Shrine there were olive trees, aloe vera, succulents and other plants. Gardeners removed them and the topsoil for later relocation to the outer areas of the upper terraces. They also took away the remaining loose rock and stones so that they could form rockeries way up towards the summit.

There were delays on the roadwork, caused by winter rains and the termination of the involvement of the main contractor, but the team rose to the challenge, and with the new management structure the work began to accelerate. By mid-year the excavation of the northern side of the road was finished. After the completion of the 250-metre retaining wall there, a team of Turkish masons affixed local stone on it and also installed curbing stones.

The MCBP team and the contractors, working from the courtyard of the Information and Security building under Terrace 11, had raised the columns for the bridge, and by November they were erecting scaffolding for the main slab of the bridge. On that same south side a 15-tonne machine sat on the roof of that building and installed 53 prestressed anchors to retain the mountain behind it. A giant concrete slab was to go into a cavity between the building and the mountain to make the building independent from the retaining system.

Upper terraces

The goal was to have the complex two-storey Terrace 19 ready for the International Convention in April 1998. At the start of the year, 50 per cent of the stonework of the structure had been completed. A contingent of Turkish masons set to work and by the end of the year they had finished the job, which involved putting in place 1,100 square metres of the distinctive local *tubzeh* stone.[6]

To avoid any risk of damaging the beautiful carved stone that would eventually be put in place on Terraces 18 down to 15, one particular job took place before the masons started their work. Heavy lifting equipment necessary to install mature canary palms trundled on to the terraces. Even with the help of that machinery it required six men to shuffle into place the giant palms, which were three times the height of a person.[7]

The balustrades, pedestals and runnels were soon complete and cypress trees began to make their distinctive candle-like appearance alongside the stairways. By mid-year the landscaping on the outer western areas was close to completion and work soon began on the eastern equivalent.

Construction teams on those steep eastern areas of Terraces 18 down to 16[8] built service paths and created rockeries that recreated the natural look of the mountain. From Terrace 19 down to 16, gardeners planted succulents, oleanders, rosemary, lantana, olives, jacarandas, coral and frangipani. In addition, they planted almond trees, pistachio shrubs, rock roses, rosemary, groundcovers and native grass. The drought-resistant plants required only monthly watering, and that could be done by sprinklers rather than drippers.

In the autumn a soil-filled geoweb covering the inner slopes of Terrace 15 was growing ivy. The landscaping of the inner areas continued through the winter of 1997/98 with the goal of having plant cover in place by the time of the International Convention.

Meanwhile there was intense construction work in the demanding areas of Terraces 13 and 14 where the slope inside ranged between 45 and 60 degrees. These terraces sat over the parking tunnel for the large building to the east, the Centre for the Study of the Texts. Anchors went into place to strengthen the mountain and big backfilling operations took place.

By the end of the year, extensive concreting work was under way on Terraces 13 and 14, and major earthworks had begun on Terrace 12.

Lower terraces

A spectacular event occurred on 7 March 1997 when the giant claw of a demolition machine ripped into the last remaining building blocking the completion of Terraces 1 and 2. The demolition of the four-storey house, on the inner west of the slope, followed four years of sensitive negotiations with the two owners of the building, its tenants and the Haifa Municipality.[9]

Achieving this very difficult task at this stage of the project, allowing completion of the project before the end of the century, was very exciting for the MCBP team. Four days later, on 11 March 1997, the Universal House of Justice sent an uplifting message to the National Spiritual Assemblies throughout the world:

> With joyful and thankful hearts we announce the successful acquisition after many years of difficult negotiations and the subsequent demolition a few days ago of the building which stood as the last obstacle to the completion of the first two terraces of the Shrine of the Báb at the foot of Mount Carmel.[10]

To enable the building of Terraces 1 and 2 and the entrance plaza, the project manager had presented a modified town planning scheme proposal to cancel 100 metres of Ben Gurion Avenue that had intruded into the Bahá'í property, and to incorporate that area into the gardens. The point in favour of it, which the authorities had accepted, had been that because the Bahá'ís were now the owner of all the lots on both sides, there was no need for a public road inside such private property.

Work soon began on the bottom two terraces. After the excavation, the team built retaining walls that descended some nine metres. Those concreted-rubble walls supported the structure of Terrace 2 and connected it to the walls above. By July, Terrace 2 was almost complete and the construction of Terrace 1 had begun.

The removal of the building and the ongoing landscaping work opened up vistas of great beauty for people in and around Ben Gurion Avenue. Green lawns across the face of the lower mountain provided soothing views, and the greens, greys and dark reds of other vegetation gave a pretty contrast to the limestone terrace walls, the stairs and the balustrades. Bright reds and purples of bougainvillaea, as well as orange, purple, blue and yellow flowers brought colour to many areas. Olives with their grey-green foliage and the green-leafed tall ficus trees stood in the outer areas amidst more colourful shrubs and trees such as jacaranda and frangipani.

Planting went on through the year on the western and eastern outer areas. Gardeners bedded down many spring flowering bulbs, with colour and fragrance continuing to be criteria for selections.

Those visiting Terrace 9 could see a lotus and lily pond to the west. It was in the place which had once been an outlet for the Afnán cistern – the underground water reservoir that 'Abdu'l-Bahá had built and which remained in place under Terrace 10. In the time of the Master, rainwater from the roof of the Shrine had been collected in this reservoir and used for the garden. The outlet had provided water for the donkeys which carried earth and building material up the mountain. 'Abdu'l-Bahá had mentioned that this cistern forever would remain in the name of 'the illustrious Afnán of the sacred Lote-Tree, the honoured Mírzá Báqir'.[11] It was for that reason that even though by the 1990s it was not needed for its original purpose, it was nevertheless restored and turned to a water tank for firefighting in the garden, and its outlet was turned into a lotus pond, a small feature yet one that would delight many visitors.

Towards the end of the year there was a major refurbishing of Terrace 10, the Terrace of the Shrine of the Báb, with care taken to retain the original design of the Master and the Guardian. Gardeners removed the ornamental plants to a safe place, corrected the levels and geometry of the gardens and then returned all the plants. Then they replaced the annual rye grass with sod so that there could be permanent lawns throughout the year. Many of the old plants and trees were replaced with healthy new ones. Other staff repaired or replaced ornaments and pedestals. Subsoil irrigation replaced overhead water methods for the extensive santolina hedges.

It became clear during the year that future visitors to Haifa and local residents would have many pleasant areas in and around Ben Gurion Avenue from which they could view the terraces as they dined, strolled or shopped.

A brochure published by the Haifa Municipality's Office of the Templer colony project showed plans to create some public spaces reminiscent of the Templer gardens and also to develop a spacious pedestrian promenade on both sides of the avenue. There were also plans to restore the original facades of the historic buildings and to construct new ones in similar styles. Much of the work would be finished in time to coincide with the completion of the Terraces project, and would fulfil the Master's vision of a highway from the sea to the Shrine and beyond to the crest of the mountain.

In November the Municipality of Haifa arranged a seminar about the project, the topics including a timetable for completion, the planning and use of the colony, and the integration with the Bahá'í development. Mr Sahba made a detailed presentation to an intrigued audience of architects, engineers, city councillors and business people.[12]

Keeping in touch

The Bahá'í world had many ways of keeping up to date with the progress of the project. Regular issues of the newsletter *Vineyard of the Lord* went to all communities around the world, and the annual *Bahá'í World* volumes contained a summary. For detail, though, there was a video with an interview with Mr Sahba and the latest aerial shots. Also available were slide shows and other videos.

The Universal House of Justice was also in direct communication with the Bahá'ís. On 4 February, noting the accomplishment the previous year of a US$74 million fund for the Mount Carmel Projects, it had said that the contribution of US$10 million each year until the end of the century would be sufficient to meet the needs for the completion of the enterprise, although there could be unforeseen disturbances ahead. The House of Justice also observed that there was careful attention to economy in the project without compromising the high standards of construction befitting the edifice and terraces.

17

1998: AN EXPERIENCE FOR DELEGATES

The most important event at the Baháʼí World Centre in 1998 was the International Convention at the end of April, when delegates from throughout the Baháʼí world poured into Haifa to elect the Universal House of Justice.

Work had speeded up in the previous months to prepare as many of the terraces as possible so that these men and women, these representatives of the global Baháʼí community, could experience the beauty and return home to spread the excitement.

The work led to the completion of significant architectural and landscaping work on Terraces 19 down to 15, the completion of the structures of Terraces 14 down to 12, and the beginning of the work on Terrace 11. In addition, the main terrace of the Shrine had been refurbished, Terraces 9 to 3 had been fine-tuned, and work had begun on Terraces 1 and 2. A building under Terrace 1 was complete and the contour wall and geometric curves defining it were in place. The Hatzionut bridge had been newly concreted, and the stonework on the retaining walls below was almost complete, as was the relocation of underground services. The effort had been enormous but the reaction of the visitors excited the MCBP staff, who felt that all the hard work and long hours were well worth it.

Before the Convention began, the delegates and the members of the Continental Boards of Counsellors toured the upper terraces. They began from Panorama Street (Yefe Nof) at the crest of Mount Carmel where they admired the spectacular view ahead and below. Terrace 19 alone was a wondrous sight for them, with its grand entrance, its matching stone staircases on both sides, the balustrades, planters and lampposts.[1]

As they descended they admired their immediate surroundings on all five of the completed levels, which culminated in Terrace 15. One of the delegates, Marjorie Tidman of Australia, described her reaction: 'The terraces were breathtakingly beautiful and we knew we were witnessing the creation of heaven on earth on the mountain of God.'[2]

Then they walked through the construction sites of Terraces 14 down to 11, detoured eastward to the Centre for the Study of the Texts on the Arc, and then returned to finish their visit by standing on the concreted[3] Hatzionut bridge, which had yet to be adorned with its decorative elements and gardens. A small section was left without concrete so that they could see something special. Underneath the bridge was a 30-metre long five-pointed star created by the 90-cm deep structural beams. They could have been laid in a straight line but instead were placed in an artistic pattern which matched the 'Haykal', the star the Báb used as the symbol of His faith.

It was a stunning experience for the Bahá'ís to be in a spot where they could look back to the steep, wondrous terraces which they had descended, and then look ahead to the famed circle of cypresses where Bahá'u'lláh had stood 107 years previously and had pointed out to 'Abdu'l-Bahá the site for the future Shrine of the Báb, which was now there before them in all its majesty. As reported in *Vineyard of the Lord:* 'The eagerness and excitement of these esteemed guests of the Universal House of Justice was thrilling beyond words.'[4]

The visitors had other delights as well. They experienced the grandeur of the lower terraces, all but two of which were completed. They enjoyed being among the exquisite plants and flowers on the terraces and seeing the splashes of colour amidst the green in certain outer regions. The central focus was the Shrine itself, and after they walked slowly through the captivating charm of its garden terrace, designed by the Guardian, they entered with great reverence that holy place built by 'Abdu'l-Bahá, crowned by His grandson, cared for by the Universal House of Justice, and forever a place of supplication, contemplation and inspiration.

There was much to see, because so much effort had been put in to adhere to the 'divine deadlines' that the project manager had constantly stressed. The Universal House of Justice in its Riḍván message that April told the Bahá'ís of the world: 'We are gratified by the marvellous speed with which the construction projects on Mount Carmel proceeded to fulfil the schedule which had been set for the year just ended.'[5]

The progress was also a talking point in Haifa. The Mayor of Haifa, Amram Mitzna, told Mr Sahba that the people of Haifa were amazed at the speed of the project.

Upper terraces

By September 1998, Terrace 19 was largely complete and, at the request of the Mayor of Haifa, the Universal House of Justice approved its opening to the public. This was conducive to good relations with the local residents and authorities, and it had the additional effect of acting as a milestone for the MCBP team.

Large numbers poured through the entrance, which was an ornamental gate flanked by columns on which sat life-size sculpted eagles. The people exclaimed with delight at the beauty around and before them.

Leading up to that significant event, there had been much intense work, with final touches to the planting in the inner and outer areas of Terraces 19 to 15, except for Terrace 17, which had its own requirements. Ancient olive trees, the silver grey native sage, centaurea and santolina seemed to accentuate the blue, violet, yellow, red and orange of the large flowering trees and shrubs in the outer areas where there was also an attractive combination of colours as bougainvillaea and juniper merged with native plants.

Closer to the inner areas, the small trees and shrubs had muted colour accents. The lilac of vitex and the red, burnt orange and maroon of acalypha provided a colour contrast against the cream stones.

There were more plants to come. A nursery established to the west of Terrace 18 would provide some of the plants required in each of the next two years for 50,000 square metres of gardens.

During the year the work had accelerated on Terrace 14, which sat on a metre-thick slab on the roof of the entrance tunnel to the Arc on the extension of Crusader Road. Work also accelerated in the Terraces down to 11. Italian-made gates and pedestals were installed. An underground mechanical room, like the one on Terrace 6, was constructed under that terrace to house a large transformer.

Planting of the eastern outer areas of Terraces 13 and 14 took place as grading continued on the western side of Terrace 13 to allow the building of the curved stairs which mirrored the already completed steps on the east. On Terrace 11 a skylight in the shape of an eight-pointed star emerged from the roof of the information centre building below.

Before the winter's typical drenching rains arrived, work had been under way to connect the kilometres of underground drainage pipes to manholes, which were up to 11 metres deep behind the southern retaining wall lining Hatzionut Street.

Lower terraces

One special event on 5 July brought pleasure to the Guardian's widow, Amatu'l-Bahá Rúḥíyyih Khánum, by then 88 years old. On Terrace 9 gardeners had bedded down two of the seedlings propagated from the original orange tree that the Báb had planted in the courtyard of His house in Shiraz. In 1979, enemies of the Faith had destroyed His house along with the orange tree, but the seeds were saved. After gardeners had used techniques involving budding onto rootstock, and had employed a root hormone, the new trees grew from the seeds of those oranges.[6]

When Rúḥíyyih Khánum heard the news that the trees were in place, she wrote a note to Mr Sahba in which she said, 'What could be more, one might say, romantic in the true sense of the word than this!'[7]

The team did a lot of work that year behind and to the east of the Shrine. They had to incorporate large sections of the old level of Hatzionut Avenue into the boundary of the gardens. The gardens southeast of the Pilgrim House became a hive of activity. Distinguished by the four triangular sections planted with cacti, this area had become known after the death of the Guardian as the 'Arizona gardens'.[8] The team upgraded the lawns and flower beds and regraded the paths with steel edgings to keep their ochre tile chips from spilling out. The opportunity to do this work had arisen because it had become necessary to dig deep trenches there to install ducts for electricity and phone systems.[9]

Around the grove of cypress trees behind the Shrine, they cleared the existing plants in preparation to realign the gardens with the centreline of the terraces. They relocated two decorative stone urns and the pedestals, each weighing a tonne, to another position there.

Meanwhile, down below, the construction teams were concentrating on the platforms on Terrace 2 and Terrace 1, the platforms that ascending visitors would reach after leaving the expansive entry plaza. Paving was by now complete on the roundabout at the junction of Ben Gurion Avenue and Hagefen Street.

Hatzionut bridge

It was an intensely satisfying year for those who had worked for so long on the design, preparation and construction of the Hatzionut bridge. After the pouring in March of 1,000 cubic metres of concrete on the 150 tonnes of steel reinforcement, the team tested the result and found the operation had been successful. By July, they had begun to remove the formwork in an operation conducted at night to avoid excessive disruption to traffic.

By September, all the scaffolding was gone. The bridge was now a self-supported, free-standing structure that had passed all the required structural tests. By the end of the year the traffic was flowing along the new traffic lanes underneath, the work on the face of the bridge was under way, and pedestals and balustrades were being put in place on top of the walls of the bridge.

Reminiscent of the times in the early 1950s during the construction of the superstructure of the Shrine, cargo loads of stone were on their way from Italy to Haifa. In the 18 containers was carved sajur stone. Some was intended for the double curved arch leading from the bridge into the courtyard on the south side of the bridge, some for the smaller single arch on the north with a view to the Shrine, and some for the remaining columns on the upper terraces and for pools on Terraces 13 and 15.

VIPs

Increasing numbers of ambassadors, politicians and officials from around the world were visiting the project. For example, when United States Ambassador Ned Walker and his delegation arrived, accompanied by the Mayor of Haifa, his hosts were Mr Sahba and the deputy Secretary-General of the Bahá'í International Community, Murray Smith, both of whom accompanied their guests down the Terraces from the Shrine.

Publicity

The drumbeat of publicity began picking up. Several major news-papers reported the opening of Terrace 19. The Municipality of Haifa, with the support of Israel's Ministry of Tourism, published a 20-page glossy brochure on the Terraces and the Arc buildings called *The Eighth Wonder of the World*. It said that the 'luxuriant gardens open out all around the golden domed Shrine, forming a shining landmark in the Mount Carmel landscape'. Photographs of the project and some of the Shrine in the time of the Guardian and the Master illustrated the text. It was the first time the local authority had published such comprehensive information about the Faith. First published in English, the brochure later appeared in a Hebrew translation as well as in French, German, Russian and Spanish. Distributed initially to locals and visitors to Haifa, the brochure also became popular with Bahá'ís throughout the world.

The media gave the project some publicity when they covered the presentation to the Bahá'í World Centre from the City of Haifa of the 1998 Ephraim Lifshitz award for 'designing and erecting the "Hanging Gardens" Project which provides Haifa a prime tourist attraction'.

18

1999: BEAUTY RECOGNIZED

Recognition of the beauty of the Shrines reached another level in 1999.

An award

In a ceremony on 25 May at the official residence of the President of Israel, the architect of the Terraces, on behalf of the Bahá'í World Centre, received from President Ezer Weizman the Magshim 1999 Award for the final stages of their development and in particular its environmentally friendly design. While presenting the award, the President told the audience that in the last few years he had flown over Mount Carmel several times when the project was under construction and the mountain was bare. He added that he had become increasingly concerned, until he saw the outcome and realized the beauty it had brought to the mountain and city.[1] The previous year the gardens had won the same award.

Presented by the Council for a Beautiful Israel, the awards committee noted that the 'innovative design employs hanging gardens to create an appropriate setting and approach for the Shrine, as beautiful as it is functional'. The citation said: 'To the Terraces of the Shrine of the Báb, Haifa, for their splendour, their beauty and their exquisite integration into the landscape of Mount Carmel.'[2]

Media

As progress on the project accelerated, the publicity in Israel likewise picked up pace, a phenomenon that confirmed the 1994 statement of the Universal House of Justice that the edifices and terraces under construction were a 'manifest expression of the emergence from obscurity' of the Bahá'í Faith.[3]

The Hebrew national newspaper *Yediot Akhronot* gave some detailed instructions to readers planning a visit. It advised its readers that 'to achieve the most amazing effect' they should start their visit with closed eyes: 'Let the wind and sun stroke you lightly and only then open your eyes.' The newspaper promised that they would then behold below them 'the Hanging Gardens, multi-coloured flowers arranged in row – it is really festive to behold.'[4]

Another example of the increasing media coverage was an 11-page article in *Itzuv*, a publication of the widely circulating *Ma'ariv* newspaper. It carried the headline 'The Eighth Wonder of the World'. Quoting an outline by Shoghi Effendi of the Faith's principles, it also described the history of the Terraces and the design principles of the current project.

For a six-page article in its Hebrew edition, the *National Geographic* also used the 'wonder of the world' description but expanded on its heading, 'The Wonder of the Hanging Gardens', to point out that the difference from the garden in ancient Babylon was that the 'magnificence of the Bahá'í gardens is expressed by the restraint of their design'.

In China, the widely circulating newspaper in Beijing *Youth Daily* reported on a presentation about the Terraces that their architect gave in the Chinese capital to the Congress of the International Union of Architects. The newspaper said the Terraces were not only decorative but 'an instrument to create an environment of serenity, peace and meditation' and that they prepared pilgrims for the 'spiritual experience ahead of them'. In those times in China, it was very unusual to bestow such praise on a spiritual place.

In May, media representatives toured the Terraces in preparation for a visit by dignitaries who would be attending a major agricultural conference, Agrictech '99, in Haifa. In a colourful description, the *Ha'aretz* newspaper said: 'At present one can only peep, but on September 9, 1999 the gates of heaven will be opened wide and a chosen group of professionals will be able to enter the Baha'i Hanging Gardens on Mount Carmel . . .' When the big day arrived, more than 200 dignitaries from around the world descended from Terrace 19 to the Shrine and later walked down some of the lower terraces. Among the Bahá'í ushers assisting the visitors were several wearing their national costumes.

Major announcement

In its Riḍván message of April 1999, the Universal House of Justice, referring to the 'unfolding magnificence of the Terraces', issued a 'chronology of expectations' in which it said the Mount Carmel projects would be complete by the time of the Counsellors' Conference at the end of November in 2000.[5] This had an historic parallel 46 years earlier when in his Naw-Rúz message of 1953 the Guardian had written of his hope that the superstructure of the Shrine would be finished by October that year, a hope fulfilled.

On 14 September 1999 the House of Justice set an opening date for the Terraces:

> The final work on the current construction projects on Mount Carmel is scheduled to end in December 2000. The Universal House of Justice has, therefore, decided to proceed with preparations of the official opening to the public of the Terraces of the Shrine of the Báb. The ceremonies to take place in May 2001 will mark the completion of these projects.[6]

In November, the Office of the Project Manager referred to the message and announcement of the House of Justice, and described the 'excitement and feverish activity gripping the Mount Carmel Projects team with just less than 12 months left to wind-up the Project':

> What keeps us going is the warm and encouraging support from Bahá'ís around the world and loving and inspiring words from the Universal House of Justice such as these . . . 'the entire Bahá'í world stands in admiration at the manner in which this monumental task is being executed through the selfless and consecrated labours of the dear friends serving in the Mount Carmel Projects Office'.[7]

Lower terraces

The final frontier of the Terraces project, the last remaining area of construction, opened up in the first half of the year when excavation began for the entrance plaza. With the busy intersection of Ben Gurion Avenue and Hagefen Street just behind them, the team started the year by digging into the mountain below Terrace 1. By the time excavations had finished in July, trucks had hauled away more than 1,000 cubic metres of earth, most of which went to various other places on the Mount Carmel sites.

This work was necessary to provide the wide, open, flat area which would house an exquisite central fountain. That centrepiece would have two concentric bowls, which would appear as eight-pointed star-shaped flowers. Water would spout from the top and then fill an upper bowl before overflowing into a second one and then into the surrounding pool. That pool would be surrounded by 16 diamond-shaped pools set in paving marked into a star and backed by landscaped gardens. Ahead of the fountain would be a marble ladder of 15 pools cascading down between two sets of stairs leading to Terrace 1.

By the end of the year there had been very pleasing progress. An underground mechanical room to support the fountain and the water cascade was complete, the concrete structures for the fountain and the cascade were in place, and the whole area had been backfilled in preparation for paving.

Tests in a full-scale mock-up of the two concentric bowls of the central fountain had helped the fine tuning of the design. Italian artisans were now working on its production. Orders had been placed in Italy for the highest quality white Carrara marble for the cascade.

Terrace 1 had been paved, the base for the balustrades on the contour walls was fixed and the inner areas were readied for landscaping.

Meanwhile, behind the Shrine the emerging refurbished gardens – distinguished by a series of rectangles, eight-pointed floral stars and monuments – made a lovely carpet, one whose fringes touched the circle of cypress trees once graced by the presence of Bahá'u'lláh.

Crowning the year's work in the precincts of the Shrine was the reinstallation on Hatzionut Avenue of the gate designed by Sutherland Maxwell and first put in place more than 50 years previously.[8] While work had been under way lowering the road and building retaining walls, the iron gate was being refurbished at the Bahá'í World Centre's workshops, the place of work of master blacksmith Daryoush Haji-yousef, who had been in charge of fabrication of all the other gates and steel works of the Terraces.

Replicas of the stone columns were being made in the stone factory to replace the originals, now weather-beaten and worn. Careful examination of the originals provided the required dimensions, stone colour and design.

The three-year wait for the reinstallation of the gate was well worth it. Pilgrims could now enter through this magnificent entrance, its columns decorated with coronets. From there they would walk directly ahead to the newly-paved courtyard of the Pilgrim House.

Upper terraces

The top terraces were largely complete, so most of the stonework during the year was on Terraces 14 down to 11, on items such as the pools, the paving and the stairs. By the end of the year, that work had narrowed down to Terrace 12.

Terrace 11 was virtually complete by then. Underneath it, the security control room displayed the latest monitoring equipment, and the public information side had an auditorium, a marble visitors centre, and two large eight-sided pyramid skylights. Four smaller skylights provided natural illumination for the office area.

At the start of the year most of the landscaping and planting had been finished on the eastern side of the terraces, so attention then focused on the vast western side. By March, after the required grading, backfill had gone into the western outer areas of Terraces 12 to 15, a big operation requiring two excavators working constantly. The team laid extensive sewage and drainage lines connected to the city system, and installed some 26 manholes. By mid-year the entire outer area on the western side of Terraces 15, 14 and 13 had topsoil, and at the end of August rockeries, olive trees, smaller flowering trees and groundcovers were in place.

Once planting had been finished on the steep slope above the tunnel over Crusader Road, and also to the west of Terrace 11, the entire western extension was complete. Most of the scars that had once covered that part of the mountain were gone, and the green line of terraces with its transitions on both sides stretched right down to a few metres from Hatzionut Street, a 35,000-square-metre coverage.

The three-zone design of the landscape was now more apparent. The formal areas in the centre near the pathway had lawns, annual flower beds, hedges and pruned bushes and trees. The next zone contained drought-resistant flowering trees, olives and oaks, and perennial bushes. The outer area then merged into the natural forest.

Wildlife corridors

The design had envisioned a gradual transition of pristine landscaped terraces to a medium-size zone of drought-resistant shrubs. That zone would then merge into the existing original native forest. Later on, it was decided to establish 'wildlife corridors' within this forest zone. They would run down both sides of the Terraces, from top to bottom.

It would be an uninterrupted band of vegetation, established without the need for landscaping, irrigation maintenance or expensive input. It would solve several pest problems by protecting the native animals and beneficial insects, which would otherwise leave the site, disturbed by the construction. It would also remove the need to irrigate the outer terraces. There would be no maintenance requirement.

Horticulturalist Andrew Blake, who managed this part of the project under Mr Sahba's direction, said it required a complete change in culture for many of the garden staff:

> They were used to the formality of the mown lawns and trimmed hedges of the inner Terraces but now had to cope with a mixture of disparate native plants, which were not allowed to be titivated, boosted or mulched. We also found it necessary to manage the human–animal interaction, because most of our staff and visitors – mostly city dwellers – were afraid of, and reacted negatively to, animals in the gardens.[9]

With the ending of the massive grading and filling work, birds began to return, including the kingfishers in their striking blue jackets, iridescent sun-birds, finches and quails. Creatures such as ladybirds and praying mantis also arrived. Andrew Blake said this project became even more successful over time:

> After some years, populations of native birds, bats, lizards, tortoises, jackals, mongoose, snakes, frogs, terrapins, and boars built up to a level where they started to help with garden pest control. The star performers were the hooded crows which became expert at finding lawn grubs; the jackals which kept feral cats away; and the birds and bats which greatly reduced the flying insects. We developed methods to both encourage this beneficial wildlife as well as to use

them as bio-indicators – to indicate the biological health of our garden ecosystem.[10]

The edging forest not only became a sanctuary for mammals, and offered the hope that birds, insects and wildlife would be a natural deterrent to pests and make redundant the use of chemical pesticides. It also had another advantage. It provided a visual and sound buffer between the residential areas and the gardens.

Hatzionut bridge

The huge project to build the Hatzionut bridge came to a dramatic conclusion on 17 August 1999 following weeks of intense work by staff.

It was time for the commemoration, based on the lunar calendar, of the Declaration of the Báb. It would be the first time Bahá'ís had observed a Holy Day by proceeding along the newly completed pathway to the Shrine. What they did that day would set an example for the commemoration of Holy Days in Haifa for the decades ahead.

After recitation of the Tablets of Visitation while facing the Shrine, members of the Universal House of Justice, the International Teaching Centre and other Bahá'í institutions, pilgrims, Bahá'í visitors and World Centre staff left the concourse of the Seat of the Universal House of Justice and walked down the steps in front of it, turned left along the Arc path, passing the International Archives Building to the left, and then crossed the Hatzionut bridge, through its lovely gardens and between its recently completed ornamental edges.

They proceeded down the steps to the east and took the paths through the gardens until they reached the Shrine, where they circumambulated that sacred place before entering to pray to their Creator.

2000–2001
Completion

19

2000: YEAR OF COMPLETION

The year 2000 was the final year of the Terraces project. During all 12 months, the end-of-year deadline for the completion of the Mount Carmel Projects drove the team forward towards their goal.

Work continued at feverish pitch. In January, the Office of the Project Manager wrote of 'many anxious moments on the road to completion'; in July of expectations of 'intense and hectic activity'; in November of the 'final massive rush towards the finish line'.

In the first month of the year, joy and sadness were intertwined. The joy came with global television coverage that included a vision of the Shrine and its Terraces. The sadness descended with the passing of the much-loved and respected Amatu'l-Bahá Rúḥíyyih Khánum.

Media

The year had begun with the Shrine of the Báb and its Terraces appearing on global television to an estimated audience of close to one billion people during the worldwide Millennium celebrations.[1]

The Universal House of Justice said that, crowning the media coverage of the Faith in the world, was 'the independent choice of international media establishments to use the Shrine of the Báb and the Terraces as the site for the telecast of the Holy Land's segment of the worldwide media programme celebrating the arrival of the year 2000'.[2]

The British Broadcasting Corporation (BBC) and the American Broadcasting Corporation (ABC) screened a segment from Haifa in which six members from the Carmel *a cappella* choir sang 'Hallelujah' in Hebrew as they stood on the steps of one of the lower terraces, while behind them the Shrine of the Báb stood in all its majesty. Young people performed Arabic and Jewish dances on Ben Gurion Avenue, the Shrine and its Terraces again the backdrop. The lyrics of the accompanying

Disney song 'Small World' were in harmony with a key teaching of Bahá'u'lláh: 'The earth is but one country, and mankind its citizens.'

In the United States, the commentator for the screening of the Public Broadcasting Service's coverage of that event spoke about the Báb, the persecution of His early followers and His tragic execution, moving on to mention the name of Bahá'u'lláh before introducing the principles of His Faith and its aim of uniting all the peoples of the earth. The Shrine had yet again played its mysterious role of proclaiming the teachings of the Faith.

Passing of Amatu'l-Bahá Rúḥíyyih Khánum

Rúḥíyyih Khánum, the beloved widow of the Guardian and the last link to the faithful members of the Holy Family of Bahá'u'lláh, passed away in Haifa on 19 January 2000 aged 89 years. The Universal House of Justice paid her an eloquent tribute:

> For all whose hearts she touched so deeply, the sorrow that this irreparable loss brings will, in God's good time, be assuaged in awareness of the joy that is hers through her reunion with the Guardian and with the Master, Who had Himself prayed in the Most Holy Shrine that her parents be blessed with a child. Down the centuries to come, the followers of Bahá'u'lláh will contemplate with wonder and gratitude the quality of the services – ardent, indomitable, resourceful – that she brought to the protection and promotion of the Cause.[3]

Rúḥíyyih Khánum's association with the Shrine of the Báb had begun even before her birth, as the House of Justice mentioned. It had resumed when she was a toddler in Montreal and was cuddled in the arms of 'Abdu'l-Bahá, Who had built the original mausoleum. Her connection resumed in the 1920s when, as a 12-year-old girl, she had visited the Shrine after arriving with her mother, May Maxwell, on pilgrimage.

After marrying Shoghi Effendi in 1937, Rúḥíyyih Khánum assisted him with his work. Among her contributions to the completion of the Shrine and its surrounds was to arrange for her father, Sutherland Maxwell, to come to live in Haifa after he was widowed, and then to encourage the Guardian to call upon his talents as an architect. That led Mr Maxwell to receive the commission to design the superstructure and to be the project manager for its construction. Rúḥíyyih Khánum was also closely involved in that project, working closely with the Guardian and attending to administrative details.

After the tragic early death of Shoghi Effendi, Rúḥíyyih Khánum had become one of the 'Custodians', a body of nine Hands of the Cause elected 'to conduct and protect the affairs of the Faith from its World Centre'. Among their duties was to 'maintain the Bahá'í Shrines and Holy Places in 'Akká and Haifa . . . and continue their expansion'.[4]

As a member of the hosting party for the increasing number of visits to the Bahá'í World Centre by prominent local and international figures, Rúḥíyyih Khánum often escorted them to the Shrine. The overall responsibility for the cleanliness and maintenance of the internal ornaments, carpets, lights and other aspects of the Shrine remained her responsibility, and she trained some of the wives of the Universal House of Justice and, later, too, of International Council members in how to undertake that important task. She continued her close attention to the Shrine for the remaining years of her active life.

Rúḥíyyih Khánum had participated in the official prayers in the Shrine at the very start of the Terraces project and continued to show great interest, to Fariborz Sahba's delight, occasionally visiting the architect in his office and on several occasions the construction site. Rúḥíyyih Khánum told Mr Sahba that she closely followed the progress from a window of her house.[5]

In 1999 she undertook her last visit to the Terraces when Mr Sahba drove her to the upper terraces via the service access road in the company of his wife, Golnar, and Mrs Violette Nakhjavani.[6] Mr Sahba recalls that on that particular day, Rúḥíyyih Khánum was tired and had initially planned to view the Terraces from a car window but changed her mind and joined the others.

> It was a very beautiful day, and the gardens were in their full beauty. From the balcony of the Terraces, we could all see the precious Shrine sitting in the bosom of the heavenly garden, and we could view the Arc and all its completed buildings. Looking at this magnificent sight made Rúḥíyyih Khánum very excited, and with much joy she said she now understood the vision the beloved Guardian had for Mount Carmel. She said this is exactly what he had often spoken about, and said Shoghi Effendi is very happy with the

fulfilment of his vision. The next morning Mrs Nakhjavani told me that Rúḥíyyih Khánum for hours that night had spoken with excitement of her experience. Mrs Nakhjavani said she had never seen 'Amatu'l-Bahá so moved.[7]

On 23 January, four days after her passing, and after a funeral service attended by diplomats, Israeli officials and Bahá'ís present in the Holy Land, Rúḥíyyih Khánum was buried in a garden facing her home, the House of the Master where she and Shoghi Effendi had lived. From that garden, those present could gaze to the south and see glimpses of the Terraces adorning the Shrine of the Báb.

It seemed fitting that the MCBP team was honoured with the responsibility of preparing her burial ground – a very challenging project due to flooding rains and the resulting mud[8] – as well as the establishment of the surrounding garden.

Upper terraces

The early focus in the upper terraces in 2000 was the completion of Terraces 11 and 12, a goal achieved with the completion of the stonework by March. Then followed the landscaping of the inner and outer areas of the terraces. With the rugged patches being increasingly covered up and red service paths curving across the slopes, the work was mostly complete by September. The eastern side looked harmonious and colourful with the different hues of the bougainvillea, dark-green carissa and red pennisetum.

Another construction job was the creation of a viewing area, measuring 6 by 10 metres, to the west of Terraces 17 and 18, where visitors could obtain a view that at once encompassed the Shrine, its upper terraces, and the Arc buildings. It had not been part of the original plan, but the excellence of this vantage point had become clear during the construction process and after a site office had been established there.[9] Prior to the Terraces project, and in fact from the time of its purchase by the Bahá'ís, the Israeli army had been using this land for a workshop and for storage, but Mr Sahba successfully negotiated for the site to be vacated.

The installation of an automated gate to the side of the terraces from Crusader Road allowed emergency and service vehicles to obtain access to Terraces 16 down to 14, and to enter the tunnel to an underground parking area on the eastern side of the Arc.

Lower terraces

All eyes were on the entrance plaza as the fountain arose, as the geometric green curves on the side lawns appeared and as the intensive landscaping began, with jacaranda, bougainvillea and bright green grass providing a show.

There were three major water features to complete – the cascade, the fountain in the entrance plaza and the one set in the retaining wall under Terrace 1. To ensure they would all be ready on time, contracts for production of the marble parts went to three contractors in Italy rather than to just one, all three of them committing to complete their work by August. The carved marble arrived in September. Soon skilled French stonemasons were installing the pieces, completing the work by the end of the year.

Mr Sahba had spent about six months designing the plaza, including the fountain and cascade. His vision was for a green crystal mirror at the foot of the Shrine that reflected the beauty and perfection that emanated from everything associated with the Báb. The concept that came to him was of a plain of fine, silky, emerald green grass[10] that would merge into a complex of diamond shaped crystal mirrors – although he did not intend to use grass as such. He was inspired by the mirrors in the beautiful historic architecture of Shiraz, but in this case they would be green. He drew on the constant references to mirrors in the Báb's Writings.[11]

The main pool of the fountain was built of green granite, but when filled with water it would be the water rather than the granite that would be visible, and the surface of that water would appear as a series of green mirrors. Water would overflow from a beautiful white flower into the green water without disturbing the peace of the mirrors. The pattern of the green mirrors would continue into the pattern of stone floor of the plaza, suggesting, as Mr Sahba said, that the 'water of life' would continue expanding forever and cover the entire universe.[12]

The Biblical quotation that read: 'Then the angel showed me the river of the water of life, as clear as crystal, flowing from the throne of God and of the Lamb'[13] – the one that had inspired him to design the runnels along the stairway – also inspired the idea of water coming out of the wall on the southern side of the plaza. Mr Sahba designed the fountain so that water would emerge from the wall and enter the cascade. It would then appear as if the water goes underground before coming up in the centre of the fountain. The water of life that came from the Shrine would now reach humanity via this fountain. He noted that the Master had spoken about fountains with reference to the Terraces of the Shrine.

In *Vineyard of the Lord*, the writer Eliza Rasiwala provided a lovely word picture of the scene:

> The cascade is a beautiful sight; the water originates from a fountain set below a triple arch in the retaining wall of Terrace 1, and flows over white Carrara marble basins into a large pool set in the landing above the cascade. From there it appears to bubble up, spring-like, into the topmost pool of the cascade, and falls in glassy sheets through each of its fourteen pools. The culmination of the water's journey comes when it bursts forth like a geyser from the central fountain of white marble shaped like an 8-pointed star. Interestingly, the pool below this fountain is made from deep green Indian granite, which serves as a still, reflecting base of water. The entire effect is quite stunning.[14]

The view from Ben Gurion Avenue of the Shrine and its lower terraces opened up in September after a demolition crew levelled a building which the Bahá'í World Centre had obtained after years of patient negotiation.[15] The work enabled the expansion of the area east of Terrace 1 and gave direct access to the spot where Bahá'u'lláh once pitched His tent at the base of Mount Carmel, now a Bahá'í-owned area adorned with cypresses and lawn.

The Shrine

Work began during the year to upgrade the lighting system of the Shrine, employing a computer program which controlled the lights on the Arc, Terrace 10 and the Shrine itself. An automated dimming system allowed control of the outer floodlights, bringing them on gradually and fading them before and after each sunrise and sunset, and enabling

Steep slopes in the upper terraces required stairways in the shape of brackets

In May 1997, work was advancing with steps leading up from Terrace 13

The beautiful and complex design of Terrace 19 in its incomplete, unadorned state

View up Mount Carmel from the uncompleted Hatzionut bridge

Soil-filled geowebs covering some steep inner slopes of the upper terraces

Working flat out, vegetating the upper terraces

Many hands are required to insert a canary palm

Greenery adorns part of the upper terraces (rear left) before the Seat of the International Teaching Centre rises from its site to the northeast of the majestic Seat of the Universal House of Justice. The Arc (centre left) is clearly visible in this remarkable photograph, and at right centre, the Shrine of the Báb shines amidst her exquisite gardens

An aerial view shows the lower terraces almost completed. Priority given to those terraces at the start of the project gave Haifa residents more reason to be patient with the dust and noise as they saw the beauty unfold close up

Incomplete lower terraces, and completed upper terraces leading over the Hatzionut bridge to the Queen of Carmel

Beauty at its peak: Terrace 19 at the summit of Mount Carmel

the Shrine to remain lit throughout the night. The lighting panels in the rooms adjacent to the Shrine now controlled only the lights around the colonnade and the rooms of the Shrine itself. All other services were relocated to minimize technical visits.

In the weeks leading up to 21 March, the Holy Day of Naw-Rúz, gardeners planted many flowers in the reconstructed garden behind the Shrine, and placed ochre-coloured tiles on the Hatzionut bridge. On the Holy Day, pilgrims, Bahá'í visitors and staff left the Concourse of the Seat of the Universal House of Justice and passed through freshly enhanced garden vistas to the bridge and then down and through the gardens to circumambulate the Shrine.

The completion of the garden behind the Shrine and the work on the bridge meant that heavy equipment was no longer necessary in the area, so by September the surface of Hatzionut Avenue could safely receive its final layer of asphalt.

In June 2000 the Department of Security and the Office of Public Information moved into the building under Terrace 11, occupying respectively the east and west wings of the 2,000-square-metre building. Gracing the public information area was a marble reception area under a star-shaped skylight, and to its rear a space for a museum exhibit about the Faith. A 164-seat auditorium and other displays completed the public area, with offices for staff set off to the west. Large automated iron gates created a beautiful, impressive entrance for visitors from Hatzionut Avenue to the forecourt of the security and information building.

As for Bahá'í pilgrims, a new reception facility in two adjacent buildings opened on Hatzionut Avenue to the southeast of the Shrine, nearly opposite the entrance from that street to the resting place of the Greatest Holy Leaf. Once serving as a hospital during the British Mandate and later as medical laboratories, the refurbished buildings had their exteriors restored and interiors remodelled to create large spaces, including a hall for 350 pilgrims.

Gardens

Unusually torrential winter rains at the start of the year provided a good test of the drainage system on the Terraces and of the stability of the planted slopes. The work passed with flying colours – there was hardly any erosion. Nevertheless, the team continued to look at ways to strengthen the established gardens as they waited for planting season in the spring.

The maintenance of the gardens relied heavily on scientific horticultural practice. It had already produced spectacular results by resurrecting the original geranium variety that Shoghi Effendi had planted. After five decades, disease had taken its toll, viruses turning the once rich vermilion to a dull pink. Careful work in a local laboratory specializing in plant tissue culture produced a plant of the original colour and strength, and so now people looking at the geraniums in the gardens could appreciate the Guardian's eye for colour.

An automated climate station helped predict the arrival of pests and diseases, and an integrated pest management system reduced the need to rely on pesticides through the use of natural predators and other options. The team used special human-made soils for the gardens on the bridges, conducted tests on plant growth to find the most suitable plants for the steep slopes, and employed biomechanical tree analysis methods to check the health of the older trees.

They made sure they used environmentally friendly methods. The recycled waste went to compost, which laboratory technicians checked before use, as they did with manure. The team also established a bio-monitoring programme with the local university, and employed harmless monitoring methods of animal species in and around the Terraces area as a way of checking the biological health of the gardens.

Experiments with mowing the steep terrace lawns, some at 40 degrees, did not produce any miraculous results. The best method, and one that attracted a lot of attention from visitors, was having three men use a rotary mower, two of them holding ropes to keep the machine working steadily on the slope. Specially designed metal profiles enabled those trimming trees, shrubs and hedges to obtain the exact shape required.

The Terraces had several climatic zones, each requiring specialized attention. Although the three zones of the Terraces were diverse in their elements, the garden specialists treated the multi-coloured floral carpet as the one great, living organism that it had become.

The gardeners carefully nurtured the original gardens around the Shrine, those first established by the Master and then developed and expanded by the Guardian. They had to ensure, too, that the circle of historic cypress trees behind the Shrine grew naturally and not at speed, as would happen had they used fertilizers or excessive irrigation.

Attention to water conservation was a priority in the selection of vegetation such as special groundcover and drought-resistant, deep-rooted plants. Watering was done mainly during the early hours of the morning or at night when there were lower levels of evaporation and there was less demand on the city water supply. After consultation with experts, they had selected a multi-regime irrigation system involving sprinklers, sprayers and drippers to ensure that the gardens used only the amount of water required and no more. Recycling of the water in the fountains and running down the runnels meant little was wasted,[16] and in fact the fountains lost only a couple of cubic metres a day, mainly due to evaporation.[17]

Staffing arrangements saw a handful of horticultural professionals supervising local Israeli staff – mainly from the Arab community – and Bahá'í volunteer staff. Due to adherence to principles of good communication and non-competitive methods, a teamwork culture arose in which the skill and devotion of the whole team became evident to all.

Towards the end of the project, the MCBP was entrusted with responsibility for the maintenance of all the Bahá'í gardens in Haifa, the aim being to lift the quality of all the gardens in Haifa to the standard of the Terrace gardens.

Budget

The budget for the combined MCBP projects, the Terraces and the Arc buildings had been US$250 million, but through careful financial management, the use of value engineering, and the direct supply of building materials after assuming construction management, the final cost came in at US$200 million. The 20 per cent saving was a staggering achievement and was recorded in an itemized account on a detailed report to the Universal House of Justice. The $50 million dollars in savings became the foundation of an endowment fund which, when combined with donations from Bahá'ís throughout the world, would pay for the future maintenance of the Arc buildings and Terraces.

The cost of the actual construction of Terraces was about $60 million. The estimate saved on the Terraces project alone was $16 million.[18]

20

2001: GRAND OPENING

The year of the grand opening of the Terraces began with a major conference marking the inauguration of the seat of the International Teaching Centre and attended by members of the Continental Boards of Counsellors and 849 members of their Auxiliary Boards from 172 countries, nearly 1,000 Bahá'ís in all. It was the first gathering of the entire membership of 'the Institution of the Counsellors', which has the responsibility to encourage the spread of the Faith worldwide.[1]

They reverently ascended the lower terraces and circumambulated the Shrine of the Báb. One of them, Dana Hudson of Taiwan, recalled later: 'When each of us started to ascend we had no choice but to bow our heads in utmost humility. It was a feeling which most of us had to express in the form of tears.'[2]

They then proceeded along the Arc path, past the International Archives Building, viewing the glorious marble circular portico of the Centre for the Study of the Texts to the right, then the majestic Seat of the Universal House of Justice and, there, ahead of them the stately columns of the Seat of the International Teaching Centre. By happy coincidence, and not because of the intention of the architect, that building faces in the general direction of the Shrine, although not facing it exactly.[3]

In a message marking the inauguration, the Universal House of Justice expressed its gratitude to Bahá'u'lláh: 'The very earth of Carmel is astir with the wonders of His grace as she responds to the redemptive call He raised in the Tablet bearing her name.'[4]

What the participants saw on their visits to the Terraces they later related to Bahá'ís around the world, increasing the excitement about the forthcoming opening.

Terraces

Members of the Mount Carmel Bahá'í Projects team set about in early January to complete the stone paving around the central fountain. Then, on 8 March 2001, the members of the Universal House of Justice inspected the exquisite entrance plaza in the company of the architect. It was some 15 years since the architect had been appointed, and more than six decades since Rúḥíyyih Khánum, on behalf of the Guardian, had asked her father, the Hand of the Cause Sutherland Maxwell, to design an entrance plaza, although that was not built.

Publicity

Civil authorities played their part in publicizing the Terraces project. In April, at the suggestion of Mr Sahba, the Israeli Post authorities issued a special stamp to commemorate the completion. The well-designed nine-centimetre-long stamp, illustrated by a photograph of the Shrine and its Terraces – as well as one of a balustrade – came with a souvenir leaf, illustrated similarly. On its reverse there was a description of the Holy Place published in more than ten languages. To encase each numbered leaf with its stamp, the Bahá'í World Centre provided a blue velveteen cover, embossed with a golden title noting the opening of the Terraces and the date.

The Municipality of Haifa, in close cooperation with the MCBP Office, published *Bahá'í Shrine and Gardens on Mount Carmel, Haifa, Israel: A Visual Journey*, a high-quality large-format 128-page hardcover book with more than 100 full-size photographs of the Terraces by the Bahá'í photographer Ruhi Vargha, with text in English and Hebrew. The book also included detailed interviews with the architect.

The newly-inaugurated website for the *Bahá'í World News Service* published a series of stories leading up to the event, and the Office of Public Information provided extensive information on the Terraces and Arc projects to the local and international media.

Arrivals in Haifa

In its Riḍván message, one month before the official opening, the Universal House of Justice wrote that the significance of the inaugural events lies principally in the pause it will allow for a review of the remarkable distance the Cause has covered in its development during the twentieth century. It will be time, too, for considering the future implications of the phenomenal accomplishments symbolized by the rise of the monumental structures on God's holy mountain – a rise that opens the spiritual and administrative centres of our Faith to the gaze of the world.[5]

Excitement had been building up in Israel. On one day during Passover in the previous month, public visits to the gardens near the Shrine soared from the usual 2,000 on a Jewish holy day to 12,000.[6] The managing director of the Haifa Tourist Board, Moshe Tzur, said the city considered the gardens a gift and hoped it would become one of the main tourist attractions in the world. Days before the event Haifa residents received in their mailboxes a leaflet about the Terraces that the Municipality of Haifa and the Bahá'í World Centre had jointly published.

In the days leading up to the inauguration event on the evening of 22 May, the 158th anniversary of the Báb's declaration of His mission, more than 2,500 Bahá'ís from 182 countries and dependent territories began arriving in Haifa in response to an invitation from the Universal House of Justice.[7] It followed the selection of most of them as representatives by their national communities, some for their exemplary service. Others had their names picked out of a hat.

The programme coordinator for the inaugural events, Douglas Moore of the United States, said the people attending 'represent the kind of world we are working for as Bahá'ís, a unified community of people from every nation, religion, race, ethnic group and culture. And they are people, by and large, who have been working towards this goal, whether in Africa, Asia, the Americas, Europe or other regions of the world.'[8]

The Bahá'í World News Service reported that those attending spanned the gamut of professions, social and economic class, and racial and religious backgrounds. They ranged from a New York investment banker to a young woman from the Fulnio people in northeastern Brazil, from a Nepalese journalist to an architectural student from Belarus.

Some had never left their home countries before, such as Henrietta Josias, a flea market saleswoman who came from an economically disadvantaged community in South Africa. 'I feel I am part of this great process where people are trying to become citizens of this whole wide world and so that we see one another as brothers and sisters,' Ms Josias said.[9]

To explain his 'great happiness', Claudio Limachi, a Quechua from Bolivia, drew on imagery used in the Bahá'í Writings: 'I feel like I am next to God, with people of different colours, from different places, and that we are flowers of one garden.'[10]

Many of the participants brought gifts for the Universal House of Justice. Staff volunteers formally accepted and registered them, however small, and gave the donors a letter of thanks from the House of Justice. One volunteer, Josephine Hill from Australia, recalls: 'One gift came from Argentina and was a small toy truck containing a tiny sack of the herbal drink maté and a tiny sack of sugar. Another came from India in a large cardboard box. Inside were dozens of packets of tea, one from every family in the village it came from.'[11]

To accommodate the participants, the Inaugural Events Office booked virtually every hotel room in Haifa and in surrounding cities from Nahariya to the north of Acre down to the hilltop of Zichron Ya'acov on the southern end of the Carmel mountain range.[12]

Preliminary gatherings

On Monday 21 May, the Bahá'ís attended a devotional event at Bahjí. They heard prayers and scriptural excerpts read or chanted in Arabic, English, French, Persian and Russian, including one chanted by Hand of the Cause 'Alí-Akbar Furútan. They then circumambulated the Shrine of Bahá'u'lláh, the One who had directed the establishment of the Shrine of His predecessor, the Báb, and had selected its very spot on Mount Carmel.

On the morning of Tuesday 22 May they convened at the Haifa Congress Centre where the Hands of the Cause 'Alí-Muḥammad Varqá and 'Alí-Akbar Furútan addressed them on the significance of the occasion and on the importance of conveying to others the atmosphere when they returned home. Haifa Mayor Amram Mitzna welcomed them, and musicians from diverse places around the globe, such as Spain and the Democratic Republic of the Congo, lifted their hearts even higher through song. There was a message from the Samoan head of state, His Highness Susuga Malietoa Tanumafili II, the first reigning monarch to become a Bahá'í. The Bahá'ís of Iran, whose representatives could not be present due to the persecution in their country, sent long-stemmed red roses with their message.[13]

In an address to the gathering, a speaker from the Bahá'í International Community's Office of Public Information, Matthew Weinberg, said: 'the dedicated and selfless efforts of Bahá'ís across the decades of the twentieth century to raise up and adorn the Shrine of the Báb – as well as the great Administrative Centre in its shadows – is undoubtedly a triumph of the unheard peoples of the world.' It was, he said, 'a momentous victory of the meek'.[14]

There had been sound checks on site at the base of Mount Carmel for the evening's inauguration ceremony. Supervising was the event's music director, Jack Lenz, a Canadian composer who had written the opening music for the 1992 Bahá'í World Congress. In an interview, he spoke of the historical and Biblical significance of the musical performance, which would comprise three-quarters of the programme, referring to the Prophet Isaiah talking about songs of 'everlasting joy' on Mount Carmel. There were individual microphones on each instrument in the orchestra to compensate for the lack of acoustic benefits that are provided by concert halls. Windsocks were placed over the microphones, to ensure protection against breezes.

For nearly two weeks before the inauguration event on Tuesday 22 May 2001, the city authorities blocked off the major intersection of Ben Gurion Avenue and Hagefen Street at the foot of the mountain to give enough time for the construction of a temporary amphitheatre, right on the intersection of those two important roads.[15]

Arrivals at the amphitheatre

On the day of the main inaugural event, the local authorities closed to traffic Ben Gurion Avenue right down to Allenby Street, except for more than 60 buses bringing in the Bahá'ís and the limousines transporting the dignitaries.

The 16-metre-tall amphitheatre, with capacity for 4,500, provided easily enough seats for the more than 2,500 Bahá'ís and the 650 special guests, who included ambassadors from more than 30 countries, Israeli government ministers and deputy ministers, members of the Knesset and three Supreme Court justices. Other dignitaries who accepted invitations were the mayors of Haifa and Acre, as well as local political and religious leaders.

Before taking their seats, the VIPs mingled with the Hands of the Cause and members of the Universal House of Justice at a pre-event reception in a big marquee on the western side of Ben Gurion Avenue. Among the guests was Israel's Foreign Minister, Shimon Peres. One of the guests at the event later recalled that as they walked up to the amphitheatre, local people lining the Avenue called out 'congratulations' to the Bahá'ís.[16]

An usher, standing ready at the top on the amphitheatre, looked down the avenue and saw members of the Universal House of Justice informally walking from the marquee up to the site of the event to mark the completion of a project for which the institution on which they served had for so many years worked and planned.[17]

More than 100 members of the national and international media were there to report the event, including television networks such as the BBC, CBC, CNN and China TV. The wire services Associated Press, Agence France Presse, the DPA German News Agency, Reuters and UPI sent their staff, as did individual newspapers such as *Frankfurter Allgemeine Zeitung*, *Le Monde* and *The New York Times*. It was some years before the arrival of social media and the use of smartphone cameras.

It took some planning to get all the busloads of participants seated in time for the 6.30 p.m. commencement of the event. They began to arrive from 3.30 p.m. when the weather was still warm. This large gathering of diverse members of the peoples from all over the world, many wearing national dress, shaded their eyes from the westering sun to take in the breathtaking view that encompassed the exquisite marble entrance plaza, the Pathway of the Kings with its flower-adorned terraces flanked by emerald lawns, cypresses and palms, and then, in the centre of the middle ground, the gold and white Shrine, which rose imposing yet beautiful, massive yet delicate, and whose dome, because of the perspective, appeared to be above the crest of the holy mountain itself.

Statement by the House of Justice

The centrepiece of the event was the statement by the Universal House of Justice for the occasion. No member of that institution addressed the gathering. Instead, the Secretary-General of the Bahá'í International Community, Dr Albert Lincoln, stood on the entrance plaza and delivered the statement, which spoke of the One whose Shrine the Terraces now adorned:

> With joyful and thankful hearts, we welcome all who have come from near and far to join us on this auspicious occasion for the Bahá'ís of the world. We acknowledge with deep appreciation the presence of so many distinguished guests.
>
> A century and a half have passed since that unspeakable tragedy in the northwest of Persia when the Báb faced the volley fired at Him from the rifles of 750 soldiers. The soldiers had followed the orders of the highest authorities in the land. The Báb's mangled body was then thrown on the side of a moat outside the city, abandoned to what His cold-blooded persecutors thought would be a dishonourable fate. They had hoped thus to put an end to the growing influence of His teachings on masses of people throughout the country. These masses had accepted, in the face of intense persecution, the Báb's claim to prophethood, and their lives were being transformed spiritually and morally as He prepared them for what He said was the dawn of a new age in which a world civilization would be born and flourish. The expectations that stirred countless hearts were heightened even more sublimely by the Báb's announcement that One greater than He would soon arise, One who would reveal the unparalleled character of the promised world civilization that would signify the coming of age of the entire human race.
>
> We are met not to lament the tragedy of the Báb's martyrdom and the persecutions that followed; rather have we come to celebrate the culmination and acknowledge the meaning of an unprecedented project that had its beginning over a century ago. It was then that Bahá'u'lláh, Whom the Ottoman authorities had banished to Acre to serve out His days in confinement, visited Mount Carmel and selected the spot where the remains of His Herald would be interred. We humbly trust that the wondrous result achieved by the completion of the nineteen terraced gardens, at the heart of which rises the Shrine of the Báb, is a fitting fulfilment of the vision initiated by Bahá'u'lláh.

The sufferings sustained by the Báb so as to arouse humanity to the responsibilities of its coming age of maturity were themselves indications of the intensity of the struggle necessary for the world's people to pass through the age of humanity's collective adolescence. Paradoxical as it may seem, this is a source of hope. The turmoil and crises of our time underlie a momentous transition in human affairs. Simultaneous processes of disintegration and integration have clearly been accelerating throughout the planet since the Báb appeared in Persia. That our Earth has contracted into a neighbour-hood, no one can seriously deny. The world is being made new. Death pangs are yielding to birth pangs. The pain shall pass when members of the human race act upon the common recognition of their essential oneness. There is a light at the end of this tunnel of change beckoning humanity to the goal destined for it according to the testimonies recorded in all the Holy Books.

The Shrine of the Báb stands as a symbol of the efficacy of that age-old promise, a sign of its urgency. It is, as well, a monument to the triumph of love over hate. The gardens which surround that structure, in their rich variety of colours and plants, are a reminder that the human race can live harmoniously in all its diversity. The light that shines from the central edifice is as a beacon of hope to the countless multitudes who yearn for a life that satisfies the soul as well as the body.

This inextinguishable hope stems from words such as these from the Pen of Bahá'u'lláh: 'This is the Day in which God's most excellent favours have been poured out upon men, the Day in which His most mighty grace has been infused into all created things.' May all who strive, often against great odds, to uphold principles of justice and concord be encouraged by these assurances.

In reflecting on the years of effort invested in this daunting project, we are moved to express to the people of Haifa the warmth of the feeling in our hearts. Their city will for all time be extolled by the Bahá'ís everywhere as the place in which the mortal remains of the youthful Prophet-Herald of their Faith finally found refuge, and this after half a century of having to be secretly moved for protec-tion from one place to another in His native land. The patience and cordiality shown towards the Bahá'ís throughout the most difficult years of the construction work exemplify the spirit of goodwill in which so much of the world stands so greatly in need. Haifa is providentially situated on Mount Carmel, with its immortal associations with saintly visionaries, whose concern throughout the ages was largely focused on the promise of peace. May Haifa achieve wide renown not just as a place of natural beauty but more especially as the city of peace.

Let the word go forth, then, from this sacred spot, from this Mountain of the Lord, that the unity and peace of the world are not only possible but inevitable. Their time has come.[18]

Musical presentations

It was a momentous statement on a momentous occasion, and accompanying it were musical presentations to uplift the soul.[19]

In place on the plaza were the Israel Northern Symphony, Haifa, under the baton of Stanley Sperber, and the 70 members of the Transylvania State Philharmonic Choir of Cluj, Romania, and its conductor Cornel Groza. Also present were three Canadian soloists: mezzo-soprano Patricia Green, tenor Stuart Howe and baritone Brett Polegato. In contrast to the black suits and gowns of the singers and musicians behind them, the white tuxedo jackets of the men matched that of the conductor. The blue gown of the soprano added iridescent colour. On the plaza and above were Austrian violinists Bijan Khadem-Missagh, his son Vahid, and his daughter, Martha.

As the air began to cool, birds soared over the terraces, and the music began.[20] The audience thrilled to the performance of a symphonic composition by Tolibkhon Shakhidi of Tajikistan, which the Universal House of Justice had commissioned. Entitled *O Queen of Carmel*, the cantata was based on an eloquent eulogy to the Shrine written by Shoghi Effendi for Naw-Rúz in 1955.[21]

The first movement was exquisite, the piano and later the strings producing a santour-like sound and together suffusing the atmosphere with a distinct and entrancing oriental flavour, evoking notions of rose-perfumed Shiraz, the birthplace of the Báb. The second movement opened with rolling kettledrums preceding and then underpinning a dramatic fanfare of trumpets. The strings joined in with enthusiasm but then softened in preparation for the tenor to begin the verbal salute to the Shrine.

Soon the soloist was employing the beautiful words of the Guardian with which he had addressed the Báb and celebrated the beauty of His Shrine: *'Thy glorious throne, attired in thy white raiment, crowned with thy golden crown resplendent with the lights shining within thee and around thee . . .'*

The third movement began softly and beautifully, the soprano continuing with the poetry, and the orchestra producing, among other effects, a shimmering sound. Eventually the tenor joined with her as they sang of how blessed is the person who glorifies the Báb's station *'for the love of God, thy Creator, in this hallowed and radiant, this great, august and wondrous age'.*

After the singers retreated, the orchestra introduced elements of swirling music calling to mind dancers in the heart of Persia, and then quietened before its firm conclusion.

Then came *Terraces of Light*, an oratorio by prominent Norwegian composer Lasse Thoresen.[22] Also commissioned by the Universal House of Justice, it was based on Bahá'u'lláh's Tablet of Carmel that had been revealed on Mount Carmel 110 years previously, and it employed most of its text. The Tablet, revealed in the form of a conversation between Bahá'u'lláh and Mount Carmel, contains passages that relate to the establishment of the world centre of the Faith, and which address the Bahá'ís.[23]

The composer wrote the oratorio for soprano, tenor and baritone soloists, solo violin, symphony orchestra and an 80-voice choir. There were five parts to its single uninterrupted movement. The soloists' voices recreated the dialogue, interwoven with choral passages and fanfares.

Bahá'u'lláh had revealed his Tablet with great volume and majesty, and the oratorio was soon to honour this in the first part. However, it started with ethereal strings, evoking spirituality, and then came the deep, rich sounds of the cellos, until the tenor burst in with the opening words of the Tablet: *'All glory be to this day . . .'* His voice rose and fell, and soon the chorus was repeating and amplifying some of the text. The climax came when at full volume the choir chanted, with great power and drama, the words attributed to all created things and the Concourse of High (holy departed souls). They began with the words *'Haste thee, O Carmel . . .'* Fanfares accompanied the injunction. Ethereal strings returned to conclude the part.

The tenor introduced Part II, the text starting with *'Seized with transports of joy . . .'.* Singing in the voice of Mount Carmel itself, a soprano answered, accompanied by a wistful violin. The orchestra began accompanying the violin, that instrument moving into melancholy as the singer sang about how remoteness from God had '*well-nigh consumed*' her. Appropriately a fanfare introduced the final words of that part, which referred to the voice of the Manifestation of God as '*a trumpet-call amidst Thy people*'.

The tenor returned for the introduction to Part III, and a baritone, accompanied by the choir, sung in the voice of Bahá'u'lláh, uniting in a layered injunction to Mount Carmel to rejoice because God had '*established upon Thee His throne*'.[24]

Part IV opened with the solo baritone, in the voice of Bahá'u'lláh, the chorus answering as Mount Carmel. This was the climax of the piece, and it occurred just after the sunset, as the sky turned a rosy hue on the threshold of dusk. As the music reached its crescendo, to the delight of all watching, lights illuminated each of the 19 terraces, one by one.[25] At the conclusion of this section, the solo violin became especially poignant, and then to conclude came a vocal trio, a solo violin and a chorus singing a lyrical ending. These last words referred to the establishment of the Universal House of Justice: '*Ere Long will God sail His Ark upon thee, and will manifest the people of Bahá who have been mentioned in the Book of Names.*'

In Part V, the finale, the vocal trio and chorus, accompanied by solo violin and orchestra, sang the powerful last part of the Tablet of Carmel.

Once again the mighty words of Bahá'u'lláh had resounded on the Mountain of God.

A sea of lights

A little more than 87 years previously, on 14 February 1914 while 'Abdu'l-Bahá was seated at the window of the Eastern Pilgrim House, He said: 'Mount Carmel itself, from top to bottom, will be submerged in a sea of lights.'[26]

During the performance of the oratorio, that vision had come to life before the peoples of the world, a microcosm seated in Haifa and others watching on television and via the Internet in many countries around the globe.

The *Bahá'í World News Service* reported that the 'brilliant flourish' of that moment 'will be remembered by participants for a lifetime'. It quoted a Bahá'í from Zambia as saying: 'It was stunning. I felt myself in a different world. In the Bahá'í writings, it is said that music gives wings to the soul. And I felt that.'[27]

British Bahá'í Thelma Batchelor said she felt proud and honoured to be there. 'Why me? Such an honour and a bounty to be sharing this moment with so many nationalities reflecting the cultural diversity of the human race. Everyone began to sing "Alláh-u-Abhá"[28] and other Bahá'í songs just because they felt moved to do so and it was a very moving and inspiring occasion.'[29]

The Shrine and the Terraces remained illuminated until late, thrilling the residents of Haifa. It had been a long, noisy and often inconvenient wait for them while the construction went on, but now with this vision of loveliness constantly before them it had surely been worthwhile.

Media coverage

Living up to the observation by the Universal House of Justice that the Faith was moving out of obscurity,[30] the event became the focus of worldwide coverage, so extensive that *The Bahá'í World* could provide but a sample in its report. There was coverage by CNN International, and the major United States networks NBC and CBS, there were stories by *The New York Times* and *Le Monde*, radio coverage in Germany, and news agency reports by UPI, Associated Press, Agence France Press, the Religion News Service and PTI India News Agency.

The Israel media provided extensive coverage. The whole programme was broadcast live on cable television and then rebroadcast four times due to popular demand.[31] A classical music station broadcast the programme. The nationally-circulating newspaper *Ha'aretz* published a 24-page insert about the Terraces in its 22 May edition, and other newspapers also carried it. In all, there were inserts in about 400,000 copies.

The reports later spread throughout the world. *Vineyard of the Lord*, which had chronicled the project since January 1994, produced its last edition in July, with a stunning edition that featured a breathtaking cover photograph and many others inside, with the events described in lively yet concise text.

In an interview, an excerpt published in a *Bahá'í World News Service* report, Dr Lincoln said the completion of the structures on Mt Carmel and the associated ceremonies represented a message of hope to the world:

This extraordinary work of art that we are seeing on the mountain is visible expression of inspiration that comes only from the Creator. It is the same spirit of faith that built the great cathedrals of Europe, the great mosques, monasteries and religious monuments of the East. We think the world should consider the great vitality of this force and consider setting aside some of the negative stereotypes which have in this modern era come to characterise religion. In other words, we see these terraces and this event as an opportunity to see the positive force of faith at work.[32]

Ascent

The next day dawned warm again. Volunteer staff were at the amphitheatre at 6 a.m. and quickly used towels to dry the dew from the seats before the first people arrived.[33] Some 3,000 Bahá'ís then assembled for a devotional programme before their opportunity came to ascend the Terraces.

There were prayers and readings in different languages. The Hand of the Cause Dr 'Alí-Muḥammad Varqá chanted one of the Tablets of Visitation associated with the Shrines, and a member of the Universal House of Justice, Mr Douglas Martin, recited the other. An international choir comprised of Bahá'ís serving at the Bahá'í World Centre, joined by Indian soloist Vivek Nair, sang uplifting songs and added splashes of colour with their scarves over their white shirts. Rhythmic singing and drumming from a youth choir from the Democratic Republic of Congo in their multi-coloured distinctive costumes inspired and energized the Bahá'ís for the climb ahead.

In preparation for this event many had read the descriptions in the Bahá'í Writings of the kings and rulers ascending the terraces at some future date. With bare heads and bare feet, the Writings said, these leaders would approach the Shrine of the Báb with all due humility. The climb of these kings and rulers would be no procession of comfort and ease, but one founded upon an understanding of the suffering endured by the Herald of their Faith, one that would be carried out with physical effort and with outward signs that they, the rulers of the world, were His subjects.

As the time came closer on Wednesday 23 May 2001 for the 3,000 Bahá'ís to climb the lower terraces to the Shrine, the sun beat down on them with a burning intensity not usual for a spring morning in Haifa. The camera operators were ready to broadcast the event around the world via satellite and the Internet.

As the Bahá'ís began their ascent, it was clear by their reverential attitude that they were well aware of the spiritual significance of the event. Led by the members of the Universal House of Justice[34] and their wives, they started slowly up the steep stairs, past the cascade and up to Terrace 1. Above them, ushers, volunteers from the staff at the Bahá'í World Centre, waited on each terrace, ready to provide assistance to those stepping steadily up the slope.

Many of those ascending wore the traditional costumes of their own lands, expressing the reality that people from all over the planet had converged at this sacred place. Most of the others wore conventional western clothing. Some had hats, others had not brought anything to protect them from the heat, which seemed to redouble in its strength as their efforts to keep climbing increased.

Up and up they went. Pausing to admire the stunning beauty all around them, they caught their breath and drank more water. The design of the staircase meant that their golden goal was always in sight.

As they arrived at the Shrine on Terrace 10, there was universal exhilaration. They renewed their energies and circumambulated the Shrine, which, because of such large numbers, was not open for prayer. They then walked to the east and through the gardens established by their beloved Guardian, Shoghi Effendi, and ascended the steps to the bridge over Hatzionut Avenue, the structure so painstakingly built in difficult conditions, and then walked along the path to the Arc.

The *Bahá'í World News Service* quoted Leslie Serrano, a 20-year-old Bahá'í from Mexico, who, like many there on that historic day, recalled the Biblical prophecy of Isaiah, reciting the passage from memory:

> I thought of where it says, 'And it shall come to pass in the last days, that the mountain of the Lord's house shall be established in the top of the mountains, and shall be exalted above the hills; and all nations shall flow unto it.' And when I saw all those people from all these nations, climbing up Mount Carmel, I felt that was the fulfilment of that prophesy. It is a privilege without words to be part of that.[35]

A 65-year-old sugarcane farmer from Kenya, Samuel Benjamin Obura, said he thought of many things as he climbed:

> I thought of the suffering of the Báb. He was put in prison and He was mocked and He was martyred and everyone thought that was the end but now we see the glory that surrounds His Shrine and the adoration people feel when they visit it.[36]

Peace pervaded the thoughts of Galina Iefremova, a 23-year-old teacher from Belarus:

> The idea that more than 3,000 people can come together to do this is an example that can show the way the world can be, without any problems or prejudice. All over the world, people are waiting for this.[37]

Evening event

That night at the Haifa Congress Centre, after an introduction by a member of the Universal House of Justice, Mr Hushmand Fatheazam, the architect of the Arc buildings, Hossein Amanat, and the architect of the Terraces, Fariborz Sahba, received warm applause from the Bahá'ís gathered before them. Mr Amanat told the audience: 'This was not an ordinary project. This was a kind of sacred task for us. We really look on it as a prayer.'[38]

It was time for Mr Sahba to review the project, but he touched only briefly on the 'challenges, the problems, limitations, difficulties' of the past 15 years. Instead he spoke of what he had been thinking the previous evening:

> Last night I thought the Báb and Anís were standing at the top of this heavenly mountain and the whole of humanity – people representing the entire planet – was at the feet of the Báb begging for His forgiveness and blessings. At the conclusion of that shameful event [the execution] at the end of that day, the entire city was shrouded in dust in a storm of heaven's anger. At the conclusion of last night's event, I felt the light of heaven was returning to humanity.[39]

Then the architect-project manager paid tribute to his wife, his children, the MCBP team of almost 150 and his deputy Steve Drake in particular, to Mr Amanat for his friendship and collaboration,[40] to the consultants and the 'army of Jewish, Christian and Moslem workers and contractors', and above all to the Universal House of Justice.[41] He also expressed his indebtedness to Amatu'l-Bahá Rúḥíyyih Khánum.

He said that at the opening ceremony he had recalled the 'majestic words' of Shoghi Effendi which the Guardian had recorded during a wave of persecutions. Mr Sahba recited the passage, including this excerpt:

> In this snow-white Spot, and in other lands, the immutable Will of Him Who has stretched out the earth and raised up the heavens, shall be fulfilled, the cherished desire of longing hearts will emerge from behind a myriad veils in the realm of existence and the highest aspiration of the people of Bahá will be fully, perfectly and conclusively realized.[42]

The audience viewed a 38-minute video documentary of the Mount Carmel Projects, titled *Not Even a Lamp*. They also were able to show their appreciation of composers Tolibkhon Shakhidi and Lasse Thoresen.[43]

After a morning when Bahá'ís had displayed the diversity of the worldwide community by their costumes, came music with a similar effect – the selections were from American, Arabic, Chinese and Indian native traditions. For the events on that day and the next, the variety of musicians included a Latoka flutist from the United States, Kevin Locke; a Tunisian vocalist from Paris, Atef Sedkouai; and a group of Roma musicians from Spain, the Tabarsi Group.[44]

Message to participants

During the next day, Thursday 24 May 2001, the Bahá'ís could again visit the Shrines and the gardens, and also the resting place of Amatu'l-Bahá Rúḥíyyih Khánum, whom many had met either on pilgrimage or when she had visited their countries. Her grave's beautiful curved marble monument, designed by Mr Amanat, was installed shortly before the inauguration ceremony of the Terraces. It faced the Shrine of the Báb.

Attending the evening's event were the two surviving Hands of the Cause, 'Alí-Akbar Furútan and 'Alí-Muḥammad Varqá. Following a musical interlude, the audience stood in respect and then applauded as the members of the Universal House of Justice took their places on the stage. One of the members, Mr Glenford Mitchell, read the institution's message to those Bahá'ís gathered for the events marking the completion of the projects on Mount Carmel:

> The majestic buildings that now stand along the Arc traced for them by Shoghi Effendi on the slope of the Mountain of God, together with the magnificent flight of garden terraces that embrace the Shrine of the Báb, are an outward expression of the immense power animating the Cause we serve. They offer timeless witness to the fact that the followers of Bahá'u'lláh have successfully laid the foundations of a worldwide community transcending all differences that divide the human race, and have brought into existence the principal institutions of a unique and unassailable Administrative Order that shapes this community's life. In the transformation that has taken place on Mount Carmel, the Bahá'í Cause emerges as a visible and compelling reality on the global stage, as the focal center of forces that will, in God's good time, bring about the reconstruction of society, and as a mystic source of spiritual renewal for all who turn to it.[45]

That event also included a drama by Ann Boyles of Canada drawing on the book *Century of Light* that the Bahá'í World Centre had recently published. 'Our idea was to juxtapose news events happening in the world at large with dramatic episodes from the Faith's history, and how the Faith offers hope to the world,' Ms Boyles said.[46]

Prayers on the Arc

The next day, Friday 25 May, saw a dramatic sight on the bow-like path that joins the buildings on the Arc on Mount Carmel, stretching from the newly completed Centre for the Study of the Texts right around to the International Teaching Centre building.[47] The Bahá'ís, some wearing traditional costumes from their native lands, some holding parasols and many wearing hats as protection against the sun, assembled all along the path and on the steps of the mighty buildings. Out of the stately entrance of the Seat of the Universal House of the Justice appeared the two elderly Hands of the Cause, whom helpers escorted to the path below. Then, one following the other, the House of Justice members also exited the doors.

As all present faced the Shrine of Bahá'u'lláh across the bay, a House of Justice member, Mr 'Alí Nakhjavání, chanted the longer of the two Tablets of Visitation and another member, Mr Ian Semple, read the other Tablet. Then in a spontaneous expression of their feelings, which evoked tears among many present, the Bahá'ís from one end of the Arc to the other began singing 'Alláh-u-Abhá', finishing with a soft, resonant humming of the melody.

The members of the Universal House of Justice moved back up the stairs and into the building behind, moving across the concourse and towards the rear stairs that led to the Council Chamber.

The formal events of the completion of the Mount Carmel projects were over.

As the Bahá'ís were leaving the Holy Land, they reflected on their experiences of an historic few days in the history of their religion and their own lives. Virginie Montiel, a 25-year-old medical student from Belgium, for example, described how encounters with so many people from so many different cultures had changed her. 'In the Bahá'í Faith we always say that we are one. We saw this in practice here, with all these different people from different backgrounds working for the same thing. We saw that it is possible for everyone to be equal.'[48]

Reflection

On 1 June, a week after the events ended, the Universal House of Justice issued a message to the Bahá'ís of the world:

> Our hearts overflow with joy, our heads are bowed in gratitude to the Blessed Beauty, as we contemplate the astonishing success of the ceremony that inaugurated the Terraces of the Shrine of the Báb. The awe-inspiring, worldwide effects are reflected in the many messages being received here from different parts of the planet where telecasts of the event via satellite were seen.[49]

The House of Justice said it was too soon to assess the immediate impact of this unexampled global proclamation of the Bahá'í Faith or the implications for its progress, but there was no doubt it would accrue towards the process of many more people becoming members of the Faith.

The completion of the structure on Mount Carmel had profound spiritual significance for the Bahá'ís, as had been explained at the Conference of the Continental Counsellors in January and reported by the *Bahá'í World News Service*:

> The scriptures of the Faith foreshadowed this achievement and prophesied that it would coincide at the end of the 20th century with two other significant developments, one within the community of believers and the other in the world at large. The first would be the emergence of vibrant, self-governing Bahá'í communities in all parts of the world, and the second would be the laying of the foundations of international peace through agreements among the nations of the world.[50]

For some observers, it was interesting that in the United Nations Millennium Declaration adopted by the General Assembly on 8 September 2000, just before the December completion of the Mount Carmel Projects and their inauguration some five months later, the nations of the world said:

> We solemnly reaffirm, on this historic occasion, that the United Nations is the indispensable common house of the entire human family, through which we will seek to realize our universal aspirations for peace, cooperation and development. We therefore pledge our unstinting support for these common objectives and our determination to achieve them.[51]

It could be said that the nations had, in effect, publicly affirmed a teaching expressed by Bahá'u'lláh more than a century previously that humanity was one family and its unity was vital for world peace. That did not mean that Bahá'ís saw a smooth path to peace, believing as they did that there were two parallel process taking place – the integrative factors bringing humanity together that would lead to world peace, and the destructive processes associated with the out-of-date or negative activities of humanity.

21

FOOTSTEPS ON THE TERRACES

The public demand for visits to the Terraces was overwhelming. A public opinion survey in February and March of 2001 showed that about 95 per cent of Haifa residents planned to visit them 'in the near future' and that 75 per cent of Israelis as a whole had similar plans.

The Bahá'í World Centre had always intended that the Terraces and their gardens, sacred in nature, would be shared with the world at large, and would be open to the public with no admission fee. There were also no souvenirs on sale, a constant policy at the Bahá'í World Centre.

The plan was to establish a programme of pre-reserved guided tours for those who wanted to walk down the Terraces from end to end. Drop-in visitors would be able to visit special viewing areas at the base, the middle, and at Terraces 18 and 19.

The goal was to accommodate the public desire to walk on the Terraces while at the same time ensuring that their experience matched 'the kind of care and dignity that went into creating the site', said the director of the Bahá'í International Community's Office of Public Information, Douglas Moore: 'We know that one reason people are so attracted to our terraces is because of their beauty, their orderliness and their cleanliness. And so we felt a guided tour programme would be the best way to preserve that atmosphere.'[1]

It became clear that there were not enough staff or tourism expertise for the Bahá'ís to handle the job by themselves, so they reached out to two local organizations. The Haifa Tourist Board would take on the management of the telephone reservation system and the Beit Hagefen Center, an Arab-Jewish cultural centre that promoted co-existence, would recruit and train the tour guides. The centre, which organizes cross-cultural events and tours in Haifa, would recruit the guides mainly from university students.

There were two options for the tours, each accommodating between

40 and 50 people. One tour went down the top nine terraces, and the second started at the Shrine of the Báb and went down to the entrance plaza.

On the Saturday after the opening, the number of people from the general public coming to visit the Shrine was unprecedented. They were mostly Israelis of all backgrounds, but there were other nationalities too. During the regular public opening hours, from 9 a.m. to noon, 2,756 people entered the Shrine, far more than the previous record of about 1,500. The queue was so long that it reached back to the Pilgrim House. Bahá'í staff worked hard to ensure the process was orderly. The visits involved people walking along the pebble and tile paths to the arcade, removing their shoes, entering and exiting the Shrine, finding their shoes – not one shoe was lost that day – and walking back to the Pilgrim House and to the exit from the gardens.[2]

Beginning on 4 June, the tours quickly became popular. On the first day 11,000 visitors came. Within the first nine days of the opening more than 23,500 people had made bookings for the tours, 54,000 taking them by August, and others virtually booking them out until December. Each day there were more than 20 tours, each lasting 45 minutes to an hour. During those initial months, by far the majority of visitors were Israelis, there being a downturn in the number of international tourists in the Holy Land at the time.

Some 35 guides had received three days of training, which included meeting the architect and a Bahá'í Holy Places official, Jamsheed Ardjomandi. They learned about the purpose of the gardens as well as about the design and special characteristics. One of the guide supervisors, Gad Zorea, said visitors remarked on the guides of different backgrounds working together. They were Christian, Druze, Jewish and Muslim, together with some Bahá'í volunteers from the staff serving at the Bahá'í World Centre.

'Israel is a difficult country,' Mr Zorea said. 'People are stressed and nervous because of the things that are happening. Our guides are the first people they encounter when they enter the gardens, and slowly we try to show them a different perspective, give them a glimpse of the way the Bahá'ís view the world – in a way educate them that the world can be a better place.'[3]

The guides would describe the Terraces and how they were built, point out aspects of the gardens, and tell the story of the Báb, and how and why the sacred remains of the young Prophet came to be buried on Mount Carmel in a Shrine built at the direction of Bahá'u'lláh.

The *Bahá'í World News Service* reported that the tours were giving many Israelis their first glimpse of the Bahá'í community. It noted that since the time when Bahá'u'lláh had arrived in 1868, there had been a strict policy under His direction of not seeking or accepting converts in the Holy Land, a policy that is ongoing. As a result, virtually the only Bahá'ís who lived in Israel were elected and appointed members of Bahá'í institutions and the staff of the Bahá'í World Centre, some 800 adherents from more than 75 countries who had offered temporary volunteer service.

The guides noted the general reaction of visitors: they admired the high quality of maintenance, the dedication of the volunteers and other staff, and the beauty and harmony all around them. The questions from visitors were characteristic of those that thousands of people would put to the guides in the years to come; such as, 'How are the lawns cut?', 'Who paid for the gardens to be built?', and 'Are there symbolic meanings in certain items?'

One of the visitors who came with her family was Haifa resident Lynn Taubkin, who said the gardens were a wonderful contribution to the city. 'If I may speak as a representative of the people of Haifa, I have never heard anything but positive remarks about the gardens,' Ms Taubkin said. 'And knowing that it is all based on voluntary contributions and the work of volunteers adds to our appreciation. There is beauty here – harmony, balance and symmetry – and there is a spiritual element that even those of us who do not belong to the religion can pick up on. The gardens have a personality that seems to personify the religion.'[4]

Huge numbers visited the three drop-in visiting points, 400,000 in just two months. Newly-wed couples began flocking to the entrance plaza for their wedding photographs. The restaurant precinct on Ben Gurion Avenue, previously quiet during weekdays, gained a new lease of life as visitors flocked there to enjoy a meal with a view of the gardens, which were illuminated for a couple of hours after sunset. As predicted, the economic vitality of the city took off.

Many visitors on tours asked why they were permitted only to descend, not ascend, the upper terraces, while Bahá'í visitors have the choice – but the steep slope soon answered that question for them when considering also the numbers in groups and the range of age and physical fitness. The staircase divides from some terraces, so visitors had the choice of alternating sides to take in the views of the lawn, groundcover and trees on both sides. Sometimes they saw gardeners going about their work, using metal forms to clip the cypresses into candle-like shapes, and sometimes they witnessed the intriguing sight of staff using a lawnmower held on the horizontal by colleagues gripping ropes attached to the machines.

Guides often noticed a lift in mood among many visitors as they left the usual city life, with its concrete environment, speed and frustrations, and started their slow walk down a path of harmony and beauty. Any grumpiness usually changed to expressions of delight, and questions sometimes faded to silence as the people bathed in special feelings, unexpected before their tour.[5]

Bahá'í visitors

Bahá'ís, who were permitted to start their visit from the lower entrance, would first pass through towering, ornate gates and arrive in a place of water, marble, shiny granite and paving, with emerald green lawns ahead and to the sides. As they paused by the fountain with its pleasing star-shaped basin they would then marvel at a marble ladder of mini-waterfalls before ascending a stairway to the first Terrace. This would be their first experience of being on these platforms of wonder, these sanctuaries of beauty featuring lawn, flowers, shrubs and trees set in an oasis with low fountains and their pools.

The purpose of the Terraces was as an approach to the Shrine. This was evident as people moved up the stairway, seemingly urged on by the parade of cypresses. Always in sight above was the dome of the Holy Place and the ornate structures on which it rested.

The slope is steep, so when going uphill visitors pause to catch their breath before ascending to the next sanctuary, there to be surprised by a different creative version of the one theme, with the colours, shapes, fountains, and designs of the paving and gates being a subtle variation of those previously witnessed.

Sometimes the human mind needs a change from contemplating a wide view and will narrow its focus. People would view the layered tops of the pedestals on which the vases sat, the circled ends of the balustrades, the shape of the central quadrangles, the subtle designs of the benches, and the gilded lampposts.

The path over Abbas Street seemed a mere flat continuation of the walkway, not so much the top of the bridge that it in fact was. By the time the visitors reached Terrace 9, just below the Shrine, many would, after an inspection of what lay before them, turn and lean on the balustrade to gaze out over where they had been. This position allowed for a more complete view than the generous yet limited glimpses they had over the hedges and to the sides of terraces on the way up. Terrace 9 with its lovely low twin fountains and, to the west, the beautiful pool near the cistern, were reason enough for a long pause.

The next climb, though, was special because the wide steps took the people to the level of the Shrine itself where the unique feeling created by Shoghi Effendi in the gardens and the spiritual power of the Holy Place would cause most to stand in silence and then slowly approach the arcade.

The experience of those entering through the ornate gates at the peak of the mountain began with a spectacular panoramic view of the Terraces in the foreground, then the golden dome in the middle ground before the view widened over the city and the bay to Acre beyond. This view of mountain slopes, town, sky, bay and the white city beyond was the very one that the Master had praised so highly. Stairs leading down from the roof of a substantial edifice which houses a tunnel under Yefe Nof Street, led down to another viewing balcony and then to the spacious Terrace 19.

As the visitor descended the Terraces, it seemed as if the water, flowing down the runnels at the side of the stairway accompanied them, distracting them from any noises from the city spreading out below. As the architect said, the sound of the water – and the song of the birds[6] it attracts,

> creates the best camouflage for the noise of the city, provides the tranquillity that is needed for a separation from the day-to-day reality of life. When you are in the gardens, you feel you are in a different world. The environment enables you to become detached from your mundane activities.[7]

The architect intended for the water in the runnels to also attract birds, their song also helping to block out the city sounds.[8]

On some terraces, spacious pools enclosed in exquisitely carved marble sent wide waterfalls into pools below, and metal peacocks seemed to be witnesses to the spectacle. Few other places, perhaps none, presented such tranquil scenes.

After Terrace 11, as the people crossed Hatzionut Avenue, most only dimly recognized that they were walking over a bridge, because it was the garden with its twin eight-pointed stars that captured their attention. They usually stopped at the northern balustrade for a special view of the southern side of the Shrine and dome, the wooden door named after Hand of the Cause Leroy Ioas clearly visible in the octagon. The circle of cypress trees was not far away, at the northwestern end of a magical garden that resembled a patterned Persian carpet.

The path the Master had established from Mountain Road (now Hatzionut Avenue) appeared to the left, but for visitors to get to the Shrine they took the steps to their right and proceeded along an eastward path until they could turn northward again, and walk through the gardens established by Shoghi Effendi.

Soon they reached their destination.[9] It was the resting place of the Báb, the young Prophet Who had told humanity of One Whom generation after generation would address as the Blessed Beauty.

ANNEX I

LOOKING BACK

The stories in this annex come from questions put 17 years after the inauguration of the Terraces to Bahá'ís who were involved in the project. They were selected using the criteria of availability or recommendation by others for their specialist contribution. There are many others whose stories also deserve telling.

The overwhelming feeling expressed by those who responded to the questions was that of gratitude for the privilege of serving on the project, an experience they said they would remember for the rest of their lives.

When previously ordinary people do extraordinary things in the service of others or humanity as a whole, we call them 'heroes'. Shoghi Effendi called two Hands of the Cause 'Hercules and 'Titan'. Many would surely agree that it is fitting to describe those Bahá'ís who volunteered and served on the project as 'heroes'.

Project manager

by Eliza Rasiwala (see a short profile about her later in this chapter):

> Fariborz Sahba comes across as a reserved and dignified person to those briefly acquainted with him. To those who know him well, he can be charming, expressive and humorous. But the overriding impression he gives is that of a strong personality, a man with a mind of his own. Mr Sahba is passionate about his work and absolutely dedicated to his profession, an architect par excellence. He also has a remarkable understanding of structural engineering.
>
> As the chief architect of the Terraces of the Shrine of the Báb, and as project manager for their construction, Mr Sahba led from the front his team of architects, engineers, designers, horticulturists

and others, numbering nearly one hundred. He drove his team hard. A perfectionist to the core, Mr Sahba would not tolerate substandard work.

Generally Israelis are assertive by nature and dealing with them is no mean task. But at the end of the projects some 13 years later, Mr Sahba had gained their respect and appreciation. To his credit, Mr Sahba never allowed his authority to be undermined and always drove a hard bargain. He particularly demanded quality work at reasonable prices, and always maintained a tight grip on quality control. If time was lost getting clearances and permits, he would make up for it by speeding up work, and working overtime, to get the tasks accomplished. If work needed to be finished in twelve hours, he made sure it was done in eight.

The scale of the projects was such that it was inevitable that the citizens of Haifa were inconvenienced by the dust, noise and disruption. Here Mr Sahba's excellent skills in public relations came to the rescue by minimizing adverse reactions.

Mr Sahba was able to extract commitment from the volunteer team members to complete tasks before finishing their term of service, thereby ensuring that no delays would occur because of the changing workforce.

Fariborz Sahba always worked with the maxim that 'divine deadlines must be met'. A major triumph was the completion of the projects on time and well under budget.

Deputy project manager

Steve Drake became very busy in Haifa in 1989. He had been appointed the sole quantity surveyor for the Mount Carmel Bahá'í Projects (MCBP), also known as MCP. That organization was tasked with the construction of the Terraces for the Shrine for the Báb as well as the 'Arc' buildings southeast of the Shrine near the Seat of the Universal House of Justice.

A registered quantity surveyor from New Zealand, Mr Drake had worked in the 1980s on the Samoan Bahá'í Temple, a beautiful structure designed by Mr Hossein Amanat. Quantity surveyors primarily calculate the amount of materials needed for building work, and how much they will cost. They invariably administer contractual payments.

After the completion of the Temple in Samoa, Mr Amanat went on to design the magnificent buildings for the Arc. Steve was recruited for the project. He was contracting out the first wall work for the Terraces, while also writing tender documents and doing value engineering and cost estimates for the Arc buildings. As the work picked up, he was soon supervising other quantity surveyors.

Over the next few years, work accelerated to include 15 different construction activities happening at any one moment. Then came the time when the Terraces needed more and more attention. Mr Sabha decided he needed a deputy project manager, and in 1995 he promoted Mr Drake to the position.

'In essence I was directly responsible for anything related to contracts and money, and in Mr Sahba's absence, the management of the project and the team,' Mr Drake says. Asked specifically about the work on the Terraces, Mr Drake makes sure to praise the workforce. 'There was a loving camaraderie and support for each other. Mr Sahba set the tone, the work ethic, and inspired all to do the best for the project.' He refers affectionately to Mr Sahba as 'my brother'.

One of the project's slogans, Mr Drake says, was: 'Never say it can never be done.' That applied, for example, at the beginning when an overseas construction company said the project could not be done in time, or when it was said that a particular type of stone was unavailable, or when they were told no suitable canary palm trees for the Terraces could be found. All were difficult, seemingly impossible problems. All were solved.

Mr Drake's office was near Mr Sahba's in the historic building, the 'minor archives' near the resting place of the Greatest Holy Leaf.[1] Working a minimum of ten hours a day, five and a half days a week, he and his team had a dispensation to work on Holy Days, a time when construction noise was not conducive to the commemorative gathering: 'We did have to stop the rock breakers just before the official observance programme began.'

On one memorable day off, the team participated in an 'Olympics' sports day. 'Each department at the Bahá'í World Centre had to make up a flag. We won the prize. I came up with the theme "Builders of the Last Arc", based on a popular movie at the time, and you can guess whose face was superimposed as Indiana Jones on the flag cracking the whip.'

Dealing with contractors was part of his job. Mr Drake said he worked hard – as did Mr Sahba – to make sure both sides were happy. He said he took his cue from Mr Sabha, who said he had never seen in a successful project a happy contractor and an unhappy client and vice versa. Either both were happy or both were unhappy: 'I would say that all the contractors who worked with us would say that the Bahá'ís were exacting but extremely fair.'

He said that while working, he was so busy he did not have much time to reflect about the significance of the project:

> I guess if I thought about it too much it could have been paralyzing and would have made me feel totally inadequate. I felt it was for most of its life a building site until the day of the inauguration when it became a sacred gift to the Bahá'í community and then took on a whole new meaning that day. It's not often you get a chance to work on a project that is designed to last for a minimum of 500 years or to be an active part in the fulfilment of Bahá'u'lláh's prophecy.

Mr Drake and his family returned to New Zealand where he took up a role as manager of a division at the Auckland City Council supervising a team of project managers with a portfolio of more than NZ$350 million.

Designer

Evidence of the devotion and artistry of the late Golnar Sahba can be found throughout the Terraces of the Shrine of the Báb.

Carried out in collaboration with her husband, Fariborz Sahba, the architect of the Terraces, Golnar Sahba produced designs for the gates, fountains, ornaments, paving and other features. She passed away, aged 55, from an illness on 25 March 2005, in Canada.

In a message of condolence, the Universal House of Justice said that Golnar Sahba's 'devoted and selfless services', including her artistic collaboration on the Temple project in India and the Terraces on Mount Carmel, left 'a lasting testimony to her love for the Blessed Beauty [Bahá'u'lláh] . . . Her radiant heart and saintly character left an indelible impression upon all who crossed her path.'

Born in Isfahan in Iran, Golnar Sahba obtained a Bachelor of Arts

Amatu'l-Bahá Rúḥíyyih Khánum, a portrait, and (above) gazing in the direction indicated by Fariborz Sahba during a visit to a terrace behind the Shrine

Left: *At the dome of the Shrine of the Báb. Her late husband Shoghi Effendi, Guardian of the Baháʼí Faith, climbed up to the dome on Naw-Rúz in 1953 and placed behind a tile a silver box containing plaster from the prison cell occupied by the Báb in Máh-Kú, Persia*

Below, left: *The last resting place of Amatu'l-Bahá Rúḥíyyih Khánum. The grave monument was designed by Hossein Amanat*

Below, right: *Solemn duty as pallbearers for Amatu'l-Bahá Rúḥíyyih Khánum, 2000: members of the Universal House of Justice (those visible left to right) Mr Hushmand Fatheazam, Mr Glenford Mitchell, Dr Peter Khan, Mr Douglas Martin, Mr Ian Semple*

Construction of the entrance plaza to the lower terraces well under way in 2000

Members of the Universal House of Justice visiting the entrance plaza with the architect in March 2001

The entrance plaza

Among more than 3,200 waiting for the inaugural ceremony to start are Fariborz Sahba (at front, left in grey suit turning to his left) and his wife Golnar Sahba, eminent Norwegian composer Lasse Thoresen (second from right, front row), and his wife Britt Strandlie Thoresen in Norwegian costume. The Universal House of Justice commissioned from Mr Thoresen the oratorio Terraces of Light, *which was performed at the ceremony*

The musicians who performed Terraces of Light: *the Israel Northern Symphony, Haifa, under the baton of Stanley Sperber; 70 members of the Transylvania State Philharmonic Choir of Cluj, Romania, and its conductor Cornel Groza; and in front three Canadian soloists: mezzo-soprano Patricia Green, tenor Stuart Howe and baritone Brett Polegato*

The beautiful fountain was a stunning foreground for the musicians, who had as a backdrop a marble ladder of mini-waterfalls

Detail of the bench design harmonized with the garden design on a terrace

A fountain plays on a beautiful lower terrace

An upper terrace with a view over the Hatzionut bridge

A fountain plays on an upper terrace

Different colours combine to create a natural harmony

A lovely path to the east of the lower stairway

In all her magnificence, the Queen of Carmel is embraced by her garden terraces

This pool, very popular with pilgrims and other visitors, is next to the wall that conceals the Afnán reservoir built by 'Abdu'l-Bahá

Shoghi Effendi first managed the difficult feat of entwining bougainvillea on a jacaranda tree near the Shrine, producing a stunning display of colour

in graphic design from the College of Decorative Arts and then went on to produce animated films for children at the Center for Intellectual Development of Children and Junior Youth.

In 1970, when Golnar and Fariborz were engaged to be married, they started a Bahá'í children's magazine called *Varqá*. It was soon to circulate worldwide and appear in nine languages, including Persian, English and Hindi. Motivated in this service by her love for children, Golnar Sahba's main role was illustration and art direction, with her husband serving as writer and editor.

At the opening in New Delhi in 1986 of the Bahá'í Temple designed by Mr Sahba, the architect praised his wife's support during the ten-year project: 'As a designer, [she has] been of great help to me and I have consulted with her on every aspect.' She contributed to the design of fences, gates and benches of the Bahá'í House of Worship in New Delhi, and worked on the content and graphic design of the panels in the Temple's information centre.

Summarizing his wife's role with him in the project to build the Terraces of the Shrine of the Báb, Mr Sahba said that they worked together, in particular in the final detailing and production of different elements of the design.

'Goli was a natural artist,' he said. 'It is interesting that the last illustration she did for *Varqá* was the cover design in which a beautiful little girl is flying in the sky side by side with Varqá, the white dove, freed from our material world. In my opinion, in this picture, without knowing it, she has illustrated herself so naturally and modestly.'

A long-time friend, Mrs Shafiqih Fatheazam, drew on poetic language to describe her: 'Beloved Goli was like a peaceful sea, in whose clear waters the coral and pearls are visible to the beholder . . . Her charming, beautiful eyes revealed the true, radiant essence of her being. She was a peaceful and pensive person, an exquisite flower, who herself created beauty all around her.'

After her passing, the Universal House of Justice directed the National Spiritual Assembly of the Bahá'ís of India to hold a memorial service in her honour at the House of Worship in New Delhi.

A project architect

For Robert ('Bob') Pilbrow, involvement in the project to build the Terraces was a time of unparalleled intensity, sustained for more than a decade. As an architect, Mr Pilbrow's primary role was the design development of construction documents for the upper terraces. From May 1991 to June 2001, he experienced something quite different from the other major projects in which he had been involved in his homeland, Canada.

'Participation in the design and construction often felt as if we were working in a time machine,' he said.

> We worked diligently day by day, and week by week, concentrating wholly on a multitude of incremental demands and then, every once in a while, we would raise our heads and discover that the project had leaped ahead, seemingly far in advance of what our daily efforts could account for. It often felt like the projects were at the centre of a hurricane of both physical and spiritual energy. There was a sense of massive forces operating just outside the sphere of the intensely focused activity at the centre.

Mr Pilbrow recalls the intensity of the atmosphere of the office and the commitment of the team: 'That intensity was maintained, remarkably, for the full ten years we were there and it was due to the unfailing support and prayers of the Universal House of Justice,' he said.

> The challenges were constant, endless and daunting from all perspectives: design, contracting, engineering, construction, project management, logistics, local resources, authorities, and quality control. These are challenges associated with all major architectural projects, particularly those of such a scale as the Terraces, but they were magnified by the time and place of this project.
>
> There was, however, a common thread to overcoming the difficulties, and that was, from month to month and year to year, the unfailing support, in all respects, of the Universal House of Justice. The completion of the Terraces at that time and in that place was a physical miracle born of a spiritual destiny.
>
> An enduring memory was of a hot afternoon spent climbing

along the centreline of the upper terraces during my first summer in Haifa. I was climbing through the trees, bushes, brambles and rocks along with the geotechnical engineer looking for what might be an understanding of the raw physical fabric of our site, a site that had waited millennia for this day.

Asked to single out a colleague for special mention, Mr Pilbrow did not hesitate. 'We were all fortunate to work alongside Mrs Goli Sahba whose commitment and contribution to the graphic and decorative elements of the Terraces was truly inspiring.'

Mr Pilbrow said he found the work on the Terraces immensely satisfying: 'There was a clear vision of the goals and time lines, the teams were lean, professional and committed, and the design itself was inspiring from an architectural perspective. There was a sense of responsibility to the Bahá'ís of the world, there was the unfailing and creative leadership of Mr Sahba and there was the constant loving support and guidance of the Universal House of Justice.'

Before he joined the Terraces project, Mr Pilbrow was working as a project architect in Calgary. He had previously assisted the construction of the House of Worship in Apia, Samoa. After returning from Haifa, he became engaged in project management, building embassies for Canada, and is now semi-retired and living in Ottawa.

Journalist

When this author thinks of Eliza Rasiwala, it is her smiling face, her happy demeanour, her graceful Indian attire, her professionalism, and her devotion to service that come to mind. A highlight of staff meetings in the Office of Public Information at the Bahá'í World Centre between 2003 and 2006 was her professional, methodical reporting, studded with telling statistics. Eliza described with great clarity and precision all aspects of the guided tours operation on the Terraces, which she founded and managed. Her sister, Yasmin, also served in Haifa.

Eliza wrote a newsletter, established and edited by MCBP architect and project manager Fariborz Sahba. A chronicle of a major part of the Terraces project and known as *Vineyard of the Lord,* this bimonthly publication went to Bahá'í communities worldwide. It provides an invaluable written and photographic record.

Before her premature passing in her homeland of India in 2012 Eliza wrote to the author saying: 'I will be very happy to answer questions about the construction of the Terraces as that is a subject close to my heart.'

Eliza had also worked with Mr Sahba as supervisor of the Bahá'í volunteer guides after the completion of the construction of the Bahá'í Temple in India. Later she was invited to join his team in the Holy Land. Of her, Mr Sahba says: 'My collaboration with Eliza goes long back to India when she was very young. I trained her to be the head of the volunteers at the Temple. Later I brought her to Haifa. She was a very bright and dignified lady and a very devoted Bahá'í. It was very sad and unfortunate she died so young.'

Construction engineer

At a social event two years after the inauguration of the Terraces, Hooshang Yazdani was explaining to this author the background to his role in the project to build them. He said that many years earlier he had asked Bahá'u'lláh to let him use his engineering expertise to serve the Faith but instead found himself building roads in the mountains of Iran.

After he joined the project in 1992, he realized that his prayers had been answered. Here he was, building a road up a mountain. Maybe he had been trained for it.

Fifteen years later he provided more memories:

For the first few years I was in charge of supervising the structural work of the Terraces, controlling the accuracy of its implementation. In 1996 the contractor of the Terraces declared bankruptcy, so after that we worked like a contractor under the supervision of the Project Manager, Mr Sahba.

At first when I saw Mount Carmel, it seemed to me it would be an easier site than what I was used to in Iran, but when I got involved with the project I realized how wrong I was. To get to the bedrock of the mountain, metres of rock and top soil had to be removed. In many areas we would be facing huge boulders which had to be broken in pieces by excavators with heavy duty hammers. Then metres of clay were removed to reach the bedrock before the base of the walls could be prepared.

Mr Yazdani said the working conditions were testing, being extremely hot in the summer, and then four months of rainy conditions not appropriate for earthworks. And the hours were long. 'Very often we would pour concrete till late night. Once there was a report that a stranger was intruding in the Bahá'í gardens before dawn. The security department investigated and discovered that it was me working early.'

He said much of the work required great precision: 'To get the exact shape of the terrace designs, we allowed for a tolerance of plus or minus five millimetres. Surveyors were constantly checking.'

Mr Yazdani said one of the most challenging parts of the project was building the entrance terrace in the rainy season only six months before the inauguration. 'We covered the entrance plaza with several huge tents. We could hardly believe that in that particular winter there was the least rainfall ever recorded there. It gave us a chance to complete the job without delay. The following year, the rainfall was extremely heavy.'

Mr Yazdani fondly remembers two architects supervising the terraces work – Saad Al-Jassar and Bob Pilbrow – and many other colleagues, too many to name. 'An Arab foreman working under my direct supervision said that in the future his grandchildren and great grandchildren would be proud that their grandfather was involved on this project.'

Mr Yazdani, together with his wife Manzar, went back to live in Canada after their service. He said that working on this project was the fruit of his engineering and personal life. 'I hope I did justice to it. I am so thankful to Bahá'u'lláh that he provided me this opportunity and helped me till the end.'

Horticulturalist

Andrew Blake worked as a horticulturalist in the final years of the Terraces project, but his role extended into a far wider range of duties than his professional title conveys. Perhaps the most fascinating was his role in establishing habitats for mammals, birds and insects in the wildlife corridors of the Terraces.

The benefits of the idea for the corridors were many. They would be a sanctuary for all sorts of wildlife, the creatures could assist with pest control, and the trees and plants provided a visual and sound buffer for nearby residents. This project, described in an earlier chapter, had its moments, such as trying to vaccinate jackals against rabies. The animals were not keen to cooperate.

Before moving to Haifa, Mr Blake ran a horticultural consultancy business in Western Australia. He arrived in the Holy Land in July 1998, filling a gap left when a landscape supervisor on the uppermost terraces left Haifa. That role involved supervising a crew of local workers who were landscaping the slopes on which the final topsoil levels had just been completed. This required transposing the landscape design onto the bare soil, planting, watering-in, mulching, and working with the irrigation engineer (also from Western Australia).

By the next year Mr Blake was multi-tasking by:

◆   training and supervising the tree care crew;
◆   establishing and supervising the horticultural laboratory;
◆   developing and delivering horticultural training materials for the general garden staff;
◆   establishing the wildlife corridors; and
◆   redeveloping the pest and disease control crew into an IPM (Integrated Pest Management) team.

His duties later broadened to include general problem-solving, horticultural experimental work and wildlife management.

Mr Blake also researched the history of the Bahá'í gardens. He saw that as important because he felt he was maintaining a 'living museum'. He later gave many presentations on this topic.[2]

One of the challenges was to try to control a serious outbreak of algae that had turned some of the terrace fountains into a dark green pea soup:

> After trialling different solutions, we solved the problem by adding a small amount of anolyte (salty water which had been activated by an electrical charge) to the underground pipework where bacterial biofilm had become a catalyst for the algae outbreak. Removing the biofilm in this way resulted in complete control of the algae which lasted for many months – without the use of any chemicals or damage to the fountains.

One of the most moving and significant events for Mr Blake was the funeral of Amatu'l-Bahá Rúḥíyyih Khánum in January 2000. He was

involved in the preparation of her resting place: 'For me, just as signifi-
cant were the heartfelt condolences delivered to me personally by my
Arab workmates who mourned the passing of the person they called the
"Bahá'í queen".'

The team spirit was the best he has ever experienced: 'I can remember very few arguments or real tension between people.' Overall, he
found the work itself a joy:

> It provided a deep sense of satisfaction, as the direction was clear, the
> goal challenging but achievable, and the outcome infinitely reward-
> ing. I felt grateful every day for the opportunity to work in such a
> place, at such a time, with such good souls – but only now, after a
> gap of many years, can I begin to understand the significance of the
> task in which I was allowed to participate.
>
> For me the Mount Carmel Projects did not end with the opening
> of the Terraces in 2001. I had the blessing of participating in the
> transition from a somewhat frenetic construction period into a
> calmer, and yet at times just as intense, maintenance regime – a
> process which took several years.
>
> Even after 2001 I felt as if I was still in MCP – because the
> forward-thinking, quality-oriented, hard-working culture instilled
> during construction continued quite naturally through this transi-
> tion period to become a hallmark of the Haifa Gardens Department.

Work with wildlife resumed for Mr Blake when he returned to Western
Australia. For ten years he was curator of horticulture at the Perth Zoo.

A project architect

Saad Al-Jassar was one of the first to be involved with building the Ter-
races. He was working as a project architect and manager in St Louis,
Missouri, United States when he received the invitation to come to
Haifa.

He became involved in the early development of Fariborz Sahba's
conceptual design for the Terraces. His role moved on to the detailing
and construction phases of the work, coordinating with all the other
engineering disciplines on the Terraces. He was also involved in the
design and detailing of the Offices of Public Information and Security

under Terrace 10, as well as the bridges over Abbas Street and Hatzionut Avenue, storage buildings along the terraces, and tunnels under Hatzionut Avenue and Yefe Nof.

'The work atmosphere was unique,' Mr Al-Jassar said. 'We were a team of Bahá'í professionals, of different experiences and backgrounds and from countries around the world. We hired both local Israeli and international consultants. Our local contractors were Jewish, Christian and Muslim Israelis.'

Mr Al-Jassar travelled with an American passport, but his name and place of birth, Baghdad, led to questions from the Israeli airport authorities. It was the time of the political turmoils that culminated in the first Gulf War in 1990. Iraqi missiles landed not so far away, but the work on the projects continued, the team resolutely focused on achieving its mandate.

His Iraqi background might have delayed him at the airport but it was also an asset: 'Though we all used English to communicate, I was lucky to speak Arabic, my mother tongue, to the Israeli Arab workers and contractors. That helped a lot with negotiating a good price and with controlling the quality of work.'

He said it was hard to single out any particular colleague, but two distinguished, dedicated and highly professional members come to mind when he recalls the team: 'Mr [Husayn] Banani was the electrical consultant for the Terraces and the buildings of the Arc. He was stationed in Canada, but he used to make frequent visits for consultations. The second is Mr Rohullah Kashif, a mechanical engineer who worked with the team in Haifa and led the design and execution of the mechanical and plumbing elements for the Terraces and all associated buildings.'

Mr Al-Jassar said it was special to be in Haifa in 1992, the Holy Year of the commemoration of the centenary of the Ascension of Bahá'u'lláh, when 3,000 Bahá'ís from around the world walked up the lower terraces – on what were then plain concrete steps – to the Shrine of the Báb. He said he found his involvement not only satisfying but exhilarating:

To work on such an historic and important project and under the shadow of the Shrine of the Báb and with continuous guidance of the august institution, the Universal House of Justice, was such a bounty. We witnessed the fulfilment of the prophecies of the Central

Figures of our precious Faith unfold in front of our eyes. We were so privileged to be part of that process.

I left in 1996, after the work on the lower terraces was completed and the upper terraces were ready for finishing work. My family and I went to Botswana, Africa for seven years where I worked with a local architectural firm for couple of years and then started my own architectural practice. We returned to the United States in 2003 and I assumed a new position as a professor of Architecture and the director of the urban design program at Savannah College of Art and Design. My wife and I were invited to attend the inauguration in 2001, where we witnessed the memorable celebrations.

Irrigation engineer

Samandar Milani has strong family links with the Shrine of the Báb through his great-grandfather, who was instrumental in concealing the sacred remains of the Báb in 1850.[3]

In March 1992, 142 years after the service of his illustrious ancestor, Mr Milani joined the project aimed at embellishing and drawing attention to the resting place of those remains, a Shrine which is now a focal point for Bahá'ís around the world.

'I had been working with the Department of Agriculture in Western Australia as an irrigation designer,' said Mr Milani, who was born and brought up in Rabat, Morocco. 'But on a trip to Macau to investigate moving to China, I met a Malaysian Bahá'í who told me that Mount Carmel Projects was looking for an irrigation engineer. He suggested I apply, and I did, and I served there from March 1992 to December 1998. The task given to me was to design and install the irrigation system for all the gardens on Mount Carmel.'

Mr Milani said the main challenge on the Terraces was due to the site and topographical conditions:

The challenge with the Shrine gardens was due to the fact that the integrity of the original gardens – the design and look – needed to be preserved, and all equipment valves and controllers had to be concealed and camouflaged. This had to be done in an area of the world where water is a precious resource, where summers are long and temperatures regularly soar above 40 degrees. Then add to this the steep topographical conditions, and the need to obtain a balance between the focus of the engineers on the practical aspects and the architects' focus on the look.

Mr Milani's tasks included undertaking the technical hydraulic design of all the outdoor water supplies – the irrigation, fountains, tap and drinking water, and the fire protection pipe network. 'It also involved', he said,

> the selection and procurement of all the required material, the supervision of the installation of the systems, the production and recording of all the drawings and producing the operation and maintenance manuals to be left to the future maintenance team. In the construction and supervision area I was assisted by Bahá'í staff members Bernard Devera, Benjamin Pastores and Ben Costino from the Philippines, and Joseph Guicheru from Kenya.

There were many technical design issues associated with topography, water and soil conservation, water distribution uniformity, high pressures, automation and control:

> In drought-stricken areas of the world every drop of water counts and water distribution efficiency is of the utmost importance. To achieve high water distribution efficiency on steep slopes such as the Terraces was very challenging. The design was also made complex due to the complexity of the different plant arrangements and the microclimates created by the higher plants, and the need for a design of an irrigation system to cover the various water regimes. To incorporate all these variables and keep the system as simple as possible was challenging.

Mr Milani said there were also regular changes to landscape designs, often after the irrigation and plants had been installed, so the irrigation had to be re-designed and the installation altered accordingly. 'These challenges were overcome with lots of prayer, meditation and drawing on patience,' he said.

He named many contributors to the great enterprise, including Hooshang Yazdani, the site engineer who, he said, was calm, devoted, had great technical skills and experience, and worked non-stop. 'I was also greatly helped in the design work by the late Dr Jack Keller, a

Bahá'í from the United States – he was a world-renowned irrigation engineer, who visited three times.'

Mr Milani said the role required him to be totally focused and to work 12 to 14 hours daily, six days a week. He said the site conditions were so difficult and dangerous that it was surprising nobody was seriously injured or died during the construction period on the Terraces: 'I witnessed a grader tumble down 45 degrees and then stopped by a small rock. The driver emerged unharmed from the crushed cabin. I myself was spared many times from real harm when working on the slopes.'

He said that when he looks back on those days full of challenges, he is very grateful to Bahá'u'lláh: 'I feel I was the recipient of the gift to participate in this historical project, and it was because of the dedicated services that my father, grandfather and great-grandfather rendered to the Faith.'

There were other gifts too: 'I married Nasrin Yazdani shortly before I started on the project. Our first three children were born in Haifa. Our fourth was born a few months after we got back to Australia.'

Bridge builder

When Abdul-Rahman Jarrah these days looks at pictures of the Terraces, he does not see flowers and stone work: 'I always remember the retaining walls, the underground pumping stations and the 'dozers moving earth. And yes, I always remember my friends I worked with – that brings a smile to my face.'

Abdul-Rahman Jarrah served at the Bahá'í World Centre from 1991 to 1994, initially as contracts manager in the Works Department, and then transferred to Mount Carmel Projects in 1992. He remained there until July 1994.

His parents were Palestinian Arabs from Acre. They went as Bahá'í pioneers to Libya in 1952 at the direction of the Guardian. Mr Jarrah was born and grew up in Libya, and moved to Maryland in the United States in 1982. His forebears served Shoghi Effendi and the Universal House of Justice.

Abdul-Rahman is an engineer and a lawyer by profession. He was construction supervisor for the earthmoving and underground structure works on Terraces 2 to 4. His responsibilities included supervising the demolition of the Abbas Street bridge and building a new one, as well as building the retaining walls along Abbas Street (named after the Master). That included installing all the stone cladding now visible along that street. The work also included the building of gravity walls under Terraces 2 to 4 and all the earthworks up to the levels just below the landscaping levels. He said:

> Most of the people I interacted with were Israelis, Arab and Jewish. Generally the supervisors were Jewish and the workers Arab.
>
> The work conditions were very hard. We were exposed to the elements all day. I had to walk up to Terrace 8 to go to the toilet. I remember a period when I was chronically dehydrated. I was very tired and fatigued all the time. On the advice of a friend at the World Centre who was a physician, I forced myself to drink large amounts of water. The problem went away with time.
>
> However, my work conditions were nothing compared to the Arab workers, especially the ones who were building the retaining walls. That was all manual work. These were gravity walls essentially made of layers of concrete mix on layers of natural stone placed by hand. They did that all day with me demanding quality and clean work, and their supervisor shouting in the background.
>
> The Arab workers became my friends. I don't remember their names now but I knew every single one of them. We often had lunch or coffee together. We drank a lot of Turkish coffee!

Mr Jarrah said that of the Israelis he especially remembered David (Dodo) Cohen, owner of one of the contracting companies working on the Terraces, and his field supervisor Ovadia.

> Dodo was a Syrian Jew and owned the earthmoving company working in my area. He spoke fluent Arabic like a Palestinian, a lovely person and clever. He was always amazed that the Bahá'í supervisors were so diligent and hardworking even though we were volunteers.
>
> Of the Bahá'ís I remember, of course, Mr Sahba, and having lots of laughs with the deputy project manager Steve Drake, who was an expert mimic, and with Mr Sahba's secretary Nancy Markovich. I also fondly recall one of the main architects on the project, Saad Al-Jassar, an Iraqi-American.
>
> I worked six days a week. My commute every day involved

walking around the Shrine. I started at 5.30 a.m. and finished on site around 3 p.m. My walk home was up the mountain. There were no stairs when I started work there.

My work was very satisfying. Every time I looked up, there she was – the Queen of Carmel shimmering in the sun. How could this not be satisfying?

Landscaper

Ernie Lopez served on the Terraces project from 1991 to the summer of 1999:

> After seeing a small design I did at the residence of one of the members of the Universal House of Justice, Mr Sahba asked to meet me and then inquired about my experience in landscaping.
>
> I was at that time serving as the team leader of the 'Outlying Gardens' maintenance crew that covered Bahá'í properties in Haifa, Acre and the Sea of Galilee. Before that I had spent from 1972 to 1982 as head of the Office for Landscaping and Hardscape maintenance at the Bahá'í House of Worship in Wilmette.
>
> Mr Sahba brought me into MCBP to help source ornamental horticultural plants and materials. Then he would select the botanicals – he was very particular about the features and colour palate for his design. Mr Sabha asked me to work on the landscaping design for outer extensions of the formal central descending terraces, assisting him to fulfil his design of the gardens extending out from the central axis of the terraces.

Mr Lopez said he had left home at 16 unable to finish the sophomore year of high school, due to family reasons, but he did not stop learning. He took courses in biology, earth sciences and botany, and mastered three languages. Although he did not obtain academic qualifications in horticulture or landscape architecture, he became a specialist in those areas. In his MCBP role, he said, he located nurseries and found groundcover plants and large limestone slabs for rock outcropping features: 'I then supervised their installation throughout the Terrace project.'

The workforce on the project was a complex combination of professional and skilled workers rarely seen anywhere else, he said:

My group often worked in unison with Israeli contractors, Bahá'í engineers and architects. I consulted with the horticulturist and Bahá'í volunteer staff, and trained and managed Israeli staff working on the experimental garden terrace, which was used to test plant materials in the microclimate of the site. I was also in charge of the mostly local staff who worked in the preparation stages of the sections and the maintenance afterwards.

He said the Israelis saw Mr Sabha as audacious, tackling challenges many probably would not have taken on: 'I spoke with Israeli engineers who would state their concerns about opening several fronts on this massively challenging project on a mountain of fractured limestone bedrock on an incline of 10 to 15 degrees and more.'

Mr Lopez, who returned to the United States at the completion of his service on Mount Carmel, remembers the MCBP team as united, with 'no space between our souls':

The tasks I found arduous, but never fatiguing, challenging but exciting, fraught with risks but they generated no fear because I knew the outcome was ultimately not in our hands. To me, it was heaven or as close a man can get.

We never worked less than eight hours a day and often ten. At the weekend the Bahá'í staff would often provide service at the World Centre. They were volunteers in the best way possible.

Gardens manager

One night in May 2003, Tony White and his wife Wendy Marshall were enjoying a farewell dinner on Ben Gurion Avenue on the eve of their departure from their roles in the Holy land. During the meal, Mr White, who had just finished his role as Coordinator (manager) of the Haifa Gardens Office, looked up at the illuminated Terraces. He immediately withdrew from the conversation and reached for his cell phone. After a short conversation he resumed the socializing.

Mr White had spotted that one of the many lights on the Terraces was not functioning and could not help himself from urging somebody to remedy the situation. His devotion to duty while almost on the aircraft home is some indication of what was required of him during the project – maintaining high standards of presentation of the Terraces.

A New Zealander, Mr White had been assisting the Gardens Office in Haifa when invited by Mr Sahba to establish Mount Carmel Project Gardens, which he did in 1994. Three years later, his wife, Wendy, joined as Gardens Quality Controller. The role of the MCBP Gardens Office was later extended to cover all Bahá'í gardens in Haifa. 'We accepted that challenge, the ultimate purpose of which was to raise the horticultural and aesthetic standards everywhere to the same level as was envisaged for the Terraces on their completion,' Mr White said:

> My primary role was to build a gardens maintenance organization to take over and maintain the various stages of construction as they were completed, so that by the end of the project, MCBP would be able to hand over to the Universal House of Justice a 'turn-key' operation. This we managed to achieve.
>
> Additionally, I was to supervise the ornaments manufacturing operation, which had two staff, Oliver Stretton-Pow and Murray Dunn. Because the establishment of the MCBP Gardens was necessarily a slow build-up coinciding with the programme for completions, I was also asked to undertake all payroll management for local employees. I also helped plan the eventual demolition of the seven buildings situated on Ben Gurion Street Extension.
>
> By the time of the opening of the Terraces in 2001 there were 100 Haifa Gardens staff comprised of 80 per cent local staff and 20 per cent Bahá'í volunteers.

Mr White said the result required an initial big turnover in local staff, and a significant struggle to establish consistent standards of behaviour and performance over the years of the construction:

> We based our operating standards on Bahá'í principles, asked all staff to take individual responsibility, and gave them the opportunity to go to college and study horticulture.
>
> We initiated weekly planning and reviews of outstanding work, and promoted individual development, consultation, cooperation, appropriate behaviour on a holy site, unity within the entire group, and consistency in the work and garden quality standards. We encouraged a sense of pride and ownership within the local staff.

Mr White said the conditions were usually hot and always dusty for all site staff for most of the construction years, and there was constant climbing on very steep gradients. The site was fenced, and many nearby locals were hired as security guards. Those guards communicated in Hebrew and Arabic. They helped prevent graffiti and other damage, and built community respect.

The temporary offices for supervisors were remodelled containers, as were staff break-rooms and tool sheds. He worked 10 to 12 hours a day, five-and-a-half days a week.:

> Cooperation where supervisory paths crossed on a daily basis was essential for timeline completions, a difficult challenge in the pressure situation, but it was largely achieved. There was little certainty of completion on time until about 1999. The introduction of cell phones to the site was a huge improvement to efficiency and productivity in the work and possibly the most influential contribution to the projects being completed on time.

Mr White and Ms Marshall stayed on for two years after the inauguration to ensure the operations were properly bedded in and that the management handover was smooth.

Mr White said he constantly thought how fortunate he was to contribute to such a unique project: 'It was a great privilege to serve the Universal House of Justice on such a mighty project and work alongside such highly skilled and competent Bahá'í staff. The exhausting hours over ten years were greatly outweighed by the immense satisfaction of getting the job done.'

Secretary

From 1991 to 1998, Nancy Markovich served as secretary to Mr Sahba. She tells her story with enthusiasm, affection and nostalgia. Nancy, who had come from the United States to her post in Haifa, said her boss was an 'absolute perfectionist':

> He had no patience for slackness. He wanted things done right and on schedule. I often worked late at night, weekends, and on several occasions even had permission from the Universal House of Justice

to work on Holy Days, due to the workload.

Mr Sahba demanded perfection, but that is what made him who he was, and the results prove it. We all loved and admired him. In one of our staff meetings he said he knew it required a lot of hard work and dedication and sacrifices for families, his own included.

Our office was on the corner of Hatzionut and Hillel next to the Monument Gardens. You walked up the path and around the building to what would seem like the back, and there was an entry door into a small reception area.

We had a wonderful Israeli receptionist to help with communication with our Israeli contractors. Directly across from me was Mr Sahba's office, which had a picture of the Ashqabat Temple on the wall. Offices for Steve Drake and Les Marcus, and secretaries, were nearby. There was also a door that went out onto a deck facing Hillel and Hatzionut Streets.

Drawings were filed in the basement of our building, where there was also a kitchen, bathroom, an office for Eliza Rasiwala and a storage room, down a beautiful winding staircase. The model of the Terraces, which was for a time kept on display in the office, needed lights so I donated my sewing pins with white heads.

Because I was Mr Sahba's secretary, I had the distinct privilege of taking dictation from him, often directed to the Universal House of Justice, dealing with interactions with the Israeli community, and permissions needed or granted by the local government officials. My work included secretarial functions such as typing, filing, and communications, but a big part of my place there was to keep unity flowing during the rough times.

Mr Sahba met contractors in his office where he had a table and chairs in addition to his desk:

Sometimes when voices began rising in discussions with contractors I would bring in a glass of water and valerian, and things would soon continue in a calmer tone. I was never sure why things got so heated, but the contractors respected Mr Sahba and did a good job for us, or they were gone. They appreciated the fact that they would get paid fairly, which was not so common at the time.

Nancy said Mr Sahba would often leave those meetings in a hurry and run up the mountain to get to a meeting in the Seat of the Universal House of Justice: 'One day as he ran out he said, "I feel like an elephant charging from place to place!" After that I saw an ivory elephant in an antique shop and bought it for him.'

She also recalls morale-boosting events – wonderful dinners and parties held periodically for the entire staff:

> At these events, Mr Sahba took a back seat and often had me organize games to make people laugh. The staff needed that, they all worked so hard. One time we had a beach party with the staff, and I got the team to make a big banner that read: 'Ali Sahba and his band of 40 thieves.' Everyone cracked up and we had a great time together, off the job having a fun time!

One of her favourite things to do was host dinners for the youth. 'I often invited a member of the House of Justice to come and speak to the group, and sometimes it was a sharing of "Where are you from and what is your culture like?"'

She was exhausted, she says, when she left Haifa in her mid-fifties to return to the United States, but she says being involved in the Mount Carmel Projects was the greatest honour of her entire life. 'I am so grateful to have been a part of it. I would not have traded those years for anything.'

Draughtsman and supervisor

Frenchman Daniel Caillaud, an architectural draughtsman, served on the Terraces project from December 1992 until the inauguration in 2001. Mr Caillaud had become a Baháʼí in Nice in 1967 and later lived in Canada, New Caledonia and Guadeloupe before joining the staff at the Baháʼí World Centre. From 1988 to 1992, he was with the Department of Holy Places providing architectural documentation for the holy places by measuring and producing drawings.

Shortly after he arrived in Haifa, Amatuʼl-Bahá Rúḥíyyih Khánum invited him to reside at the Master's House, and he remained there until October 2000. 'We always spoke French together,' he said.

In December 1992 I was transferred to Mount Carmel Bahá'í Projects, first to make a few models of the terraces under the direction of Mr Sahba. Those models were on display at the Seat of the Universal House of Justice for the pilgrims to see during the construction of the Terraces, and also for visiting dignitaries like Shimon Peres. The models were on display at the Haifa 2000 exhibition organized by the city of Haifa.

Mr Caillaud said a large billboard, with a colour photograph of the model of the garden bridge over Hatzionut was put up on Hatzionut Avenue to inform the general public of the nature of work being undertaken. 'I carried out supervision on site for the construction of the underground buildings along the terraces, pump rooms, mechanical rooms, public toilets, storage buildings, the two bridges, and tunnels.'

He said he could never have dreamed he would play a part in such a project. 'All my nightmares vanished during the inauguration ceremony in May 2001. For me, it was hard to believe it got done, and done in time.'

He remained in Haifa to continue the maintenance on the Arc buildings and the Terraces, and supervise the full renovations of the staff apartments. 'After 28 years in Haifa, at the age of 69 I retired and went back to France where I had just purchased a flat at the former Grand Hotel du Parc in Thonon-les-Bains on the shore of Lake Geneva where 'Abdu'l-Bahá resided for two weeks in August 1911.'

Storekeeper

Bill Black served as storekeeper for the Terraces project from 1995 to 1999. He was responsible for receiving all the shipments of materials such as the lighting fixtures and stone for the Terraces and bridge. He stored them at a warehouse near the Eastern Pilgrim House with its entrance off Shifra Street.

Bill was able to hear about the eventual use of the materials he received because he shared his office with irrigation engineer Samandar Milani, who needed many items from the warehouse during the installation of the irrigation system he designed for the Terraces.

Every day was intense. Even with the constant demand for keeping up, it was the most rewarding, satisfying thing I have ever done. Many days, I had to be on site as early as 6 a.m. to receive shipments of various materials that were to be delivered directly to site.

I had to block the parking on the street where the trucks came in, but if somebody took the parking spot it was impossible to get the trucks into my storage building. It was a problem I had to work around. I also had to climb the mountain looking for some local overseers to sign for shipments, but often came back without signatures. Thankfully, no problem ever arose with the materials involved.

One of my most satisfying accomplishments was the creation of an inventory system for the storage building. I counted and entered into the system all the materials in the warehouse.

Once I had to interrupt members of the Universal House of Justice who had just finished their prayers and had gathered in the garden in front of the Pilgrim House. I approached and said: 'Mr Nakhjavání, would you mind moving your car so I might get this truck through?' He smiled and said, very happily, 'Of course,' and turning to the other members said, 'I will see you back up the mountain.' Even after all these years, I still regret that I had to do that, even though he did not mind in the least.

As the project progressed, I constantly watched the buildings and the terraces as they appeared. I made photographs of much of the construction so I could remember seeing it go together. Now, I can look at the photographs of the current terraces and buildings and recall how they looked during construction.

I was amazed that for three years Bahá'u'lláh had let me become part of such a wonderful event. After almost 20 years, I am still amazed and thankful for such a wonderful gift.

Mr Black's wife Gail served in the Finance Department at the Bahá'í World Centre, where among her tasks was attending to the payroll for the Israeli workers on the Terraces project and some associated property payments. The couple returned to their home in Easley, South Carolina, United States, in January 1999.

ANNEX II

THE RESTORATION OF THE SHRINE
OF THE BÁB
2005–2011

Overview of the decade

The opening of the Terraces had fulfilled the vision for the precincts of the Shrine of the Báb that 'Abdu'l-Bahá had proclaimed more than 80 years previously, but the interior of the Shrine itself was yet to be arranged as the Master had intended.

He wanted it to have nine chambers[1] and eight doors, but in His time managed just six chambers and five doors. The Guardian had added the three chambers and three doors to fulfil the wishes of 'Abdu'l-Bahá. However, over the decades those three extra chambers served only auxiliary purposes, such as for displaying important archives to pilgrims and later as storage and flower arrangement rooms.

The decade after the inauguration of the Terraces was to see the Universal House of Justice transform those chambers into prayer rooms for the Shrine of the Báb and open an arched entrance between the central rear room (#4) into the inner chamber (#9).

This was the outcome of a programme of restoration of the Shrine in which the Guardian's vision of a golden-tiled dome came back into being following years of the dome having an orange patina after the gold leaf had been lost.[2] That change of colour was described, for example, in 1974, by a member of the Universal House of Justice, Mr Amoz Gibson, who wrote to the original tile manufacturers: 'The . . . golden tiles on the Dome . . . are beginning to lose some of their color and luster. As you can see from the color photograph enclosed, the gold-gilded finish has eroded from some of the tiles completely and some others in part . . .'[3]

The restoration programme, which also involved major structural upgrades of the edifice to withstand earthquakes, began with planning in 2005. The work commenced in 2008 and came to its golden finale in 2011.

Shortly after the planning began, war erupted in the region, and the Shrine became a glowing symbol of peace to the people of Haifa. The Lebanon–Israel conflict raged from 12 July to 14 August 2006. Rockets fired from southern Lebanon landed in Haifa, killing people and destroying or damaging buildings.

During the conflict, the Shrine remained fully illuminated to midnight, long past the usual time for dimming. In a newspaper story published on 26 July,[4] readers received an explanation.

> 'This is our way to uplift the morale of the citizens of Haifa,' explained the Deputy Secretary of the Bahá'í organization, Murray Smith from New Zealand.
>
> 'It is symbolic in our view, to keep the lights on in the darkness of war. I hope this message comes across . . . The Baha'is understand that the world is going through a tough time. There will be tough problems or wars, until people realize the message of peace,' added Smith, 'so we need to stay here, to continue as usual and to promote the idea of peace.
>
> 'From our standpoint, this message is more important then everything else. We are not naïve and we know this involves a lot of work, but in the end the Peace will come. Perhaps the near future is hard and scary, but the distant future is bright, and that is what the lights of the Shrine symbolise.'

The conflict interrupted work in the gardens near the Shrine but by the time the fighting had finished on 14 August there had been no damage to Bahá'í property.

External recognition

In the decade after the opening of the Terraces, the Shrine and its precincts received widespread external recognition.

In 2003 the Terraces received an award from the Society of American Travel Writers. The society, comprising 1,300 members in North

America, named them as one of six recipients of its Phoenix Awards for that year. The awards honour individuals or groups which 'have contributed to a quality travel experience through conservation, preservation, beautification or environmental efforts'. In its citation, the Society said that by the creation of the garden terraces, the once barren face of the mountain that overlooks Haifa is now 'a magnificent floral jewel'.

There was extensive media coverage in that decade, but the major external recognition came in 2008 when the Shrines of the Báb and Bahá'u'lláh became the first sites associated with a religious tradition born in modern times to be added to the World Heritage list, which is linked to a convention signed by most nations in the world.

The listing came about because the UNESCO World Heritage Committee had determined that the two Shrines possessed 'outstanding universal value' and should be considered as part of the cultural heritage of humanity. The Bahá'í International Community Secretary-General, Dr Albert Lincoln, warmly greeted the decision:

> We welcome the UNESCO recognition, which highlights the importance of the holy places of a religion that in 150 years has gone from a small group found only in the Middle East to a worldwide community with followers in virtually every country. The Bahá'í community is particularly grateful to the government of Israel for putting forward this nomination.[5]

Another spokesman for the Bahá'í World Centre, Douglas Moore, pointed out in a video an effect of the listing:

> What it does is, it recognizes, it seems, a fundamental characteristic of the Bahá'í Faith which is that all of these places, all of the Faith, all of its teachings, the Shrines themselves and the gardens that surround them, are part of the common heritage of all of humanity.[6]

The following year, the Bahá'ís of the world turned their minds to the Shrine because Naw-Rúz, 21 March 2009, marked the 100th anniversary of the interment of the sacred remains of the Báb on Mount Carmel. Coinciding with that anniversary was the launch by the Bahá'í International Community of a new website, 'The Bahá'í Gardens', to assist visitors to the Bahá'í Holy Places in Haifa and Acre. The Bahá'í Shrines and gardens were by then among the most visited sites in the Eastern Mediterranean region.

In May 2011, on the 10th anniversary of the official opening of the Terraces of the Shrine of the Báb, UNESCO Director-General Irina Bokova, of Bulgaria, addressed a ceremony in the entrance plaza of the Terraces to mark the inauguration of the UNESCO Peace and Tolerance square positioned immediately in front of where the German Templer colony approaches the Terraces.

And in November that year the Bahá'í World Centre and the city of Haifa became founding members of the Green Pilgrimage network, organized by the Alliance of Religions and Conservation in association with the World Wide Fund for Nature.

Visitors

In the two years up to June 2003, nearly one and a half million people visited the Terraces, mostly at the three drop-in points. That number jumped to more than two million by the next year. By 2004 some 465,000 people had taken one of more than 12,000 guided tours conducted since the opening, the weekly average being about 3,200 people. As well as tours conducted in Arabic, English, Hebrew and Russian there were some in Armenian, Danish, French, German, Spanish and Norwegian. Their popularity continued during the decade. In 2010, some 760,000 visitors entered the drop-in points and took tours, and there were about 7,500 Bahá'í pilgrims and visitors.

In addition to visits by the general public, and specialist tours, staff at the Bahá'í World Centre's Office of Public Information hosted 'special visits', about 300 per year. Those on such visits included diplomats, parliamentarians, religious leaders, physicians, professors, researchers, military officials, educators, journalists, tour guides, business people, and members of civil society and NGOs.[7]

Prelude to the restoration

In 1963, studies and tests undertaken at the direction of the Universal House of Justice showed that there were signs of deterioration in the structure of the Shrine.[8] This was due to some inability of the edifice to withstand acid rains associated with pollution caused by a nearby oil refinery, the sand storms known as the *sharav* (*khamsin* in Arabic), salt blown in from the sea, rainfall in general, and the high humidity.

These factors combined to produce signs of corrosion on the tiles of the dome, the exterior stone cladding, the wrought-iron balustrades and gilded materials. The main concerns, though, were evidence of structural stress inside the superstructure, water leakage in the dome, and the deterioration of the stone cladding.

In the midst of the 1960s and again in the 1970s the Department of Holy Places at the Bahá'í World Centre consulted experts at the Haifa Technion and then carried out remedial action that took care of the immediate problems. That work allowed the postponement of a major fix to the main problems until a more suitable time.

In the 1970s and through to the 1990s, the Department also investigated the condition of the golden tiles on the dome with the assistance of experts from Germany, Iran, Japan, the United States and elsewhere. Many individuals and companies offered their ideas but no suggestion was fully adopted. A remedial project would have been so complex that it was also postponed to a time when substantial work could be done.[9]

In 1978, lightning struck the finial on top of the Shrine's lantern. The finial broke into pieces and tumbled down. It was replaced in 1980. When that was done a lightning rod was installed on top of the finial, with its two copper wires running down to a copper bar placed a couple of metres underground.

In the 1980s and 1990s it was necessary to restore the glass in the ogee windows of the octagon and the lancet windows of the drum and to replace their framings. By then the dome was leaking extensively, water penetrating through cracks and broken seals between the carved stone ornaments and the tiles. In 1988 the visible exterior joints on the dome were sealed.[10]

From 1991 through to 1993, Mount Carmel Bahá'í Projects undertook a major project aimed at waterproofing the dome. In 1991, subcontractors installed a sealant where the marble ribs and carved marble acanthus leaves met the grouted tile surface of the dome. Unfortunately, that sealant became affected by the sun's ultraviolet rays, and by 1994 it had deteriorated, allowing water to penetrate the edifice again.

In 1993 the Department of Holy Places commissioned a team to carry out a condition survey of the Shrine. In its report in 1994, the team that carried out the survey said that 'on the whole, the Shrine is in very fine condition' but they issued many caveats to that assessment, advising that 'the structure exhibits some serious problems that require prompt intervention'. The team pointed to a key problem: 'Much of the façade's watertight integrity has failed, primarily at the joints between stones, tiles and windows.'[11]

That was not good news. Even in its natural state rainwater is slightly acidic through the absorption of carbon dioxide. But in an environment like Haifa with its industrial pollution, the rainwater was much more acidic than usual, and that added to all the other damage that water can do when it gets into building materials, as it did with the Shrine.

The report listed many areas which had been damaged since the superstructure had been completed in 1953. Fortunately, the original stone building built by the Master was generally in good shape, but there were real concerns with the superstructure. The team even raised the possibility of having to demolish the dome and rebuild it should further investigations bring bad news.

The gilding had disappeared from most of the tiles, and there was organic growth on the cladding, brim, cornices, copings and panels, something that does not happen on clean, dry walls. There were problems with the windows in the drum, corrosion of the wrought-iron railings in the octagon, water movement in the arcade walls, deterioration in the shields and panels, and in a few places there were holes or cracks in the stone. The team also found that at the rear of the octagon, stonework was crushing the wooden Ioas door and frame. 'The building's structure and cladding systems lack flexible joints for thermal expansion and contraction,' their report said. 'Throughout the superstructure, no provisions were made to collect and disperse water that penetrated the tile or marble cladding . . . Water moving behind the cladding causes deterioration by dissolving the calcite and other cementing minerals of the concrete and the stone.'

The team noticed that on the top six metres of the dome, from the lantern downward, about 90 per cent of the gold glaze had gone from the tiles. On the bottom six metres, the remaining gold glaze was found in streaks, building in concentration towards the base of the dome.

However, this report recommending a stabilization of the façade was presented when the great priority was the construction of the Terraces and the buildings on the Arc. The House of Justice felt the scope of the necessary renovations and improvements had not yet been entirely determined and the question of the costs involved was, as always, a major consideration.[12] Although some maintenance practices were changed, no major work, including repairs and maintenance to the dome, could be carried out.

In February 2003 a team of conservation and restoration professionals from the United States, led by Robert Armbruster who had been involved in the 1993 study, came to Haifa at the invitation of the Office of Holy Places.

Their report[13] found that the cladding system on the superstructure of the Shrine was in poor condition. Failures in that system had let water into the dome and façade for decades. Water was trapped between the cladding and structural concrete, causing deterioration. The dome's condition was 'fragile and vulnerable' and it had an 'unacceptable aesthetic appearance', being no longer gold but orange. No gold glaze existed on most of the tiles. The report said they could possibly be regilded if the dome was sound and could be kept waterproof. Replacement of the tiles would require 'demolition of the existing dome and reconstruction of the dome's structure and waterproofing systems'.

The condition of the marble had worsened in the previous decade, but the stone pavers were in better condition due to the changed method of cleaning them. During the decade, holes had formed in the horizontal surface stone at the base of the dome and within its decorative crown. Cracks had been found in four brimstones in 1994 and there were now more in other brimstones, clearly visible.

Damage was also found in the stonework surrounding the ogee windows in the drum, in the parapets above it and in the anchorages for the railings. The team noticed that during a rainstorm water came into the interior of the octagon, mainly from the unfinished interior lancet window joints and corners and also from the upper joints where the dome meets the drum.

The report concluded that there were two choices – the first was to stabilize the edifice, the second to restore it. It recommended restoration. It then presented a project management proposal and a 'systematic continuous care' plan.

In July 2004, Robert Armbruster and an American Bahá'í experienced in the construction industry, Julian MacQueen, visited Haifa to examine the Shrine and conduct research. Their report recommended more intensive studies of the condition of the structure of the Shrine so as to suggest solutions.

The House of Justice initiates the project

The Universal House of Justice decided upon a different direction. In July 2005 it established the Office of Shrine and Archives Restoration (OSAR) and appointed Saied Samadi as the project architect and project manager for the restoration of both edifices.

Saied Samadi, 59, had wide experience in the restoration of the Bahá'í Holy Places. After graduating with a Master's degree in architecture from Tehran University, Mr Samadi had worked on projects to restore and protect Bahá'í holy and historical places throughout Iran. He had also been assistant architect for the restoration of the south wing of the House of 'Abdu'lláh Páshá in Acre. After obtaining another Master's degree in architecture – this time from the University of Detroit in 1981 – he had worked in architectural practices in California and in his own consulting and construction company there. He had also served as the project architect for the restoration of the north wing of the House of 'Abdu'lláh Páshá.[14]

Mr Samadi was joined the following year by Enayat Rohani, a civil engineer, who acted as site manager and deputy to Mr Samadi.

The commission the House of Justice gave to OSAR was firstly to restore the International Archives Building and then to move on to restore the Shrine. This plan was ideal for the Shrine project because the task of restoring the Archives Building provided the opportunity for OSAR to gain experience in working in Israel, to put together a team of experts and to learn about the difficult task of restoring similar stone used in the Shrine. It also gave time for the team to conduct in-depth studies on the restoration of the Shrine, including its history and its unique materials such as the golden tiles of the dome.

Preliminary studies

Starting in 2005, OSAR staff member Fuad Izadinia, an architect and former custodian of the Shrine, researched the history of the Shrine's construction, including the building raised up by the Master and the extra rooms and superstructure the Guardian had built.

Mr Izadinia looked at the materials and technologies used, as well as the repairs that had been carried out over the years. He studied the files held by different departments of the Baháʼí World Centre. He also examined the correspondence of the Hands of the Cause Amatuʼl-Bahá Rúḥíyyih Khánum, Ugo Giachery and Leroy Ioas, and of the engineer for the Guardian's superstructure project, Professor Heinrich Neumann. These letters were documented to be used in the restoration project and for future reference. Mr Izadinia also looked at past problems with the building, and read consulting studies and reports.

A range of consultants visited the site.[15] They researched materials and techniques and learned lessons from the Archives project that would assist the work on the Shrine.[16] Informed by those studies and by a detailed survey of the edifice, a comprehensive condition report of the Shrine was produced. It outlined in detail the different failures of the structures and materials which the severe weather and environmental conditions of Haifa had caused in the 50 years after the completion of the superstructure.

The reports covered the entire exterior and the interior of the building, from its highest point to its foundations. Included were descriptions of the Shrine's structure and its ability to withstand earthquakes. The reports surveyed the dome and the golden tiles, the stone cladding, waterproofing, plastering, floorings, ornamental metal work, doors and windows, gardens retaining wall, site drainage and other items.

Based on the preliminary studies and information in the condition report, OSAR staff and consultants prepared a complete restoration document based on three important objectives: preserving the original design and the beauty of the edifice, aiming for excellence, and the longevity of the implemented solution. Consultants provided assistance throughout the project.[17]

In its six years of operation OSAR had an average number of 15 staff members. A steady stream of Baháʼí volunteers from different countries and from the staff at the Baháʼí World Centre assisted the office, all of them forming a united team who kept in touch long after the successful completion of the work. The countries of origin of the volunteers included Australia, Canada, China, Ecuador, Germany, India, Kenya, Mongolia, the Netherlands, New Zealand, South Africa, the United Kingdom, the United States, Vanuatu and several other countries.

The work begins

The restoration and refurbishment work began in earnest in November 2008 while the International Archives Building project was in its last stages and near completion.

It was difficult to estimate how much the restoration of the Shrine would cost and how long it would take, but the budget available was US$5–7.5 million[18] and the original target date for completion was April 2013.[19] The budget would be far less than in any commercial operation because most of those involved in the design work donated their services, and many of those who worked on the project were either staff or volunteers.

Logistics

In this operation to restore a heavily visited and much loved Holy Place and public monument, careful attention to logistics was vital. OSAR began communicating with a range of departmental offices at the Bahá'í World Centre, in particular Facility Management, Haifa Gardens, Holy Places, Pilgrimage, Purchasing, Research and Works.

It set up its construction zone on the western side of the Shrine where there was a considerable flat area for storage and staging areas, and access for materials via a service road from Hatzionut Avenue. During the project a large area of landscaping had to be removed. The areas affected were later returned to their original state.

The aim was to keep the Shrine open to the pilgrims and visitors during the project while keeping up a normal daily work schedule and trying to keep the noise level down during the pilgrims' visits. Some restoration work inside the nine rooms of the Shrine would be undertaken in the summer, part of which was a non-pilgrimage time. At that time the Shrine would be closed.

The stone restoration work would clearly be the most time-consuming part of the project. To minimize the time when the Shrine would be covered or partially covered, the scaffolding would be raised in different sections and stages as needed. The covering of the dome and the drum would be postponed until the work was ready to begin in those areas.

Structural upgrade

The upgrade of the structure of the Shrine involved combining concrete, steel and carbon fibre-wrap technology that affected the entire edifice. One of the major aims of the restoration work was to protect the Shrine in the event of earthquakes, so a seismic retrofit project was a top priority, work directed by structural engineer Omid Tavangar.[20] There had been earthquakes in 1974 and 1976 reaching level four on the Richter scale, Although it could not be definitely proved, it seemed that those earthquakes had had some effect on the structure of the Shrine, indicated by the horizontal and vertical cracks in the rows of dome tiles that were discovered in a later inspection. That study also indicated that the tremors could have caused conditions that allowed water to penetrate the structure.

The upgrade was preceded by extensive laboratory and core drilling tests, inspections and examination of original drawings, and the production of computer-generated models. The calculations and specifications were peer reviewed[21] and then checked[22] to ensure that the plan complied with Israeli building codes.

The work had several components: the foundations and floors, the masonry walls and the roof of the nine original rooms, reinforcement of the ring beam at the base of the drum, the drum, the dome, the pinnacles, and the retaining walls on three sides.

The team removed the tiles from the arcade floor, carefully labelling them for replacement in their original position, and then proceeded to undertake concrete reinforcement of the foundation and floor slabs, including the arcade floor.

A huge project involved removing the five original interior stone walls that 'Abdu'l-Bahá had constructed and replacing them with sheer concrete walls. These were vital to provide support for the floor of the octagon level above. In conjunction with that work, the team reinforced the nine original vaulted ceilings.

The original support structure for the octagon, drum and dome was an eight-pointed reinforced concrete star which sat on eight concrete piers driven through the Shrine walls to the rock below. This star was formerly free-standing over the roof of the original Shrine building. During the restoration it was connected to the new roof, which had been changed from the traditional rubble-filled style to reinforced concrete. This gave added strength to the star as a support.

Originally, eight big steel pipes reached up from the star on the inside of the octagon to support a concrete ring beam at the bottom of the drum. The restoration team installed eight massive steel bracings alongside those pipes. They also strengthened the ring beam on top of the octagon. The pipes and bracings were painted white and curtains were placed behind the octagon windows to prevent them being seen through the windows at night.

The fabrication and installation of the complex steel structure was carried out by the metal shop of the Works Department under the supervision of Daryoush Hajiyousef, the master blacksmith who had made the gates on the Terraces. A structural fibre wrap installed around the interior drum walls, together with concentric fibre wrap strips in the interior of the dome, was aimed at making these structures much more resilient in the event of earth tremors. A seismic upgrade of the eight stone pinnacles rising above the octagon involved inserting in them six-metre long stainless steel reinforced rods, which were embedded into the structural concrete.

A study by Israeli consultants[23] of the retaining walls behind and to the side of the Shrine showed they needed strengthening. Experts reinforced the walls by drilling into the mountain and pinning 120 rock anchors in place. They clad the walls with the stone that had been used by 'Abdu'l-Bahá for the interior walls of the Shrine and set aside after those walls had been replaced. An entrance way into the western wall led to a new room under the western hill that would be used for flower arranging and electrical controls.

Waterproofing and moisture control

So that moisture would never again get the chance to damage the edifice, the team repaired and waterproofed the perimeters of the original Shrine building from its foundation walls down to the bedrock below. A new drainage system and a concrete apron surrounding that building prevented any surface water from reaching its foundations. A new underground storm system connected the Shrine's existing rain leader drains to an underground tank next to the service room where a sump pump sent that water, and the wastewater from the service room, away to the western service road. A natural ventilation system installed

*The Shrine of the Báb takes pride of place in this aerial photograph of
the completed upper terraces and some of the lower terraces*

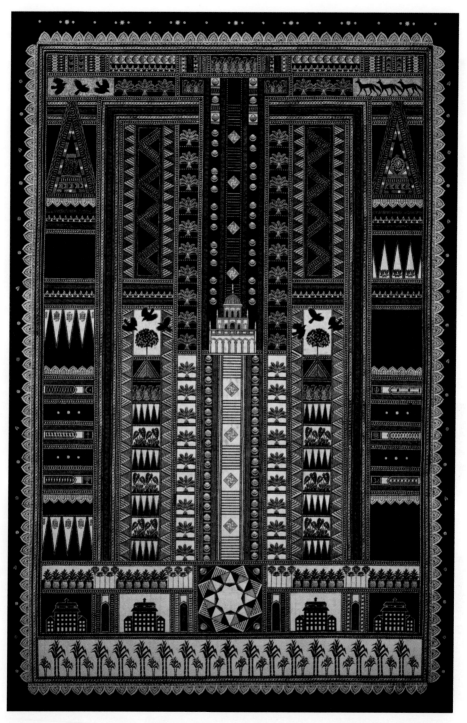

Teitei vou *(A new garden), 2009. This work by New Zealand artist Dame Robin White and Fijian artists Leba Toki and Bale Jione is a depiction of the Shrine of the Báb and its garden Terraces with a Pacific influence, addressing the history of the Fiji sugar industry. Natural dyes on barkcloth, woven pandanus, commercial wool, woven barkcloth, sari fabric mats. Queensland Art Gallery, Gallery of Modern Art*

Fariborz Sahba

Golnar Sahba

A talented creative team: Fariborz and Golnar Sahba

Terraces architect and project manager Fariborz Sahba, right, with his deputy, Steve Drake

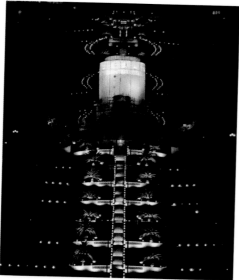

Left: *A cover was placed over the dome and drum (clerestory) of the Shrine of the Báb during its restoration.*

Above: *Saeid Samadi (left) and colleague examine the plans for the restoration of the Shrine*

Perched above the bottom lip of the dome, a worker is repairing spots damaged from 50 years of exposure to the elements

Workers restore the panels above the balustrade

Photos: Bahá'í World Centre

Photo: Bahá'í World News Service

Newly gilded pinnacles and balustrade after the restoration

The sheer beauty of the design by William Sutherland Maxwell is seen in this image showing a freshly gilded Greatest Name

Photo: Bahá'í World News Service

Photo: Arjang Pirmorady

Gilding cap

Interior lighting enables the full beauty of the windows of the drum to be visible, and the restored pinnacles to glow.

Unveiling the Queen of Carmel one glorious morning in 2011

From the southern side, the dome with its new tiles has its own magnificence, and the circle of cypress trees is a reminder that Bahá'u'lláh is the Founder of the Shrine of the Báb

beneath the concrete floor of the rooms and colonnade, and with ducts to four places on the retaining wall, created air movement and contributed to the reduction of moisture on the floors.

The mechanical upgrade also involved the installation of a new exhaust fan, thermostat controlled, which took the hot air out of the superstructure, including the dome. Supply lines for both hot and chilled water were put in, connecting the area beneath the superstructure to a future air conditioning service building to be located in the far western garden area.

To protect against the intrusion of water into the structure, new roofing was put in place on the dome gutter, octagon and original edifice; there were repairs to the parapet wall; and new roof drains were installed, changing from the old clay pipes to PVC pipes. Access hatches were installed to assist entry for future maintenance. One was to an area at the base of the dome but not visible to observers, and a new platform and ladders were installed in connection with a new hatch on the octagon roof.

Stone restoration

One of the most exciting parts of the project was the stone restoration work. A team of young staff members and several volunteers from around the world brought their energy, enthusiasm and dedication to this painstaking task. Carried out between November 2008 and April 2011, this involved 50,000 hours of detailed work.

It began with examining the causes of deterioration of the Chiampo stone which had been used for the exterior cladding of the superstructure in the period 1948–1953 but which had never been used on other major buildings for that purpose. A block of this stone was obtained and shipped to Haifa so that artisans could carve new stone pieces to replace the ones damaged beyond repair, and for any future uses.

A study at the British Research Establishment's Heritage Building Department confirmed previous reports that Haifa's high humidity had affected the expandable material found in the veins of the original stone. Two expert conservators[24] from England came to Haifa at different times and trained a small team of young OSAR staff. Israeli stone conservators, headed by Amir Genach, also assisted the team, which was headed by Canadian Jubin Nakhai.

Research into finding suitable materials to restore Chiampo stone led the team to a company in the Netherlands which shipped the materials to Haifa and sent experts to provide training in the application of the materials.

The team began by stabilizing loose stone pieces. They cleaned the stone surfaces with water. They removed stone pieces that were detached and loose, as well as clay and other materials from the surfaces of the stone veins. They then re-attached stone pieces with adhesives and in many cases rebuilt the missing pieces with carved stone of special mortar. Reinforced fibreglass pins anchored the re-attached stones in place. The team members then pointed the loose grout joints between the stone pieces, about 60 per cent of the entire grout joints of the structure.

Three rounds of reviews and spot checks by three different stone restoration teams in different conditions were undertaken. The result was a conserved and revitalized stone cladding.

Electrical upgrade

The team, led by an Australian, Hamed Sharafizad, and staff member Roderic Haake, upgraded the electrical system of the Shrine and its precincts to comply with building code requirements and to meet the needs of the edifice in the future. A new raceway – an enclosed conduit for electrical wiring – was installed to protect wiring from water intrusion, humidity, heat and corrosion. This would also meet the needs of the environmental equipment. The team removed electrical panels from a southern wall of the Shrine, and established a new system in the service rooms that had been built under the western retaining wall. They put in new wiring and new systems for lighting protection, security and fire alarms. Underground electrical raceways now serviced the lights in the gardens. Lampposts were rewired, as were the chandeliers in the prayer rooms of the Shrine.

Metals, doors and windows

The team removed the beautiful balustrades from the top of the octagon, which had been deeply corroded, and sent them to the specialist company Gvanim in Acre, which sandblasted the old paint off them and repainted them with a protective powder-coating system. Some floral pieces were too far gone and thus were replicated. A team including the staff of the gilding studio of the Bahá'í World Centre[25] and OSAR volunteers spent six months carefully re-gilding the balustrades. For any future work, the balustrades were attached into the stone so they could be removed without damaging the surrounding stone.

The railings that ran along the top of the retaining walls were reproduced in stainless steel, powder-coated, and installed so that they too could be removed easily in later years. The gilders also applied new gold leaf to such items as the ringstone symbols at the corners of the base, the central panel on the stone balustrade, the pinnacles of the octagon and the lantern on the top of the dome.

To prepare for the repainting of the metal doors and windows of the Shrine with special powder coating, they were removed and repaired and stripped of the many coats of paint applied over the decades. The carpentry shop at the Bahá'í World Centre led by Wolfgang Nieland built wooden doors that matched the classic old ones. The staff also made windows for the new openings and in the three southern rooms where doors and windows had not existed. Any broken glass was replaced after finding glass with matching colours.

Minor restoration work was carried out on the stained-glass windows of the octagon and drum, and new sealant was put around the windows to stop water penetrating the superstructure.

Plastering

The removal of the original interior cement plaster and joint mortar work of the Shrine's interior and the arcade ceiling allowed the application of a new lime-based plaster. That allowed the masonry walls to breathe and release any contained moisture. The team also repaired the plaster on the interior of the octagon and drum walls. Many Bahá'í World Centre staff participated in removing the cement plaster during their days off or after their working hours.

Flooring

A French company made new red tiles to replace most of the originals in eight of the nine rooms of the Shrine. After their installation and the application of a special coating, the team buffed them to highlight their colour and texture. The inner Shrine kept its original lime floor.

Southern rooms

Now that new storage rooms were opened through the western retaining wall, the rear rooms in the Shrine which had originally been used as an archives area could be restored, and openings made so that pilgrims could pray and meditate there.

Chandeliers similar to the originals in the prayer rooms were obtained from a Haifa antique shop and installed in the three southern rooms. Also placed there were new marble pedestals made in Italy and alabaster lamps from China, items similar to those in the other rooms. The frames for the Tablets of Visitation on the walls were similar to those in the other prayer rooms. A calligraphic representation of the Greatest Name installed over the new arch in the central southern room was similar to the one in the middle room on the western (room #6) side of the Shrine, though it was painted silver rather than gilded. New draperies and Persian rugs completed the setting.

Outside in the arcade, the original hanging and wall-mounted pendant lights were repaired, regilded – and replicated if necessary – by local artists, industrial tradespeople and glass manufacturers in the Czech Republic. Some were also purchased from a local antique shop.

The dome and its golden tiles

The effect of the restoration project most eagerly anticipated by Baháʼís all over the world was undoubtedly how the dome would look. Although most Baháʼís had little detailed idea of the damage done to the tiles, it was clear that the colour had become more orange than gold. What could the restoration experts do?

The 2006 report had described the condition of the dome, and in the following two years, OSAR consulted experts to see how to preserve the 11,000 original tiles. The office dismissed some options – such as applying leaves of gold over the original tiles – because such repair work would either change the design or last for only a few years due to the weather conditions of Haifa. There appeared to be no way to solve the problem of the water leakages on to the dome while keeping the 'golden' tiles in place. 'Therefore the decision was made,' OSAR said in its overall report,

> to remove the existing golden tiles: repair the concrete structure; restore the ornamental stone features; implement a water proofing system and install new gold tiles with higher stability and longevity while maintaining the size, shape and finish of the original golden tiles.

After a careful worldwide search, OSAR selected a Portuguese tilemaker, Porcel, and worked closely with that manufacturer to test different colours, finishes, reflections and tile compositions. OSAR's report said:

> Precise measurement of the existing tiles and the spaces between the dome's stone ribs were taken, and computer-generated design drawings of all the tiles' shapes and sizes were produced – each tile being assigned a unique number according to its size and placement on the dome. Over 12,000 shapes and sizes were ordered – this included those needed to cover the dome as well as additional tiles for future use.

On 31 May 2010 Porcel began making the tiles, starting with precision moulds. The resulting tiles were made from 100 per cent limoge porcelain covered with a compatible orange glazing applied with a solution of pure gold and a highly durable final coating. The tests showed that the tiles are five to six time more abrasion resistant than the originals. OSAR representatives conducted quality control tests to ensure the tiles met the agreed standards. Once approved, they were packed and sent to Haifa in several shipments, the first batch arriving in November 2010.[26] In Haifa, Samira Rahimi led the logistics for the tiling of the dome.

Meanwhile, OSAR staff used special tools to remove the existing tiles without damaging the dome. A few were saved for posterity but the rest, bar one, were ground up and became part of the mortar bed of the new retaining wall around the Shrine, a new role for them in protecting the sacred edifice. The one remaining original tile, facing Bahjí, was special. On 29 April 1953, Shoghi Effendi had placed a silver box containing plaster from the Báb's prison cell in Máh-Kú in a niche of the dome and sealed it with that tile.

Studies on the materials and methods for installing the tiles had begun in 2007, and a decision was taken to use Laticrete materials, which were tested on the surface of the dome for adherence and longevity.

The dome was structurally repaired and master plasterers then applied two layers of plaster to the entire dome, producing the right surface for waterproofing and installation. After the removal of the stone ornaments depicting the acanthus leaf, the waterproofing material was applied. The stone ribs were not removed – it might have damaged the dome – but were restored in place. The joints between the stone pieces were redone.

In January 2011, an experienced master mason and tile setter, New Zealander Bruce Hancock, who had worked with his father installing the new finial on the dome 33 years earlier, led a team of seven staff and some volunteers setting the new tiles in place. It took three months, the last tile being laid on Naw-Rúz, 21 March 2011.

Finale

Early in the morning of 12 April 2011, the final set of covers came off the dome, revealing the golden tiles. It was an exquisitely elegant and refined sight. The restoration project, estimated by experts to have required five years to complete, had been finished in less than three years.

The members of the Universal House of Justice visited the Shrine to offer prayers of thanksgiving, doing so in the central chamber of the three rooms that had been added by Shoghi Effendi. Afterwards the House of Justice sent a message to all Bahá'í National Spiritual Assemblies throughout the world: 'Today the "Queen of Carmel", concealed from the gaze of the public for the larger part of the project, is unveiled and resplendent again, "crowned in glowing gold" on the Mountain of the Lord.' The dome, it said, 'now shines in the plenitude of its splendour'.

The House of Justice wrote that 'a myriad details pertaining to every element of the structure . . . were attended to by highly skilled and dedicated craftspeople and a large band of other devoted volunteers from near and far, who lovingly laboured together with scrupulous care and with sensitivity to the sacred nature of the work before them.'[27]

At a celebratory reception in the former German Templer colony below, the mayor of Haifa, Yona Yahav, who had witnessed the building of the superstructure in the 1950s, said: 'To see these renovations is very touching. They are of utmost importance.'[28]

In its Riḍván message that same month, the Universal House of Justice told the Bahá'ís of the world:

At the opening of this glorious season our eyes are brightened as we behold the newly unveiled brilliance of the gilded dome that crowns the exalted Shrine of the Báb. Restored to the supernal lustre intended for it by Shoghi Effendi, that august edifice once again shines out to land, sea, and sky, by day and by night, attesting the majesty and holiness of Him Whose hallowed remains are embosomed within.[29]

BIBLIOGRAPHY

The Báb. *Selections from the Writings of the Báb.* Comp. Research Department of the Universal House of Justice. Trans. Habib Taherzadeh with the assistance of a committee at the Bahá'í World Centre. Haifa: Bahá'í World Centre, 1976.

Bahá'í Reference Library. Authoritative online source of Bahá'í writings. Available at: https://www.bahai.org/library/.

The Bahá'í World. An International Record. Vol. XIV (1963–1968), Haifa: The Universal House of Justice, 1974. Vol. XV (1968–73); vol. XVI (1973–1976); vol. XVII (1976–1979); vol. XVIII (1979–1983); vol. XIX (1983–1986); vol. XX (1986–1992). Haifa: Bahá'í World Centre, various years.

New series: *The Bahá'í World, 1993–1994; 1995–1996; 2001–2002; 2004–2005; 2005–2006.* Haifa: Bahá'í World Centre, various years.

Bahá'í World News Service. Online periodical. Haifa: Bahá'í World Centre. Available at: http://news.bahai.org/.

Bahá'u'lláh. *Epistle to the Son of the Wolf.* Trans. Shoghi Effendi. Wilmette, IL: Bahá'í Publishing Trust, rev. ed. 1976.

— *Gleanings from the Writings of Bahá'u'lláh.* Trans. Shoghi Effendi. Wilmette, IL: Bahá'í Publishing Trust, 2nd ed. 1976.

Day, Michael V. *Journey to a Mountain: The Story of the Shrine of the Báb.* Vol. 1: 1850–1921. Oxford: George Ronald, 2017.

— *Coronation on Carmel. The Story of the Shrine of the Báb.* Vol. II: 1922–1963. Oxford: George Ronald, 2018.

Drake, Stephen. *Progress of the Project on Mount Carmel.* Haifa, n.d. (1990s). A three-page report.

Esslemont, J. E. *Bahá'u'lláh and the New Era.* Wilmette, IL: Bahá'í Publishing Trust, 1980.

Giachery, Ugo. *Shoghi Effendi: Recollections.* Oxford: George Ronald, 1973.

Haifa Tourist Board (ed). *Bahá'í Shrine and Gardens on Mount Carmel, Haifa, Israel: A Visual Journey.* Haifa: Haifa Municipality, Haifa Tourist Board and MOD Publishing House, 2001. Text collated by Eliza Rasiwala.

Harper, Barron. *Lights of Fortitude.* Oxford: George Ronald, 2007.

Hobhouse, Penelope. *Gardens of Persia.* Glebe, NSW: Florilegium, 2003.

McLaughlin, Robert. *These Perspicuous Verses.* Oxford: George Ronald, 1982.

Mehrabi, Jacqueline. *Mount Carmel: Whatever is Happening?* Leuven: Brilliant Books, 1995.

Momen, Moojan (ed). *Selections from the Writings of E. G. Browne on the Bábí and Bahá'í Religions.* Oxford: George Ronald, 1987.

Mountain of the Lord. Oakham, UK: Bahá'í Publishing Trust, n.d. (1990?)

Mount Carmel Bahá'í Projects (MCBP). *Vineyard of the Lord.* Issues 1–46 (1994–2001). Newsletters published in Haifa at the Bahá'í World Centre.

Mú'ayyad, Ḥabíb. *Khátirat-i-Ḥabíb* (Memoirs of Ḥabíb). Tehran, 1961. Vol. 1. Hofheim-Langenhain: Bahá'í Verlag, 1998. Trans. and ed. Ahang Rabbani: *Eight Years Near 'Abdu'l-Bahá: The Diary of Dr. Habíb Mú'ayyad.* Witnesses to Bábí and Bahá'í History, vol. 3. E-book, 2007. Available at: http://bahai-library.com/pdf/r/rabbani_diary_habib_muayyad_2013.pdf.

New Zealand Bahá'í News. Newsletter of the National Spiritual Assembly of the Bahá'ís of New Zealand.

Office of Shrine and Archives Restoration (OSAR). *A Summary: History of original construction, restoration work & systematic continuous care program.* Prepared for the Bahá'í World Centre & Department of Holy Places, February 2012, by Saeid Samadi and Samira Rahimi.

One Country. Newsletter of the Bahá'í International Community. April –June 2001.

Rabbání, Rúḥíyyih. *The Priceless Pearl.* London: Bahá'í Publishing Trust, 1969.

Ruhe, David S. *Door of Hope: The Bahá'í Faith in the Holy Land.* Oxford: George Ronald, 2nd rev. ed. 2001.

Saiedi, Nader. *Gate of the Heart. Understanding the Writings of the Báb.* Association for Bahá'í Studies and Wilfrid Laurier University Press, 2008.

Shoghi Effendi. *Citadel of Faith: Messages to America, 1947–1957.* Wilmette, IL: Bahá'í Publishing Trust, 1965.

— *Directives from the Guardian.* Comp. Gertrude Garrida. New Delhi: Bahá'í Publishing Trust, 1973.

— *God Passes By* (1944). Wilmette, IL: Bahá'í Publishing Trust, rev. ed. 1974.

— *The World Order of Bahá'u'lláh: Selected Letters by Shoghi Effendi* (1938). Wilmette, IL: Bahá'í Publishing Trust, 2nd rev. ed. 1974.

Taherzadeh, Adib. *The Revelation of Bahá'u'lláh.* 4 vols. Oxford: George Ronald, 1974–1987.

The Universal House of Justice. *A Wider Horizon: Selected Messages of the Universal House of Justice, 1983–1992.* Riviera Beach, FL: Palabra Publications, 1992.

— *Messages from the Universal House of Justice, 1963–1986: The Third Epoch of the Formative Age.* Comp. Geoffry W. Marks. Wilmette, IL: Bahá'í Publishing Trust, 1996.

— *Messages from the Universal House of Justice, 1968–1973.* Wilmette, IL: Bahá'í Publishing Trust, 1976.

— *The Ministry of the Custodians, 1957–1963: An Account of the Stewardship of the Hands of the Cause.* Haifa: Bahá'í World Centre, 1992.

— *Turning Point: Selected Messages of the Universal House of Justice and Supplementary Material 1996–2006.* West Palm Beach, FL: Palabra Publications, 2006.

— *Wellspring of Guidance: Messages from the Universal House of Justice 1963-1968.* Wilmette, IL: Bahá'í Publishing Trust, 1976.

White, Roger. *Forever in Bloom.* New Delhi: Time Books International, 1992.

NOTES AND REFERENCES

The Story So Far

1. Bahá'u'lláh, Tablet of Carmel. In *Gleanings from the Writings of Bahá'u'lláh*, XI, pp. 15–16.
2. Reported words of 'Abdu'l-Bahá, in Mú'ayyad, *Khátirat-i-Habíb*, vol.1, p. 81.
3. Letter from Shoghi Effendi to the Bahá'ís of the East, Naw-Rúz 1955, in *The Bahá'í World*, 1995–1996, pp. 58–9.
4. Letter from the Universal House of Justice to all National Spiritual Assemblies, 4 January 1994, in *The Bahá'í World, 1993-1994*, p. 68. Available at: https://bahai-library.com/uhj_arc_1994.
5. Shakespeare, *Henry V*: 'We few, we happy few, we band of brothers . . .' And, equally, sisters.

1. Wondrous Result

1. Esslemont, *Bahá'u'lláh and the New Era*, p. 251.
2. *The Bahá'í World, 2001–2002*, pp. 65–6.
3. Letter from Shoghi Effendi to the American believers, 29 March 1951, in *Citadel of Faith*, p. 96. See Day, *Coronation on Carmel*, Ch. 18.
4. The physical work of building was not done by the Bahá'í staff, but by local contractors.
5. They were the Seat of the International Teaching Centre and the Centre for the Study of the Texts. An extension to the International Archives Building was also a major construction effort.

2. The 1960s

1. Taherzadeh, *The Revelation of Bahá'u'lláh*, vol. 4, p. 170, drawing on Mú'ayyad, *Khátirat-i-Habíb*, vol. 1, p. 81.
2. The Universal House of Justice, *Wellspring of Guidance*, p. 99.
3. ibid. p. 7.
4. ibid. p. 9.
5. See *The Bahá'í World*, vol. XIV (1963–1968), p. 87.
6. Letter from the Universal House of Justice, 18 December 1963, in The Universal House of Justice, *Wellspring of Guidance*, pp. 19–21. Two months previously, in October 1963, the House of Justice had mentioned how the plan starting in 1964 would involve the development of the World Centre (ibid. p. 17).
7. Information provided by Mr 'Alí Nakhjavání in email to the author, 16 September 2014.
8. The Universal House of Justice, Message to the Bahá'ís of the World, Ridván

1964, in The Universal House of Justice, *Wellspring of Guidance*, pp. 23–4.

9   Robert McLaughlin (1900–89) was Dean at Princeton from 1952 to 1965. He was for some time a member of the National Spiritual Assembly of the United States, served as a member of the technical advisory board for the construction of the interior of the Bahá'í Temple in Wilmette, and was Architectural Consultant to the Universal House of Justice for the building of the Temple in Panama (The Universal House of Justice, Riḍván Message 1967, ibid. p. 107, also available at http://bahai-library.com/uhj_ridvan_1967). He was also the author of *These Perspicuous Verses* (Oxford: George Ronald, 1982). He co-founded American Homes, Inc., producers of prefabricated homes, was a consultant on the design of the US Embassy in London at Grosvenor Square, and held some 30 patents for new building technologies.

10 *The Bahá'í World*, vol. XIV, pp. 87–8.

11 Email from Mr 'Alí Nakhjavání to the author, 16 September 2014.

12 *The Bahá'í World*, vol. XIV, pp. 87–8.

13 In Memoriam, Robert W. McLaughlin, in *The Bahá'í World*, vol. XX (1986–1992).

14 There was an overstatement of the extent of Professor McLaughlin's plan as described in a report in *The Bahá'í World*, vol. XV (1968–1973), pp. 174, 177 which referred to the concepts of the Master and Shoghi Effendi for the Arc and Terraces. It said: 'For a number of years a distinguished Bahá'í architect has, at the request of the Universal House of Justice, been working on a detailed plan to realize this concept. This plan has now been adopted, and is being used as a basis of a Town Planning Scheme which is to be submitted to the Municipality of Haifa.' In an interview with the author on 18 January 2015, the architect of the Terraces which were inaugurated in 2001, Mr Fariborz Sahba, said he had no knowledge of any detailed plan for terraces made by Professor McLaughlin and did not believe any such plan had ever existed. However, he had seen some very basic sketches showing the proposed location of the buildings of the Arc, which was totally different from the actual location of those edifices as they exist today. One of those drawings had proposed that the Shrine of 'Abdu'l-Bahá be situated above the Arc. He had seen those drawings when working in Iran with Mr Hossein Amanat on the design of the Seat of the Universal House of Justice.

15 The Universal House of Justice, Message to the Bahá'ís of the World, Riḍván 1966, in *Wellspring of Guidance*, p. 78.

16 Letter from the Universal House of Justice to all National Spiritual Assemblies, 7 March 1967, ibid. p. 100.

17 The Universal House of Justice, Message to the Bahá'ís of the World, Riḍván 1967, ibid. p. 105. This does not refer to the Terraces.

18 The car would be parked near the front door of the Pilgrim House.

19 Photograph and report in *The Bahá'í World*, vol. XV (1968–1973), p. 84. The film is at the Bahá'í World Centre, where the author has viewed part of it.

20 The message from the Universal House of Justice is in *Wellspring of Guidance*, p. 157: 'Grieved announce passing outstanding Hand Cause Leroy Ioas. His long service Bahá'í Community United States crowned elevation rank Hand Faith paving way historic distinguished services Holy Land. Appointment first Secretary General International Bahá'í Council personal representative Guardian Faith two intercontinental conferences association his name by beloved

Guardian octagon door Báb's Shrine tribute supervisory work drum dome that Holy Sepulcher notable part erection International Archives building all ensure his name immortal annals Faith. Laid to rest Bahá'í cemetery close fellow Hands. Advise hold befitting memorial services.' See also his 'In Memoriam' in *The Bahá'í World*, vol. XIV, pp. 291–300.

3. The 1970s and 1980s

1 The Universal House of Justice, Message to the Bahá'ís of the World, Riḍván 1969, in *Messages from the Universal House of Justice, 1963–1986*, p. 146.

2 Letter from the Universal House of Justice to all National Spiritual Assemblies, 19 December 1971, in *Messages from the Universal House of Justice, 1968–1973*, pp. 83–4.

3 Photograph of the new southwestern garden in *The Bahá'í World*, vol. XV (1968–1973), p. 175.

4 Personally witnessed by the author, who was a pilgrim in November 1980.

5 See *The Bahá'í World*, vol. XIX (1983–1986).

6 Cablegram from the Universal House of Justice to all National Spiritual Assemblies, 7 June 1972, in *Messages from the Universal House of Justice, 1963–1986*, p. 220.

7 The Universal House of Justice quoted the Guardian on this point in *The Bahá'í World*, vol. XVI (1973–1976), p. 397.

8 In the United Nations Millennium Declaration adopted by the General Assembly on 8 September 2000, the nations of the world said: 'We solemnly reaffirm, on this historic occasion, that the United Nations is the indispensable common house of the entire human family, through which we will seek to realize our universal aspirations for peace, cooperation and development. We therefore pledge our unstinting support for these common objectives and our determination to achieve them.'

9 'Abdu'l-Bahá, Tablet to Mrs Whyte, quoted by Shoghi Effendi in *The World Order of Bahá'u'lláh*, p. 206. See http://reference.bahai.org/en/t/se/WOB/wob-19.html.

10 Information from Mr 'Alí Nakhjavání.

11 *The Bahá'í World*, vol. XIX, p. 23; also an email from Hossein Amanat to the author, 6 January 2015: 'The building was to be built not only for needs, but according to Bahá'u'lláh's prophecy in the Tablet of Carmel.'

12 Cablegram from the Universal House of Justice to all National Spiritual Assemblies, 17 September 1973, in *Messages from the Universal House of Justice, 1963–1986*, p. 255.

13 It was in Shahyad ('King Memorial') Square which has been renamed Azadi ('Freedom') Square.

14 He lived and worked in Iran until 1978 (email from Hossein Amanat to the author, 6 January 2015).

15 The interior of the more modern design was not very different from the other design but the exterior was different (ibid.).

16 *The Bahá'í World*, vol. XVI, p. 403.

17 He did not consult Professor McLaughlin's plans in detail but had a general look

once when in the United States. Email from Hossein Amanat to the author, 6 January 2015.

18 *The Bahá'í World*, vol. XVI, p. 133.

19 ibid. p. 403.

20 In traditional buildings, an octagon supports most domes, and the Seat and the Shrine are in that category. Email from Hossein Amanat to the author, 6 January 2015.

21 *The Bahá'í World*, vol. XVI, p. 403.

22 Jessie E. Revell (1891–1966) was a member of the appointed and elected International Bahá'í Councils, serving as Treasurer. See http://bahai-library.com/revell_letters.

23 Shoghi Effendi quite often also referred to how the dome on the resting place of the Greatest Holy Leaf also symbolized the headship of the Administrative Order (email from 'Alí Nakhjavání to the author, 22 September 2014).

24 *The Bahá'í World*, vol. XIX, p. 24. This is the same stone as used in the Acropolis in Athens.

25 ibid.

26 Email from Hossein Amanat to the author, 6 January 2015.

27 From then on, the concourse was the venue for some Holy Day celebrations and for pilgrims to meet the members of the Universal House of Justice.

28 *The Bahá'í World*, vol. XIX, p. 23.

29 Ruhe, *Door of Hope*, p. 174. Dr David Ruhe served as a member of the Universal House of Justice from 1968 to 1993.

30 In 1985 Hossein Amanat received the Tucker Architectural Award, which is awarded for excellence in the incorporation and use of natural stone in a building or landscape project. It was awarded for his design of the Seat of the Universal House of Justice.

31 Hossein Amanat, email to the author, 31 October 2014, forwarded by Mr 'Alí Nakhjavání, who said the eventual architect of the Terraces (Fariborz Sahba) was then busy completing the Temple in India.

32 Fariborz Sahba is six years younger than Hossein Amanat. He worked with Mr Amanat for six years in Iran and later, as the Project Manager of the Mount Carmel Bahá'í Projects (MCBP), collaborated 16 years on the Arc projects. 'I believe our destinies have been closely linked together in one way or another,' Mr Sahba said in an interview with the author on 18 January 2015.

4. The Temple and the Terraces

1 For an account of the opening ceremony see *The Bahá'í World*, vol. XX (1986–1992), p. 731.

2 For these and other biographical details see White, *Forever in Bloom*, pp. 10–11. Further biographical details appear elsewhere in this volume.

3 Letter from the Universal House of Justice to the Followers of Bahá'u'lláh throughout the world, 30 April 1987. Available at: https://www.bahai.org/library/authoritative-texts/the-universal-house-of-justice/messages/19870831_001/1#842030855. The agreement was signed by Mr Shimon Peres, the Israeli Vice-Premier and Foreign Minister, on behalf of the Government of Israel, and by the Secretary-General of the Bahá'í International Community, Donald Barrett,

on behalf of the Bahá'í World Centre and in the presence of other high-ranking government officials and the deputy Secretary-General of the Bahá'í International community, Ronald Bates.

4   Prior to Mr Sahba taking on the role as project manager on the Arc, Mr Charles Grindley had been serving in this position, but there had been no construction undertaken at that time.

5   Letter from the Universal House of Justice to the Followers of Bahá'u'lláh throughout the world, 31 August 1987, in The Universal House of Justice, *A Wider Horizon*, pp. 51–3.

6   The original estimate was jointly composed in association with the independent quantity surveyor, Mr Iain Fletcher, of Dean, Murray and Partners, engaged at the very beginning of the project by Mr Amanat (email from Steve Drake to the author, 19 May 2015).

7   MCBP, *Vineyard of the Lord*, no. 1, p. 2. As summarized by Eliza Rasiwala in personal correspondence with the author, 3 March 2011, the seven phases of the Mount Carmel Bahá'í Projects were: **Phase I**. Commenced on 23 May 1990: Maintenance of the Shrine of the Báb and strengthening and restoration of the 200-metre long retaining wall below the Shrine and its extension eastwards to make it symmetrical with the western side. **Phase II**. Commenced on 17 June 1991: Earthwork for the Centre for the Study of the Texts and Archives Extension and construction of 30-metre high retaining wall behind the Centre for the Study of the Texts. Construction of Terraces 9 to 3 below the Shrine. **Phase III**. Commenced on 9 December 1992: Excavations at the site of the International Teaching Centre [Centre for International Counsellors] and construction of retaining wall and micropiles and concrete beams; and development of Terraces 15 to 19 above the Shrine. **Phase IV**. Commenced on 19 December 1993: Construction of the building of the Centre for the Study of the Texts and Archives Extension. **Phase V**. Construction of the building of the International Teaching Centre. **Phase VI**. Lowering of and building the bridge over Hatzionut Street together with construction of Terraces 11 to 15. **Phase VII**. Development of lower Terraces 1 and 2. The remaining phases of the projects were initiated during the Three Year Plan.

8   The MCBP also sent a staff member to be trained in France as a waterproof installer so that he could supervise the work (email from Steve Drake to the author, 8 February 2015).

5. Prelude and Inspiration

1   *The Bahá'í World*, vol. V (1932–1934) p. 241. The caption read: 'Tentative design of the terraces suggesting an idea of the future development of a part of this area.'

2   Interview with Fariborz Sahba by the author, 18 January 2015.

3   The model may have been a new one made by Mr Maxwell, who had great skills for such a task, or by Rúḥíyyih Khánum, who had made a model of the steps for the Guardian. See Day, *Coronation on Carmel*, p. 326, note 15, referring to Rabbání, *The Priceless Pearl*, p. 237.

4   For details and illustration, see Day, *Coronation on Carmel*.

5   Interview with Fariborz Sahba by the author, 18 January 2015. The Báb's injunction is found in the Persian Bayán, 6:3: 'For example, should one build an

edifice and fail to elevate it to the utmost state of perfection possible for it, there would be no moment in the life of that edifice when angels would not beseech God to torment him; nay, rather, all the atoms of that edifice would do the same' (Saedi, *Gate of the Heart*, p. 317).

6   Email from Fariborz Sahba to the author, 18 December 2014.

7   ibid.

8   Haifa Tourist Board, *Bahá'í Shrine and Gardens*, p. 26.

9   'In His presence, which is My Presence, there is not at night even a lighted lamp! And yet in places [of worship] which in varying degrees reach out unto Him, unnumbered lamps are shining. All that is on earth hath been created for Him and all partake with delight of His benefits, and yet they are so veiled from Him as to refuse Him even a lamp!' (Persian Bayán, in *Selections from the Writings of the Báb*, p. 87). Shoghi Effendi writes that 'in the Persian Bayán, He Himself has stated that at night-time He did not even have a lighted lamp' (*God Passes By*, p. 18).

10 Haifa Tourist Board, *Bahá'í Shrine and Gardens*, p. 26.

11 The Báb, *Selections from the Writings of the Báb*, pp. 183–6; email from Fariborz Sahba to the author, 27 January 2015.

12 The Persian Bayán included some Bábí laws, as well as references to 'He Whom God shall make manifest' (Bahá'u'lláh). Excerpts are published in The Báb, *Selections from the Writings of the Báb*, pp. 77–113, while an earlier complete translation by E. G. Browne can be found in Momen, *Selections from the Writings of E. G. Browne on the Bábí and Bahá'í Religions*.

13 Letters of the Living: the 18 who first recognized the spiritual station of the Báb. A letter of 28 July 1994, written on behalf of the Universal House of Justice to an individual believer, explains: 'While the eighteen terraces are known to be symbolic of the number of the Letters of the Living, just as the eighteen lancet windows of the drum of the Shrine of the Báb are reminiscent of His appointees, the House of Justice has not decided that each terrace should be specifically named after each of the eighteen Letters of the Living.'

The architect said: 'The word "Hai", Living, made much more sense when I read the description that the Universal House of Justice once used to describe the Terraces: "The beauty and magnificence of the Gardens and Terraces now under development are symbolic of the nature of the transformation which is destined to occur both within the hearts of the world's peoples and in the physical environment of the planet."'

14 Quoted in Esslemont, *Bahá'u'lláh and the New Era*, p. 251.

15 Rev. 22: 1; email from Fariborz Sahba to the author, 18 December 2014.

16 Fariborz Sahba in conversation with the author in San Diego, September 2018.

17 Interview with Fariborz Sahba by the author, 18 January 2015. The message from the Guardian, titled 'Spiritual Conquest of the Planet', is dated 29 March 1951; see Shoghi Effendi, *Citadel of Faith*, pp. 91–8. Mr Sahba consulted the version in the Persian language.

18 Haifa Tourist Board, *Bahá'í Shrine and Gardens*, pp. 26–8.

19 Email from Fariborz Sahba to the author, 18 December 2014.

20 ibid.

21 This appeared after the work on the eastern extension of the Shrine terrace had begun in 1990.

22 The Guardian had written in his message to the American Bahá'ís of 29 March 1951 cited above, note 17, that within the properties dedicated to the Shrine were 'gardens and terraces which at once embellish, and lend a peculiar charm to, these sacred precincts' (*Citadel of Faith*, p. 96).

23 Haifa Tourist Board, *Bahá'í Shrine and Gardens*, p. 28.

24 Email from Fariborz Sahba to the author, 18 December 2014.

6. The Design in Detail

1 In San Diego in September 2018, Fariborz Sahba told the author about this vigorous discussion in which he cited the historic and sacred nature of the Terraces.

2 Letter from Shoghi Effendi to the American Bahá'ís, 29 March 1951, in *Citadel of Faith*, p. 95.

3 See above, Ch. 5, note 13.

4 There was a ban on individuals importing canary palms but after a long time looking, MCBP found a nursery which grew them for the project in the quantity wanted. 'Many of our trees failed and we had to replace them again and again' (email from Fariborz Sahba to the author, 18 December 2014).

5 Haifa Tourist Board, *Bahá'í Shrine and Gardens*, pp. 34–63.

6 ibid. pp. 34–5.

7 ibid. p. 36.

8 ibid. p. 48.

9 ibid. The Báb was a Siyyid, a descendant of the Prophet Muhammad.

10 For a description see Hobhouse, *Gardens of Persia*, p. 8.

11 Fariborz Sahba in conversation with the author in San Diego, September 2018.

7. Dual Projects

1 MCBP, *Vineyard of the Lord*, no. 3, p. 8.

2 For further information on these roads in the time of Shoghi Effendi, see Day, *Coronation on Carmel*, p. 257.

3 Cablegram from the Universal House of Justice to all National Spiritual Assemblies, 23 January 1990. Available at: https://www.bahai.org/library/authoritative-texts/the-universal-house-of-justice/messages/19900123_001/1#234416182.

4 See MCBP, *Vineyard of the Lord*, no. 1, p. 2.

8. 1990: Work Begins

1 Cablegram from the Universal House of Justice to all National Spiritual Assemblies, 23 January 1990. Available at: https://www.bahai.org/library/authoritative-texts/the-universal-house-of-justice/messages/19900123_001/1#234416182.

2 Cablegram from the Universal House of Justice, 24 May 1990, referring to the extension of Terrace 10. Available at: http://bahai-library.com/uhj_six-year_plan_1986#69; and in The Universal House of Justice, *A Wider Horizon*, p. 83.

3 See Day, *Coronation on Carmel*, p. 328, note 17, and taking into account the caution often expressed by Mr Furútan about pilgrims' notes not being authoritative text.

4 This work was done after consultation with the city engineer. For the upper

terraces there were issues yet to be resolved involving building permits, town planning requirements and funding.

5   *The Bahá'í World*, vol. XX (1986–1992), p. 128. Notes by Eliza Rasiwala, staff writer on MCBP, *Vineyard of the Lord*, in personal email to the author, 3 March 2011. See also the video *Not Even a Lamp*, available at: https://www.youtube.com/watch?v=OKsU5MZouGg&t=1101s.

6   *The Bahá'í World*, vol. XX, p. 134.

9. The General and His Team

1   For reminiscences about the project from a sample of the volunteers, see Annex I.

2   Email from Nancy Markovich, secretary to Mr Sahba, to the author, 21 October 2014.

3   Email from Eliza Rasiwala to the author, 28 March 2011. Eliza passed away in August 2012.

4   Email from Fariborz Sahba to the author, 18 December 2014.

5   Of Mr Drake, Mr Sahba told the author in February 2015: 'Steve was not only my deputy, but a loving brother. With him on my side I could do anything.'

6   Email from Steve Drake to the author, 6 November 2014.

7   Mrs Sahba passed away aged 55 from an illness in Toronto on 25 March 2005. In a message of condolence, the Universal House of Justice said that her 'devoted and selfless services', including her artistic collaboration on the Temple project in India and the Terraces on Mount Carmel, left 'a lasting testimony to her love for the Blessed Beauty [Bahá'u'lláh] . . . Her radiant heart and saintly character left an indelible impression upon all who crossed her path.' A memorial service for her was held in the Temple in India. See *The Bahá'í World, 2004–2005*, p. 291.

8   Recalled by Steve Drake in an email to the author, 8 February 2015.

10. 1991: Working Despite War

1   *The Bahá'í World*, vol. XX (1986–1992), pp. 133–5.

2   For example, Mr Sahba and Mr Paul Reynolds kept an appointment at the district council offices when the entire city and offices were closed due to the conflict.

3   Email from Steve Drake to the author, 17 January 2015.

4   Photograph and caption in *The Bahá'í World*, vol. XX, p. 126.

5   ibid. p. 127.

6   Photograph ibid. p. 382.

7   This was a temporary measure. Nineteen years later, in 2010, the tiles were replaced; see Annex II.

8   Email from Steve Drake to the author, 8 February 2015.

11. 1992: Focus on Lower Terraces

1   See Day, *Coronation on Carmel*, p. 93.

2   Drake, *Progress of the Project on Mount Carmel*, attached to email to the author, 8 February 2015.

3   Email from Fariborz Sahba to the author, 18 December 2014.

12. 1993: Upper Terraces

1 The Universal House of Justice, Message to the Bahá'ís of the World, Riḍván 150 (1993). Available at: http://bahai-library.com/uhj_ridvan_1993.
2 MCBP, *Vineyard of the Lord*, no. 1, p. 5.
3 *The Bahá'í World, 1992–1993*, p. 175.
4 *The Bahá'í World, 1993–1994*, p. 70.
5 MCBP, *Vineyard of the Lord*, no. 1, p. 5.
6 ibid. p. 4.
7 Letter from the Universal House of Justice to the Bahá'ís of the World, 27 June 1993. Available at: http://en.bahaitext.org/MUHJ86-01/160/Securing_Building_Contractors_for_Mount_Carmel_Projects.
8 These were the extension to the Archives, the Seat of the International Teaching Centre, and the Centre for the Study of the Texts. The letter could be seen to be somewhat a parallel to those sent by Shoghi Effendi in the 1950s when completion of the Shrine was the target. See Day, *Coronation on Carmel*, pp. 186, 193.
9 Letter on behalf of the Universal House of Justice to the Bahá'ís of the World, 31 October 1993. Available at: http://en.bahaitext.org/MUHJ86: 01/171/Relative_Priority_of_the_Various_Bah%C3%A1%E2%80%99%C3%AD_Funds.
10 Email from Steve Drake to the author, 8 February 2015.
11 Such was the gratitude for the vital assistance of Mr Gurel, that he and a relative were warmly invited for a special VIP tour when the project was complete.
12 Sir Julius Chan also had consultations with the Universal House of Justice. See *The Bahá'í World, 1993–1994*, p. 78.
13 It is not true (as has been reported) that the aim was for the road to be a symbolic finger to point from the Shrine of the Báb to the Shrine of Bahá'u'lláh. Nor was it a policy or requirement of the Universal House of Justice to seek a change to the centreline of the road (email from Fariborz Sahba to the author, 18 December 2014).

13. 1994: Sacrificial Outpouring

1 Letter from Shoghi Effendi to the Bahá'ís of the East, Naw-Rúz 108, in *The Bahá'í World, 1995–1996*, pp. 58–9.
2 Letter from the Universal House of Justice to all National Spiritual Assemblies, 4 January 1994, in *The Bahá'í World, 1993–1994*, p. 68. Available at: http://bahai-library.com/uhj_arc_1994. The quotation from the Writings of Bahá'u'lláh is from *Epistle to the Son of the Wolf*, p. 145.
3 Letter on behalf of the Universal House of Justice, 12 September 1994, in MCBP, *Vineyard of the Lord*, no. 7, p. 1.
4 See *The Bahá'í World, 1993–1994*, p. 73.
5 MCBP, *Vineyard of the Lord*, no. 4, p. 7.
6 ibid.
7 ibid. no. 7, p. 7.
8 ibid. no. 1, p. 5.
9 ibid. no. 4, p. 4.

10 Information from Nancy Markovich. Mr. Noufi invited the entire MCBP staff to his son's wedding. In the video *Not Even a Lamp* Mr Noufi speaks of spiritual assistance as the reason he and his team were able to contribute as they did.

11 A division of Marmi Vicentini, the company that had worked with Mr Sahba on the Bahá'í Temple in India. See http://www.margraf.it/en/dt_portfolios/house-of-worship-of-bahai-religion/ . . .

12 MCBP, *Vineyard of the Lord*, no. 4, p. 4. The finish is called *mutabeh*.

13 Fariborz Sahba in conversation with the author, September 2018. The author is also grateful to picture framer Josephine (Jo) Hill, a volunteer staff member and mother of sculptor Oliver Stretton-Pow, who photographed the team at Bahjí.

14 Email from sculptor Oliver Stretton-Pow to the author, 6 March 2015.

14. 1995: Acceleration on All Fronts

1 MCBP, *Vineyard of the Lord*, no. 7, pp. 4 and 5.
2 Email from Fariborz Sahba to the author, 1 August 2018, and in conversation in San Diego, September 2018.
3 MCBP, *Vineyard of the Lord*, no. 11, p. 6.
4 Mr Goldschmidt and his wife, May, had built the promenade as a memorial to their late son, Louis (1952–1971). See http://www.carmelithaifa.com/GanHaemStation/LouisPromenade.aspx.
5 This was an approach that had been followed down below when the Monument Gardens had been protected while Hatzionut Avenue was being widened under the Bahá'í property.
6 MCBP, *Vineyard of the Lord*, no. 10, p. 7.
7 Fariborz Sahba in conversation with the author in San Diego, September 2018.
8 Quoted in MCBP, *Vineyard of the Lord*, no. 10, p. 7.
9 Email from Samandar Milani to the author.
10 The separate irrigation pipe came in handy after the opening of the Terraces when desalinated bore water began to be used on the gardens.
11 In about 1996 a drill was bored on the eastern side of Terrace 1, and the bore water was found to be high in salt. After the Terraces were completed in 2001, the water was pumped to a header tank on the eastern side of the Seat of the Universal House of Justice, where it was desalinated and then used to irrigate about 70 per cent of the Terraces.
12 For an explanation of the name of the Afnán cistern, see Ch. 16. According to MCBP, *Vineyard of the Lord*, the MCBP team had three underground water reservoirs to be used in case of an emergency such as if a fire broke out and there was an interruption to the city supplies, but in fact only two were so designated. Other tanks were near the Archives and the Seat of the House of Justice but were not intended to be used for firefighting (information from Samandar Milani in conversation with the author, 25 April 2010).
13 Quoted in MCBP, *Vineyard of the Lord*, no. 11, p. 8.
14 Under Bahá'í law, only Bahá'ís may contribute to the Bahá'í funds. Although individual Bahá'ís may not be approached with requests for funds, general appeals are totally within the spirit of the Faith.
15 Quoted in MCBP, *Vineyard of the Lord*, no. 11, p. 8.
16 MCBP, *Vineyard of the Lord*, vol. 12, p. 7.

17   Available at: https://www.bahai.org/library/authoritative-texts/the-universal-house-of-justice/messages/#19950421_001.

18   A local factory supplied broken tiles for the pathways. Eventually, it could not keep up with the orders using discarded tiles and had to break good tiles to maintain the supply (email from Steve Drake to the author, 8 February 2015).

19   MCBP, *Vineyard of the Lord*, no. 12, p. 5.

20   Photograph in *The Bahá'í World, 1995–1996*, p. 40.

15. 1996: Tapestry of Beauty

1   The Universal House of Justice, Message to the Bahá'ís of the World, Riḍván 1996, in *Turning Point*, pp. 21–2. Available at: https://www.bahai.org/library/authoritative-texts/the-universal-house-of-justice/messages/19960421_009/1#464347443.

2   Email from Fariborz Sahba to the author, 18 December 2014.

3   Shoghi Effendi, *Directives from the Guardian*, p. 52: 'Strictly speaking the 5-pointed star is the symbol of our Faith, as used by the Báb and explained by Him.' See also the Súriy-i-Haykal by Bahá'u'lláh, which includes his messages to specific kings and rulers of the time, in Bahá'u'lláh, *The Summons of the Lord of Hosts*, pp. 3–137; also available at: https://www.bahai.org/library/authoritative-texts/bahaullah/summons-lord-hosts/3#991628547. See also Taherzadeh, *The Revelation of Bahá'u'lláh*, vol. 3, pp. 133–46. The star can also remind some of Leonardo da Vinci's Vitruvian man.

4   Email from Fariborz Sahba to the author, 1 August 2018.

5   MCBP, *Vineyard of the Lord*, no. 12, p. 7.

6   Incident recalled by Fariborz Sahba in Skype interview and in conversation with the author in late 2018.

7   MCBP, *Vineyard of the Lord*, no. 18, p. 6.

8   ibid. no. 17, p. 8.

16. 1997: Change in Organization

1   MCBP, *Vineyard of the Lord*. no. 21, p. 3.

2   ibid. no. 22, published in July, notes on p. 3 that it was three months since the Office of the Project Manager had taken on the construction management.

3   The major savings in the project were due to value engineering and the project management in general. There were also considerable savings resulting from the tax exemptions provided by the status agreement signed by the Bahá'í International Community and the Government of Israel in 1987 (email from Steve Drake to the author, 8 February 2015; Skype interview with Mr Sahba, April 2015).

4   MCBP, *Vineyard of the Lord*, no. 22, p. 7.

5   ibid. p. 3.

6   *Tubzeh* and *mottabeh* are Arabic names for the type of the finish of stone. One has a rough finish and the other is finely bush-hammered.

7   MCBP, *Vineyard of the Lord*, no. 19, p. 6.

8   ibid. no. 20, p. 6.

9   Mr Sahba recalled that one of the owners in an interview with a local newspaper had said that only over his dead body would that property be sold to the Bahá'ís

(email from Fariborz Sahba to the author, 5 April 2015).

10 Quoted in MCBP, *Vineyard of the Lord*, no. 20, p. 2.

11 Mírzá Muḥammad-Baqír Afnán was the grandson of the younger uncle of the Báb, Mírzá Ḥasan-'Alí. See MCBP, *Vineyard of the Lord*, vol. 23, p. 7; Mu'ayyád, *Eight Years Near 'Abdu'l-Bahá*, p. 465.

12 MCBP, *Vineyard of the Lord*, vol. 25, p. 7.

17. 1998: An Experience for Delegates

1 Photo in MCBP, *Vineyard of the Lord*, no. 31, p. 5.

2 Email from Marjorie Tidman to the author, 18 May 2015.

3 The subcontractor who worked on the concreting of the bridge and tunnels was Perez GG Ltd, who also did work on the Arc. The principal of this company celebrated with Mr Sahba at the end of the MCBP work.

4 MCBP, *Vineyard of the Lord*, no. 28, p. 3.

5 The Universal House of Justice, Message to the Bahá'ís of the World, Riḍván 1998, in *Turning Point*, pp. 103–4. Available at: https://www.bahai.org/library/authoritative-texts/the-universal-house-of-justice/messages/19980421_001/1#883230825.

6 MCBP, *Vineyard of the Lord*, no. 9, p. 8.

7 ibid. no. 29, p. 7.

8 In Shoghi Effendi's many communications about the gardens, he never referred to any of them by a name, with the exception of the Haram-i-Aqdas and Haram-i-Ashraf. He once called the Rose Garden or Delonix Garden, the Japanese Garden, probably because of the Japanese sago plants he placed there. This name did not stick, probably because the roses took over as the dominant plants (information provided by gardens historian Andrew Blake in email to the author, 26 January 2014).

9 Other communications work also took place. Just to the west of the construction site of the seat of the International Teaching Centre building, the team built a two-storey structure to house phone and computer systems for the Terraces and the Arc.

18. 1999: Beauty Recognized

1 Interview with Fariborz Sahba by the author, 18 January 2015.

2 Haifa Tourist Board, *Bahá'í Shrine and Gardens*, p. 32.

3 Letter from the Universal House of Justice to all National Spiritual Assemblies, 4 January 1994, in *The Bahá'í World, 1993–1994*, p. 68. Available at: http://bahai-library.com/uhj_arc_1994. See also MCBP, *Vineyard of the Lord*, no. 35, p. 8.

4 18 May 1999 edition, as reported in translation in MCBP, *Vineyard of the Lord*, no. 33, p. 6.

5 The Universal House of Justice, Message to the Bahá'ís of the World, Riḍván 1999, in *Turning Point*, pp. 112, 116. Also available at: https://www.bahai.org/library/authoritative-texts/the-universal-house-of-justice/messages/19990421_001/1#104279438.

6 Letter written on behalf of the Universal House of Justice, 14 September 1999, quoted in MCBP, *Vineyard of the Lord*, no. 36, p. 2.

7 MCBP, *Vineyard of the Lord*, no. 36, p. 8, quoting a letter to Mr Sahba from the

Universal House of Justice, 24 October 1999. Earlier that year, in March, the Office of the Project Manager had published a statement that described the 'race against time as we draw closer to the finishing line'. It said a sense of urgency characterized the work (MCBP, *Vineyard of the Lord*, no. 32, p. 8).

8   For a description of the work by Mr Maxwell on the gate in 1946, see Day, *Coronation on Carmel*, p. 139.

9   Email from Andrew Blake to the author, 7 October 2018.

10 ibid.

19. 2000: Year of Completion

1   MCBP, *Vineyard of the Lord*, no. 37, p. 3.

2   The Universal House of Justice, Message to the Bahá'ís of the World, Riḍván 2000, in *Turning Point*, p. 128. Available at: http://bahai-library.com/uhj_ridvan_2000.

3   Letter from the Universal House of Justice to the Bahá'ís of the World, 19 January 2001. Available at: https://www.bahai.org/library/authoritative-texts/the-universal-house-of-justice/messages/20000119_001/1#491658441.

4   The Universal House of Justice, *The Ministry of the Custodians*, p. 39.

5   Fariborz Sahba told the author this in 2015.

6   Violette Nakhjavani accompanied Amatu'l-Bahá Rúḥíyyih Khánum on many overseas journeys for the Faith, and made notes which she later published in *Amatu'l-Bahá in India* and *The Great African Safari*. Her two-volume masterpiece *The Maxwells of Montreal* was completed shortly before her passing in 2012 with the assistance of her daughter Bahiyyih. Mrs Nakhjavani was a daughter of the Hand of the Cause Mr Banani, and the wife of Mr 'Alí Nakhjavání, a member of the Universal House of Justice (1963–2003).

7   Fariborz Sahba told the author this in 2018.

8   The land needed stabilizing for the funeral which was scheduled for the following day. This was achieved by covering the entire site with large panels of plywood with a thick layer of crushed stone aggregates on top. Hundreds of plants were potted to give the impression of a finished landscape. These were removed a few weeks after the funeral. The whole garden was then beautifully landscaped. Fariborz Sahba told this to the author in September 2018.

9   There were several site offices during the Terraces project: under the Shrine gardens on the eastern side; on the western side of the Shrine gardens; on Terrace 12; on the western side of Terrace 15; on the western side of Terrace 19 (information from Samandar Milani).

10 Of the kind seen in the putting greens of elite golf courses.

11 Fariborz Sahba in conversation with the author in San Diego, September 2018.

12 Email from Fariborz Sahba to the author, February 2015.

13 Revelation 22:1.

14 MCBP, *Vineyard of the Lord*, no. 43, p. 6.

15 See photograph in MCBP, *Vineyard of the Lord*, no. 42, p. 4.

16 Email from Fariborz Sahba to the author, 1 August 2018.

17 MCBP, *Vineyard of the Lord*, no. 44, p. 7.

18 Information from Mr Sahba by Skype call with the author on 17 April 2015. The cost of constructing the Centre of the Study of the Texts and the International

Teaching Centre was also about US$60 million each. In addition there were substantial costs for permits and other ancillary needs, which made up the total.

20. 2001: Grand Opening

1   *Bahá'í World News Service*, 16 January 2001.
2   ibid.
3   It had not been deliberate to face the Seat of the International Teaching Centre in the general direction of the Shrine (email from Fariborz Amanat to the author, 6 January 2015).
4   The Universal House of Justice, message to the Bahá'ís of the World concerning the Conference of the Continental Counsellors, 16 January 2001, in The Universal House of Justice, *Turning Point*, pp. 154–5. Available at: http://bahai-library.com/uhj_institution_counsellors_world.
5   The Universal House of Justice, message to the Bahá'ís of the World, Riḍván 2001, in *Turning Point*, pp. 161–2. Available at: https://www.bahai.org/library/authoritative-texts/the-universal-house-of-justice/messa ges/20010421_001/1#216251280.
6   *Bahá'í World News Service*, 21 May 2001.
7   Figures cited by the Universal House of Justice, message to the Bahá'ís of the World, 1 June 2001. Available at: http://bahai-library.com/bjuk/200105-200401/BJ200107/terraces.htm.
8   *Bahá'í World News Service*, 20 May 2001.
9   ibid. 15 May 2001.
10 ibid.
11 Email from Josephine Hill to the author, 4 September 2014.
12 Managing director of the Inaugural Events Office Gry Kvalheim, in *Bahá'í World News Service*, 21 May 2001.
13 Some elements of this description are from an account by British Bahá'í Thelma Batchelor in the *New Zealand Bahá'í News*, June 2001.
14 *The Bahá'í World, 2001–2002*, pp. 57–8.
15 *One Country*, April–June 2001.
16 Dr Janet Khan remembered the congratulatory calls (conversation with the author, 21 June 2018).
17 Email from usher Josephine Hill to the author, 5 September 2014.
18 *The Bahá'í World, 2001–2002*, pp. 65–7.
19 For a video presentation of the events see https://www.youtube.com/watch?v=9TXliGA4IDE.
20 Report by Thelma Batchelor in *New Zealand Bahá'í News*, June 2001.
21 See Day, *Coronation on Carmel*, pp. 285–6.
22 Born in Oslo in 1949, Lasse Thoresen began composing at 16, became a Bahá'í in 1971, became senior professor at the Norwegian State Academy for Music in 1988 and in 2010 was awarded the prestigious Nordic Council Music Prize for his Opus 42. written for the vocal ensemble Nordic Voices. His music has been performed by leading orchestras, ensembles and soloists. For three years he was composer in residence in Festival Présence (Paris). As a researcher he has developed a phenomenological method for the analysis of music-as-heard (published in 2015 under the title *Emergent Musical Forms. Aural Explorations*), and

has lectured extensively in Europe, Canada and the United States. Through the artistic research project 'Concrescence' he has integrated selected ethnic styles of singing and the use of microtonality with a traditional Western idiom of song, working for many years with Nordic Voices and The Latvian Radio Choir.

23 See Taherzadeh, *The Revelation of Bahá'u'lláh*, vol. 4, p. 356.

24 The Master referred to the Shrine of the Báb as the throne of God.

25 MCBP, *Vineyard of the Lord*, no. 46, p. 5.

26 Esslemont, *Bahá'u'lláh and the New Era*, p. 251.

27 *Bahá'í World News Service*, 22 May 2001.

28 Alláh-u-Abhá (God the Most Glorious) can be used as a prayer, greeting or song.

29 *New Zealand Bahá'í News*. June 2001, p. 8.

30 In several messages, see for example the 1992 Riḍván message, available at: https://www.bahai.org/library/authoritative-texts/the-universal-house-of-justice /messages/19920421_001/1#271279916.

31 MCBP, *Vineyard of the Lord*, no. 46, p. 11.

32 *Bahá'í World News Service*, 22 May 2001.

33 Email from Josephine Hill to the author, 1 January 2015.

34 Dr Farzam Arbab, Mr Kiser Barnes, Mr Hooper Dunbar, Mr Hushmand Fatheazam, Dr Peter Khan, Mr Douglas Martin, Mr Glenford Mitchell, Mr 'Alí Nakhjavání, Mr Ian Semple.

35 *Bahá'í World News Service*, 23 May 2001.

36 ibid.

37 ibid.

38 *Bahá'í World News Service*, 25 May 2001. Available at: https://news.bahai.org/ story/122/.

39 Text emailed by Fariborz Sahba to the author, 20 January 2015.

40 Mr Sahba said: 'It is my hope and prayer that we have built the buildings of the Arc to his satisfaction, and have set the highest standards for future developments.'

41 Of the Universal House of Justice, Mr Sahba said: 'I hope our efforts have brought happiness to the august body, and that we have been worthy of its trust and blessings.' On 27 November 2001 the Universal House of Justice wrote to Mr Sahba. Here is an extract: 'Dear co-worker: We entrusted into your hands a task of daunting magnitude and incalculable spiritual significance. Through the abundant outpouring of Bahá'u'lláh's strengthening grace, your ceaseless and able exertions were crowned with brilliant success. You should rest assured that the full measure of His confirmations will continue to surround you and dear Golnar throughout the years' (text of letter emailed by Fariborz Sahba to the author, 21 February 2015).

42 Shoghi Effendi, quoted in *The Bahá'í World*, vol. XVIII (1979–1983) p. 35. The complete paragraph reads:

> O people of the earth! Know you with absolute certainty, and let every wavering and hesitant soul be apprised and take warning, that whatsoever has explicitly been revealed by the All-Glorious Pen will eventually become clear and evident, even as the sun in its noon-tide glory. In this snow-white Spot, and in other lands, the immutable Will of Him Who has stretched

out the earth and raised up the heavens, shall be fulfilled, the cherished desire of longing hearts will emerge from behind a myriad veils into the realm of existence and the highest aspiration of the people of Bahá will be fully, perfectly and conclusively realized. This is that which our Lord has promised us both openly and privily, and indeed this is a promise that will not prove untrue. Therefore it beseems you to arise and exclaim: *O concourse of the earth! Die in your wrath. Ere long will the standard of His faith be hoisted in every city, shedding radiance upon all regions.*

43 The auditorium could not seat 3,000 so there was a rotation system in order that people watching on big screens in nearby rooms would see at least one evening live (email from Josephine Hill, a volunteer staff member, to the author, 1 January 2015).

44 Alex Frame, who produced the week's musical programme, said the musicians also informally jammed together and 'began to create new kinds of music'.

45 The Universal House of Justice, Message to the Believers Gathered for the Events Marking the Completion of the Projects on Mount Carmel, 24 May 2001, in The Universal House of Justice, *Turning Point,* pp. 163–4; also in *The Bahá'í World, 2001–2002,* pp. 44–5.

46 *Bahá'í World News Service,* 25 May 2001. Available at: https://news.bahai.org/story/122/.

47 For video coverage see https://www.youtube.com/watch?v=3P6gslOOvsY.

48 *Bahá'í World News Service,* 25 May 2001. Available at: https://news.bahai.org/story/122/.

49 Available at: http://bahai-library.com/bjuk/200105-200401/BJ200107/terraces.htm.

50 *Bahá'í World News Service,* 16 January 2001.

51 Resolution 55/2 adopted by the General Assembly of the United Nations. Available at: http://www.un.org/millennium/declaration/ares552e.htm.

21. Footsteps on the Terraces

1 *Bahá'í World News Service,* 31 May 2001. Available at: https://news.bahai.org/story/123/.

2 Email from the custodian of the Shrine Fuad Izadinia to the author, 28 January 2015.

3 Reported in *Bahá'í World News Service,* 30 August 2001.

4 ibid.

5 The author, who assisted his colleague Yin Thing Ming of Singapore with the hosting of many special visits, witnessed this phenomenon many times.

6 Fariborz Sahba mentioned the birdsong element to the author in October 2018.

7 Haifa Tourist Board, *Bahá'í Shrine and Gardens,* p. 42. Another reason for starting the tour from the top is that space for gathering and briefing of the visitors exists near Terrace 19. In the lower plaza it would be undignified and distracting to have those functions.

8 Fariborz Sahba in conversation with the author in San Diego in September 2018.

9 If visitors on tours, or casual visitors to Terrace 10, completed their experience with a visit to the Shrine, they may have been restricted, due to numbers, to

viewing the prayer rooms and inner Shrine from the western doorway. Should it be appropriate to enter, the guides would explain basic protocol but leave people to show their own form of respect. Some would kneel, some would prostrate themselves at the threshold, others would stand in silence. The hallmark of such visits was deep reverence.

Annex 1. Looking Back

1 See Day, *Coronation on Carmel*, p. 68.
2 The author is grateful to Mr Blake for his generous cooperation in assisting with horticultural information for all three volumes of the story of the Shrine of the Báb.
3 See Day, *Journey to a Mountain*, pp. 5, 9, 184.

Annex 2. The Restoration of the Shrine of the Báb

1 The Guardian informed a friend in December 1929: 'The construction of three additional chambers contiguous to the Shrine on Mt. Carmel will soon be completed and the plan of the Master of having nine chambers as the ground floor of the Mausoleum of the Bab realized' (Rabbání, *The Priceless Pearl*, p. 236). The Hand of the Cause Ugo Giachery writes that in 1952 'Shoghi Effendi related to me that when 'Abdu'l-Bahá undertook construction of the original Shrine of the Báb in 1900–8, He wanted to have eight doors, but He could not achieve more than five' (Giachery, *Shoghi Effendi*, p. 82).
2 Another vision of the Guardian was the engraving of excerpts from the Writings of the Báb on the stone panels of the parapet and the curved corner panels. The Universal House of Justice did not direct the team to plan or implement this.
3 OSAR, *A Summary . . .*, Appendix B.
4 See http://bahaiviews.blogspot.com/2006/07/.
5 *Bahá'í World News Service*, 8 July 2008. Available at: https://news.bahai.org/story/642/.
6 See https://www.youtube.com/watch?v=5dRwclHMFvs&t=28s.
7 For example, there were 253 special visits between April 2003 and April 2004, and 298 and 227 in the next equivalent periods.
8 OSAR, *A Summary . . .*, p. 13.
9 ibid. Appendix A and Appendix C.
10 Condition survey, 2003, Page C-2.
11 Condition survey, 1994, B-1. Two of the team members were staff at the Bahá'í World Centre – the assistant coordinator of the Department, Wendy Marshall, an experienced building project manager; and the coordinator of the cleaning maintenance office, Tony Conroy, who had already used his expertise in conservational cleaning on the Shrine. There were two members who arrived from the United States. One was David Hadden, the founder-president of the Hart Restoration Group, which had won an award for its work on the Bahá'í Temple in Wilmette from the International Concrete Repair Institute. The other was Robert Armbruster, a professional engineer who directed the preservation of the Bahá'í House of Worship and who was the general manager of the properties owned by the National Spiritual Assembly of the United States.

12 Email from Mr ʿAlí Na<u>kh</u>javání to the author, 20 November 2014.

13 The report, entitled Condition survey 2003, was prepared by The Armbruster Company Inc. and dated December 1, 2003 (email from Robert Armbruster to the author, 27 March 2014).

14 In 2011 Saeid Samadi was appointed project manager for the construction of the Continental Baháʾí House of Worship of South America in Santiago, Chile.

15 For example, in June of 2006 OSAR asked Giorgio Forti, an Italian architectural expert in the restoration of historical buildings, to study the problems of the stone and other materials used in the Shrine building, and to suggest their remedies. He followed up a 1999 report by Professor Marisa Tabasso, who had been invited to visit the Holy Places in Haifa and Acre and prepare documents on the past stone restoration of the buildings in general and the Shrine and Archives Building in particular, including offering solutions for future stone restoration.

16 Saied Samadi, quoted in *Baháʾí World News Service*, 12 April 2011. Available at: http://news.bahai.org/story/816.

17 They advised in the following areas: structural, mechanical, electrical, stone restoration techniques, materials for stone restoration, golden tiles (email from Saeid Samadi to the author, 6 May 2015).

18 OSAR, *A Summary* . . ., Appendix A.

19 *Baháʾí World News Service,* 12 April 2011. Available at: https://news.bahai.org/story/816.

20 From San Francisco, United States, Mr Tavangar had experience with seismic refit projects on historic buildings.

21 By Forrell and Elsesser.

22 By the Israeli firm Star Engineers.

23 David & Ishay David Foundation Consulting Ltd.

24 One from the stone restoration firm Hirst, and the other Mr David Jennings.

25 Nancy Barnes, Elise Parmar, Gitty van Middelaar and Grace Rychetnik comprised the BWC gilding team.

26 The previous shipment of tiles from Europe to the Shrine had taken place more than 60 years before.

27 Letter from the Universal House of Justice to all National Spiritual Assemblies, 12 April 2011. Available at: http://www.bahai.org/library/authoritative-texts/the-universal-house-of-justice/messages/#d=20110412_001&f=f1.

28 *Baháʾí World News Service,* 12 April 2011. Available at: https://news.bahai.org/story/816.

29 The Universal House of Justice, message to the Baháʾís of the World, Riḍván 2011. Available at: https://www.bahai.org/library/authoritative-texts/the-universal-house-of-justice/messages/20110421_001/1#246550054.

INDEX

ABOUT THE AUTHOR

Michael V. Day is a journalist who was editor of the *Bahá'í World News Service* at the Bahá'í World Centre in Haifa, Israel from 2003 to 2006, where he lived and worked within a few hundred metres of the Shrine of the Báb.

Born and raised in New Zealand, Michael was briefly a lawyer before becoming a newspaper reporter, leader writer and editor. He first visited the Shrine of the Báb while on pilgrimage in 1980. After moving to Australia in 1988 with his wife, Chris, and sons Thomas and George, he was a journalist with Murdoch University in Perth. He joined the staff of *The West Australian* newspaper where he was an education and feature writer before being appointed the newspaper's Asia Desk Chief, specializing in covering Indonesia. He is currently a foreign affairs advisor, while continuing to write on Bahá'í history. Michael and Chris live in Brisbane, Queensland, Australia.

www.michaelvday.com

An exhilarating read, a meticulously researched work . . .
I was drawn in and needed to continue
Dr Janet A. Khan, author of *Prophet's Daughter*

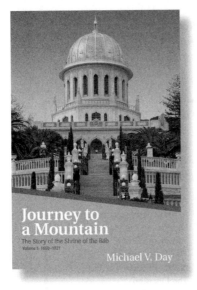

VOLUME I   1850–1921

JOURNEY TO A MOUNTAIN

The Story of the Shrine of the Báb

This is the thrilling story of the golden-domed Shrine of the Báb, which stands in exquisite garden terraces on Mount Carmel in Haifa, Israel. A UNESCO World Heritage site, the Shrine of the Báb is a symbol of the Baháʼí Faith, a world religion that envisions a peaceful global society based on the principle of the oneness of humanity.

For the first time the dramatic story of the establishment of the Shrine is told in detail. Never-before-seen photos and maps illustrate the often pulsating narrative.

By uncovering materials in English, Persian and Turkish, and by piecing together vital pieces of information, a compelling story has emerged of astounding achievement amidst great peril. It begins with the rescue of the sacred remains of the great spiritual leader, the Báb, Who had been executed in Persia in 1850 for His teachings.

Heart-stopping moments of apprehension punctuate the next 48 years as the casket containing the remains are hidden from those wanting to destroy them.

Then comes the highly secret process of carrying the casket across mountains, desert and sea to the Holy Land. Waiting for them is a prisoner of the Ottoman Empire, the commanding and charismatic ʻAbduʼl-Bahá (1844–1921).

He builds a Shrine in the heart of Mount Carmel where in 1909 He inters the sacred remains of the Báb. By so doing, He fulfilled a directive issued in 1891 by the Prophet-Founder of the Baháʼí Faith, Baháʼuʼlláh (1817–1892).

*This thrilling saga conveys the drama, excitement and challenges
associated with the completion of the Shrine of the Báb.*
Dr Janet A. Khan, author of *Prophet's Daughter*

TABLE OF CONTENTS

VOLUME 2   1822–1963

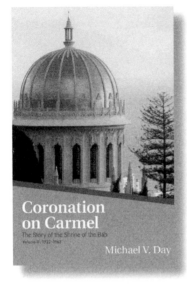

CORONATION ON CARMEL

The Story of the Shrine of the Báb

A drama opens on Mount Carmel in Haifa in the Holy Land in 1922. The new head of the Bahá'í Faith, Shoghi Effendi, begins the project to complete the Shrine of the Báb by building a domed superstructure. Aged only 24, he is faced with an almost impossible task. He has nowhere near enough money, no competent assistants, no building experience.

Undaunted by the challenge, Shoghi Effendi toils towards his goal through decades of upheaval and opposition. As time moves on, he gathers support from the growing Bahá'í community worldwide, and particularly from his wife, who becomes his tireless collaborator, an eminent Canadian architect; an Italian nobleman; a selfless donor; a Haifa construction engineer; a can-do American project manager he nicknames 'Hercules'; and an Arab called 'The Man with the Golden Touch'.

This is an inspiring, thrilling story that also includes the only woman known to have held the reins of a world religion, a member of European royalty whose pilgrimage is thwarted, and a pioneer female photographer.

In 1953 Shoghi Effendi unveils to the world the golden-domed Shrine of the Báb on Mount Carmel, set amidst gardens of a mystical charm. He names the Shrine 'Queen of Carmel'.

This true story follows *Journey to a Mountain* (1850–1921), the pulsating description of the transfer of the sacred remains of the Báb from Persia to the Holy Land, and their interment in the Shrine built by 'Abdu'l-Bahá.